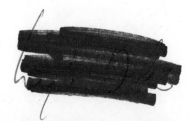

DEVELOPING PRODUCTS IN HALF THE TIME

DEVELOPING PRODUCTS IN HALF THE TIME

NEW RULES, NEW TOOLS

PRESTON G. SMITH
DONALD G. REINERTSEN

VAN NOSTRAND REINHOLD
I(T)P® A Division of International Thomson Publishing Inc.

New York • Albany • Bonn • Boston • Detroit • London • Madrid • Melbourne
Mexico City • Paris • San Francisco • Singapore • Tokyo • Toronto

Printed in the United States of America
Visit us on the Web! http://www.vnr.com

For more information contact:

Van Nostrand Reinhold
115 Fifth Avenue
New York, NY 10003

Chapman & Hall GmbH
Pappalallee 3
69469 Weinheim
Germany

Chapman & Hall
2-6 Boundary Row
London
SEI 8HN
United Kingdom

International Thomson Publishing Asia
60 Albert Street #15-01
Albert Complex
Singapore 189969

Thomas Nelson Australia
102 Dodds Street
South Melbourne, 3205
Victoria, Australia

International Thomson Publishing Japan
Hirakawacho Kyowa Building, 3F
2-2-1 Hirakawacho,
Chiyoda-ku 102 Tokyo
Japan

Nelson Canada
1120 Birchmount Road
Scarborough, Ontario
Canada, M1K 5G4

International Thomson Editores
Seneca, 53
Colonia Polanco
11560 Mexico D.F. Mexico

ISBN 0-442-02548-3

1 2 3 4 5 6 7 8 9 10 QEBFF 02 01 00 99 98 97

Contents

1

Faster and Still Faster   1

4
_____

The Power and Pitfalls of Incremental Innovation   67

5
_____

Capturing Customer Needs   85

6

Using System Design to Compress Schedules   105

7

Forming and Energizing the Team   119

8

Organizing for Communication   139

9

Designing Fast Development Processes 163

10

Controlling the Process
185

11

Preventing Overloads
205

12

Managing Risk
Proactively   221

15

Making Changes Faster
277

Biographies

PRESTON G. SMITH

For over a decade, as the head of New Product Dynamics, Preston Smith has specialized in assisting companies to make the technical and cultural shifts to shorter product development cycle times. Previously, he spent three years as a corporate staff consultant responsible for accelerating development over a range of businesses.

A Certified Management Consultant, he has helped many clients to improve their time to market. His consultation includes both focused diagnostic assessments and hands-on assistance in putting acceleration techniques into action. Client companies span the motor vehicle, power tool, medical electronics, food packaging, chemical, sports equipment, computer, telecommunications, semiconductor, and industrial equipment industries.

Preston speaks at numerous corporate meetings and professional conferences. He has given seminars and workshops in 16 countries, and he teaches product development at several universities. In addition to over a dozen published articles on rapid development, he regularly writes columns on product development and reviews books in the field.

Prior to concentrating on rapid development, Preston spent nearly 20 years in engineering and management positions with Bell Laboratories, IBM, General Motors, and companies as small as 100 employees. He holds a Ph.D. in engineering from Stanford, is a member of the Product Development and Management Association and ASME, and is listed in *Who's Who in Finance and Industry* and *Who's Who in the West*.

In off hours, Preston pursues his penchant for speed through alpine skiing and windsurfing.

DONALD G. REINERTSEN

Don Reinertsen is President of Reinertsen & Associates, a consulting firm specializing in the management of the product development process. Before starting his own firm, he had extensive consulting experience at McKinsey & Co., an international management consulting firm, and operating experience as Senior Vice President of Operations at Zimmerman Holdings, a private diversified manufacturing company.

His contributions in the field of product development have been recognized internationally. In 1983, while a consultant at McKinsey & Co., he wrote a landmark article in Electronic Business magazine which first quantified the value of development speed. This article has been cited as the McKinsey study that indicated "six months delay can be worth 33 percent of life cycle profits."

In the past fourteen years, he has gone considerably beyond this early work. He has worked with companies ranging from Fortune 500 Baldrige Award winners to small venture capital backed start-ups. He has developed a number of innovative analytical techniques for assessing, and changing, the product development process.

Don holds a B.S. from Cornell University in Electrical Engineering and an M.B.A. with distinction from Harvard Business School. He is a member of the IEEE, SME, and ASQC, and is co-author of the book Developing Products in Half the Time, which has sold more than 50,000 copies. He is also author of the book Managing the Design Factory. He writes and speaks frequently on techniques for shortening development cycles, and teaches a popular executive course at California Institute of Technology on streamlining the product development process.

Foreword

Most of the readers of this book probably associate Motorola with quality. We have worked hard to achieve leadership in this area and are very proud of our accomplishments. However, customer expectations have increased and have never been higher. Our customers expect us to demonstrate flawless quality and provide leadership products with value-added features, at lower prices, in shorter and shorter cycle times. The companies that can respond to quickly changing needs will flourish and those that can't, will be left behind. Time to market is a crucial element in being successful in the global marketplace.

For readers who are about to embark on the journey to faster development, let me offer a few observations. First, in my more than 30 years of product development experience, working with some of the best product developers in the world, I have yet to find a single magic tool for transforming a development process. Other companies may jump from fad to fad hoping there is a fast, easy way to accelerate product development. At Motorola we achieve rapid development the same way we achieved breakthroughs in quality—with old-fashioned hard work and constant management attention.

Second, many readers may wonder if pursuing development speed requires a company to compromise quality. At Motorola we have firmly rejected this option. There are abundant opportunities to improve the development process without taking the sloppy and dangerous approach of sacrificing quality. If you find yourself considering such options, you have not thought deeply enough about your choices. In fast-moving markets we often find that faster development actually provides higher quality to our customers, resulting in products delivered before customer needs begin to change.

Third, I would encourage you to question many of the deeply entrenched methods that you use for product development. Some of our greatest successes at Motorola have been a result of our engineers questioning the fundamental design of the entire process. This willingness to question the status quo proved vital to transforming quality and appears equally vital in transforming development speed.

Finally, I would encourage you to stay the course on this effort. The benefits of faster development can be substantial but they cannot be achieved instantly. Fundamental changes in your development process require careful analysis, broad involvement, and extensive effort. Not everything that is worth changing can be changed quickly. If you approach this as a short, quick journey you will not get very far.

On your journey I think you will find that *Developing Products in Half the Time* is an excellent companion. I am excited to see this new edition because at Motorola we found the original edition to be far and away the most useful book of its kind. The state-of-the-art in product development has continued to progress in the last six years and this new edition is very welcome. This book remains a vital resource for those of us interested in rapid development. I have read it more than once and I think you will too.

Neil Hagglund
Corporate VP and Director of Corporate Technology Planning
Motorola, Inc.

Preface

In this new edition of *Developing Products in Half the Time* we have replaced half the original contents with material that we consider to be more useful to our readers. The 60,000 readers of the original edition will find more and newer tools for cutting their cycle time, stemming from what we have learned in the last six years of work with our clients. New readers will find a book that makes the basics ever clearer than they were originally.

While there has been no change in the basic organization of the book or its overall message, the details have changed substantially. We have made major changes in four areas:

> Increasing the emphasis on economic analysis as a tool for guiding *all* decisions and expanding this key material in Chapter 2.
>
> Placing more emphasis in almost every chapter on the practical tools required to accelerate the development process, showing how actual companies have adapted these tools to their needs.
>
> Broadening and refining the treatment of many topics like incremental innovation (Chapter 4), product specifications (Chapter 5), and risk management (Chapter 12).
>
> Illustrating the additional power of combining the tools, such as in the case studies in Chapter 9.

Despite the new material, we have resisted the temptation to lengthen the book. We believe that a book of more than 300 pages becomes more time-consuming to read and harder to use. To keep the book at its original size we have deleted and compressed the less valuable sections and raised the density of useful material. Icons in the margin draw your attention to three types of particularly useful information in the book:

 (Wrench) A tool, something concrete that you do to shorten development cycle times.

 (Magnifier) An example of actions taken by a specific company.

 (Caution) A pitfall to watch out for as you apply a technique.

In the past several years rapid product development has become increasingly popular throughout industry. With this rise in popularity we find some companies that are pursuing rapid development simply because they believe that fast time to market is universally good. We must strongly reemphasize the message of the original book. Fast time to market is worth money—sometimes a great deal of money—but it is not universally good. The only way to determine which actions are appropriate in pursuing development speed is to know what cycle time is worth in financial terms. Since your competitors are getting faster, a sloppy approach to pursuing rapid development will become more and more expensive. In the future, the race is likely to go to those who buy cycle time at the right price. Throughout this book we stress the need to make careful choices based on the objectives of the project in question, and not to just follow the crowd.

This more deliberate approach to shortening cycle time within an organization does not come easily or automatically. For this reason we encourage you to begin now. To help you, we have expanded the tools for organizational change in Chapter 15. We find that such changes are necessary to make the other tools achieve their full potential.

We suggest that you read Chapters 1 and 2 first. Chapter 1 sets the stage, and Chapter 2, on economic analysis, is the book's logical foundation. After this, you can approach the other sections in any order. We find many cases where implementing an individual tool has had a big impact on performance. However, we are noting the increasing synergistic value of implementing supporting changes in several areas at once. For example, a more incremental approach to product introduction reduces team size and makes it easier to forecast customer needs. This reduces risk and improves accountability, making it practical to delegate more authority to the project team. We believe that in the future the synergistic integration of these tools will become mandatory to gain competitive advantage. Your competition will not be standing still.

As suggested earlier, these techniques are powerful because they are not theories, but instead tools that have been tried and proven by product developers. We are sincerely interested in how these techniques work for you and what enhancements you add to them. This edition has benefited from the experiences of readers of the first edition, and we would welcome the chance to add some of your experiences to the next edition. Feel free to contact us:

Preston G. Smith
New Product Dynamics
3493 NW Thurman Street
Portland, OR 97210
Telephone: (503) 248-0900
Fax: (503) 294-1192
preston@europa.com

Donald G. Reinertsen
Reinertsen & Associates
600 Via Monte D'Oro
Redondo Beach, CA 90277
Telephone: (310) 373-5332
Fax: (310) 373-5093
DonReinertsen@compuserve.com

DEVELOPING PRODUCTS IN HALF THE TIME

Faster and Still Faster

When the first edition of this book appeared in 1991, many companies were aspiring to cut their product development times in half, but only a few were doing it. Today this goal seems rather modest. Many companies now develop products in half of the time they did just a few years ago. What may have seemed like a fad just a few years ago is now a marketplace necessity in many industries. However, some managers now see that doubling development speed may still not put them in the competitive position they desire. They want more—and they are getting it.

This book provides the tools being used to achieve large reductions in cycle time and shows not only how these tools are applied but also *when* they should be applied. After working with many companies to apply these tools, we firmly believe that cycle-time reduction should be applied with business discretion only when it will offer a real competitive advantage, not just because others are doing it. First we will indicate the potential time savings available and then we will address the question of when these tools are appropriate.

Many Companies Have Achieved Double Speed

Figure 1-1 shows development cycle times for a variety of products. On average, these companies are developing their products twice as

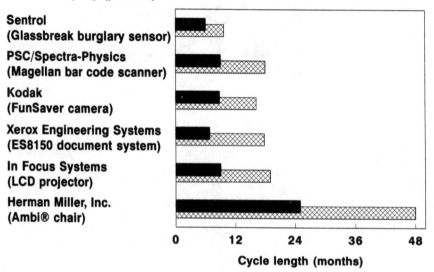

■ **This product** ⊠ **Prior experience**

In many industries, companies have been able to remove roughly half of the time formerly needed for product development.

FIGURE 1-1

fast as they did a few years ago. However, it is difficult to draw exact comparisons, for two reasons. One is that every development project is different. We do not have the opportunity to develop the same product twice, and the differences can be quite significant but difficult to measure. Even if the products were the same, the projects would not be. Some projects are blessed with more capable or better motivated people than others. Some get more of developers' undivided time. We will be taking advantage of such observed differences to accelerate our development processes, but nevertheless, they do make project-to-project comparisons difficult.

The second reason that it is difficult to make comparisons, especially between companies, is that there are no standards for when the clock should be started and stopped. Each company chooses to measure development time a little differently. Here again, we will take advantage of this observation to ask ourselves, "How would the customer measure development time?" Many managers instead choose to measure it to suit their own way of doing business. A customer-centered view will gain us real market advantage.

Fortunately, these difficulties in measurement are not an important impediment, because there are many large opportunities available for cutting cycle time. Improvements are usually clear cut, as they are in Figure 1-1.

Although a performance improvement of this magnitude is impressive, often it is not enough. A doubling of speed has become commonplace in many situations. In these cases, it is necessary to do even better than what has been considered impressive in the past.

Some Are Moving Toward a Factor of Ten Improvement

Hewlett-Packard, which used to require 54 months to complete a major new computer printer project, reduced the interval for its first DeskJet to 22 months and then to 10 months for the first color one, the DeskJet 500C. Even more dramatic, the company can now upgrade a platform in six to nine months. With this potent tool now in hand, today we are seeing many DeskJet variants. Not only has Hewlett-Packard learned how to develop products much faster routinely, it has learned the critical cultural lesson that each new product does not have to be a clean-sheet design (see Chapter 4 on incremental innovation).

As a result, the HP product line is very fresh. Figure 1-2 shows the portion of HP orders attributable to products that are less than two years old. Such charts are used as corporate metrics at this company, and the trend curve in Figure 1-2 indicates that HP continues to improve. In contrast with many companies that use such charts but define "new" to be three to five years, HP's fast-cycle capability is reflected in its two-year chart.

Intel has reduced its development cycle for motherboards from 12 months to six months, then to three months. This may seem quite fast, but the personal computer industry progresses quickly, and Intel is committed to remain a leader. One competitor in the industry, Acer Incorporated in Taiwan, develops complete notebook computers in just 6 months.

Such improvements are not limited to fast-moving markets. A major defense electronics company has cut its development cycle time from 48 months to 24 months and is heading for 12 months, the same fourfold improvement we saw in the personal computer industry in the previous paragraph. Similarly, a manufacturer of commercial electronics has shrunk its development times from 43 to nine months.

Mechanical products are showing comparable improvement, as illustrated in Figure 1-3 for Senco Products, Inc., a manufacturer of powered nailers, staplers, and the fasteners they drive. Senco is facing fierce global competition, so time to market is critical to maintaining

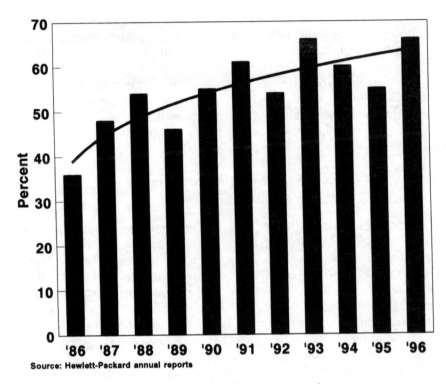

Source: Hewlett-Packard annual reports

With its fast-cycle capability, Hewlett-Packard is able to keep its product line so fresh that over half of its orders come from products less than two years old.

FIGURE 1-2

market leadership. Scott Allspaw, Manager of Product Development, attributes Senco's cycle-time reduction primarily to co-located, cross-functional, full-time teams and also to "an uncompromising obsession with understanding and meeting (or exceeding) customer needs" and to up-front supplier involvement.

Let's consider a much more mature industry, automobiles. In this industry Chrysler is now the leader in the United States. Its progress is charted in Figure 1-4. They started in the 1980s with a cycle time that averaged 54 months for a new vehicle. Several specific models in the 1990s are bringing this down through the 28-to-38 month range, and Chrysler executives are looking toward a 24-month target. This represents more than a doubling of speed over about 20 years. Already, their product line looks fresher, and this is reflected in their market share growth: up from 12.0 to 15.9 percent of the United States market from 1991 to 1996.

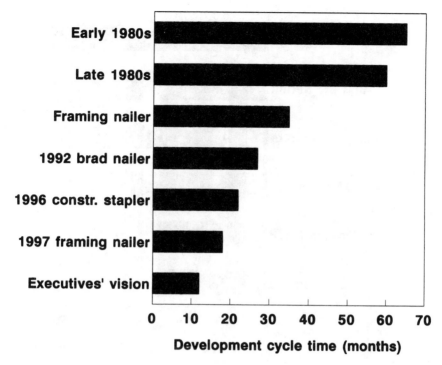

Senco Products has improved time to market several-fold and is continuing to get faster.

FIGURE   1-3

Finally, Motorola has established a corporate program to cut its cycle time by a factor of 10 within five years. This so-called 10X program is clearly aggressive, but so was its Six Sigma quality program. Six Sigma has had great impact on not only Motorola but also other related businesses worldwide. Motorola may not yet have reached its 10X goal, but reports indicate that at least one of its businesses had improved by an average of 3.8X by 1996.

What Is the Limit?

Based on our experience with many clients, we believe that there is much more potential left. We know of no company that is putting all of the tools in this book to work fully. Just shrinking the Fuzzy Front End (Chapter 3) is worth about 2X. Dedicated, co-located, cross-functional teams (Chapters 7 and 8) are good for at least 2X. And effective overload management (Chapter 11) will bring roughly another 2X.

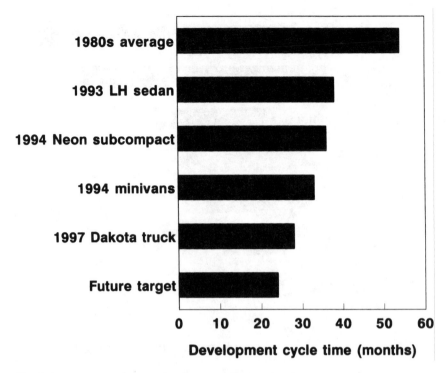

Chrysler's journey toward shorter development cycle times is quite
impressive for a mature industry.

FIGURE   1-4

Because these tools are largely independent, we have 8X right here,
from four of the 15 chapters.

Consider a related situation: writing, editing, and publishing a
book. Using a conventional approach, such a project takes 12 to 18
months. But fast-cycle publishers, such as the publishers of the popular *Dummies* books on personal computers and other subjects, can
produce a book in just three months, from idea to store shelves. This
represents a 4X–6X acceleration, and it is not the limit. Books on
major political events, such as Watergate, appear much faster. Or compare a book with a daily newspaper, which is about the same number
of words and requires similar development and manufacturing steps.
This gets us down to a matter of hours, from a project that traditionally has been considered to take a year or more.

In our training courses on this subject, we sometimes show a video
of such a related situation that is done much faster than normally. Once,
 we showed this video to a client in the motor vehicle industry that was
trying to cut its development cycle to 30 months but was stuck at 42

months. The reengineering team set aside its work and sketched out a plan for developing a vehicle in just six months. The plan required technologies, resources, and styles that the company did not have at the time, but the six-month plan has prompted the changes needed to reach 30 months. It has lead to substantial reductions in development cycles.

WHY DEVELOP PRODUCTS FASTER?

The motivation for rapid development is different for each company. It is important to know why you are accelerating the process, because your reason will determine which tools you use and how vigorously you apply them. For example, many companies start a program to accelerate their process when the real problem is that the current process is out of control. Their real need is just to deliver products according to the modest established schedule, not to go at breakneck speed. Some of the techniques in this book will be appropriate for them, but they will not be ready for many of the others yet.

Increase Sales

At the most basic level, we usually develop products faster because sales will increase. It is important to be specific about this, however, because the specifics are the key to quantifying the impact of faster development. Perhaps the most obvious but least important impact is that the product's sales life is extended. If a product is introduced earlier, it is likely to be a bigger surprise to the competition, so their lag in matching or surpassing it is likely to be larger. Consequently, for each month cut from a product's development cycle, up to a month is added to its sales life. Figure 1-5 shows this increase in sales life for the common case when our introduction does not affect the end of the product's sales life.

For some products that have high switching costs the benefit is even greater, because the early introducer gains on both ends of the cycle. If a product is introduced early, it gains customers, who maintain their loyalty due to the cost of switching to another product. Consequently, an earlier introduction can develop momentum that also carries the product's sales further into the future.

As a second benefit, early product introduction can increase peak sales. The first product to market has a 100 percent share of the market in the beginning. The earlier a product appears, the better are its prospects for obtaining and retaining a large share of the market. In some prod-

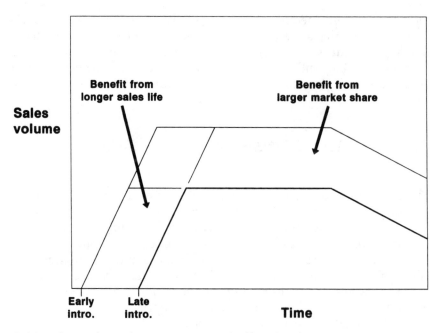

Early introduction of a product can increase its sales life and market share.

FIGURE   1-5

ucts, such as software and certain types of industrial machinery, there is an especially high premium on offering the first product of a given type, because buyers get locked into the first operating system or computer language they acquire. It then becomes difficult for them to switch.

A third benefit is higher profit margins. If a new product appears before there is competition, the company will enjoy more pricing freedom, making higher margins possible. The price may later decrease as competing products appear. By then, however, the company will be moving down the manufacturing learning curve ahead of the competition (see Figure 1-6), so there is a continuing advantage to being first.

Beat the Competition to Market

Marketing professors have written numerous papers on whether it is better to be a pioneer or a fast follower, and they have reached no clear conclusion. Ironically, being in the fast-follower mode often affords a company less time than that of the pioneer. Normally, we think of pioneers as the faster movers, but they may have started years ago, as often happens with truly revolutionary products. The clock is clearly running for fast followers, and they must be fast to succeed.

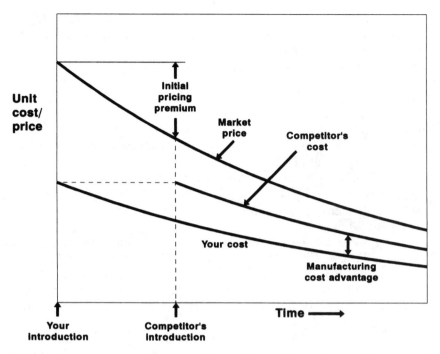

Early entrants can enjoy premium pricing and cost advantages from the manufacturing learning curve.

FIGURE   1-6
_____

In some cases, being there first does offer a substantial benefit. Producers of electronic components place a premium on being first in order to gain "design in" victories. If yours is the only component of a certain type and it thus gets designed into a larger system by a customer, the competition is effectively locked out. Even if a competitor's later component proves to be better, the switching cost to redesign the system and qualify another component can be substantial.

This contrast between pioneer and fast follower asks the wrong question. Each product has a certain cost of delay that will determine how much effort should be put into accelerating it, regardless of its pioneer or fast-follower status. Chapter 2 shows how to calculate this cost of delay.

Be Responsive to Changing Markets, Styles, and Technologies

An ability to move quickly provides a great deal of flexibility. It can enable you to get to market first, but it can also allow you to wait longer for the market or the technology to settle out before starting, still getting to market in time but with a better solution than the competition. There can be economic advantages to starting late when the underlying technology is moving down its price-performance curve rapidly.

 We once consulted for a company that was on the losing end of one of these situations. It had a durable old line of products that were entirely mechanical. The age of electronics was approaching, however, so it started developing a microprocessor-based product. Unfortunately, one of its faster-moving competitors also decided to switch to microprocessor control. The competitor waited until a chip appeared that would do the job at half the cost, but then moved quickly. Although the two products appeared at about the same time, the competitor had a strong advantage, because its manufacturing cost was significantly lower.

Besides technology issues, this flexibility applies to changes in styles, markets, and in the political and regulatory setting. Styling and design flexibility is one reason for Chrysler's current success; its United States competitors' vehicles often look dated by the time they are launched, simply because their styling and design decisions were made so much earlier than Chrysler's.

A fast-cycle capability leads to flexibility, which can be a powerful weapon in changing situations. The downside of this flexibility is that management or Marketing can abuse it by changing directions unnecessarily, which not only slows down the project but demoralizes the developers.

Maintain a Market Leadership Position

Many of the companies that are best known for rapid product development use it as a strategy for being the innovation leader in their market. These include companies such as Honda, Hewlett-Packard, Sony, and Black & Decker. They introduce a continuous stream of products responsively and sharply focused on real customer needs. This does two things for them:

- It keeps them in the forefront in their marketplace, as they are regarded as the trendsetters, and customers are willing to follow them and pay a bit more for their fresher product offerings. This is an envious market position to occupy.
- It helps them to remain customer focused. Because they are the leaders, they cannot look to their competitors for product ideas; they must understand their customers and their needs. They offer a product to customers, watch carefully how it is accepted, and then take

the next step, marching to their customers' drumbeat rather than looking back at the competition.

These companies take their product development seriously and regard accelerated development as a core competence. They have invested heavily in their product development strength and continue to do so. It is clear from Figure 1-2 that Hewlett-Packard has a long-term commitment to time to market. Thus, although the use of accelerated development as a market leadership strategy is quite attractive, actually doing it is not something to be taken lightly or done sporadically.

"More New Products" Is the Wrong Focus

On consulting assignments, we often ask client managers why they want to speed up their development. Within any given company we tend to get a variety of answers. Clearly, the management team hasn't spent enough time discussing how faster development will improve their business and forming a time-to-market rationale. If the senior managers do not have a sound, uniform position on the subject, you can imagine that those in lower ranks have an even weaker grasp of how faster development will benefit the company. Some mistakenly assume that time to market means skipping steps or quick-and-dirty, which is not what management intends.

When we probe a little deeper with management, however, what often comes out is that they figure that by developing their products in half the time, they can get twice as many products developed with the same resources. That is, they really want to double their productivity, and time to market is just a means to that end. This leads to a couple of problems. Most directly, when the employees find out that rapid development is just a ploy for working harder or more hours, the program will fall apart.

Although we will be covering many tools for accelerating development, most of them involve using resources more intensively, through heavier staffing on a project and dedicating people full time to a project, as well as making ample funds available for quick prototyping and contract services to intensify the effort. Roughly, we will be doubling the "burn rate" of spending on the project but running it just half as long, so the total resources and expenditure, per project, will be about the same. Thus, the number of projects completed per year with the same resources will be the same as before, but each one will be delivered in half the time (see Chapter 11).

It is critical to understand that if managers view rapid development as a means for squeezing more projects out of the same resources, they will be unwilling to invest in a project at the higher rate required, and without the higher burn rate, nothing much will change. Nor are they likely to be willing to make the initial investment in planning, analysis, and training that will be needed to move into the new mode.

The situation is actually better than we have presented it here. Most companies that accelerate their development find that in order to, say, cut their cycle time in half, they may not have to double their burn rate. They may only have to increase it by 60 or 80 percent, so they can actually get 10 or 20 percent more projects done than before. However, it is far more effective to go into the program assuming no gain in productivity and in fact assuming some extra start-up expenses. Then the cycle time program will get the resources and attention that it will need to get launched, and it is much more likely to take root. With a solid start, the program will not only reduce cycle time dramatically but probably also yield gains in productivity.

WHAT IS THE PRICE OF A SHORT CYCLE?

Since there is no free lunch, there must be a price for accelerated development somewhere. Where will we be paying? Will our development expenses increase? Will our manufacturing costs increase? Will our product quality suffer? It is important to understand, here at the beginning of the book, where the payment will come from. As with anything else that has enduring value, a product acceleration program will take change and up-front investment; you should be aware of where this is as you go through the remainder of the book.

The most apparent response is that development expenses will go up on a per-project basis. One can make a case for this, as we do later in this book by advocating some seemingly inefficient practices, such as "building a tall junk pile" of models and prototypes, and dedicating people full time to a project, even though they may not always be busy. However, the companies that have adopted these techniques have found that, usually, any extra expenditures on such apparently wasteful practices are more than offset by improvements in communication and working relationships, so the net effect is a savings.

Figure 1-7 illustrates the general relationship between cycle time and expense. Most companies start from a situation in which they can gain simultaneously in both speed and development expense. Then as

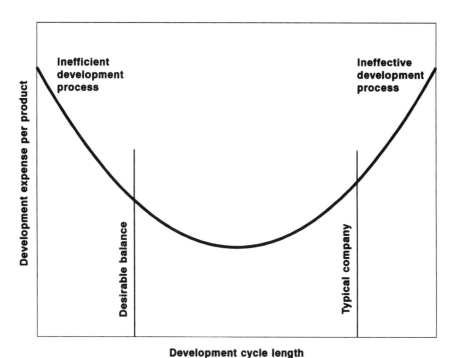

It can be expensive to develop products too quickly, but most companies are far from this point.

FIGURE   1-7

they exhaust the easy techniques, they may have to pay more to make additional progress. Because a shorter cycle pays off financially, as explained in Chapter 2, the proper balance is on the left side of Figure 1-7, in which the extra cost of speed offsets part of the extra profit that will be made from speed.

Companies that have shortened their development cycles have generally reduced expenses at the same time. For example, Rover of Great Britain has shortened car development time by 38 percent while also reducing development labor by 20 percent. Honeywell has cut development time by 50 to 60 percent while decreasing labor hours 5 to 10 percent. Deere & Company has shrunk its seven-year development cycle by 60 percent while reducing development expense by 30 percent. Figure 1-8 illustrates cycle times and expenses for three comparable United States subcompact development programs. These simultaneous improvements in both time and expenses do require an initial investment, as indicated in the previous section. We will be illustrating in later chapters the kind of investment that Chrysler has made, for example.

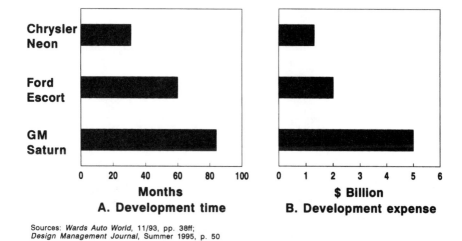

A. Development time   **B. Development expense**

Sources: *Wards Auto World*, 11/93, pp. 38ff;
Design Management Journal, Summer 1995, p. 50

Chrysler is able to develop cars both faster and less expensively than
Ford, which in turn does better than General Motors.

FIGURE   1-8

The next place one might expect to pay for accelerated development is in higher manufacturing cost for the launched product. The
reasoning is that less time will be spent fine-tuning the design for production or working the kinks out of the production system. However,
one of our acceleration techniques is to get manufacturing people involved in the early design decisions that determine manufacturability
(see Chapter 13). The net effect is shorter cycle time while also reducing manufacturing cost. The experience of many companies that
have adopted these techniques bears out these simultaneous savings.

A third place we might suffer is if product quality or performance
were compromised. The answer here depends on how you view quality. The methods presented in this book do not condone developing
shoddy merchandise or skipping development or testing steps. However, if you view quality as satisfying customer requirements, then we
do take advantage of this opportunity by understanding better what
our customers need (Chapter 5) and providing them with only what
they will value (Chapter 4). Innovation in general requires time, so providing innovation that has little or no value to the customer can waste
cycle time.

In our experience, much of the price of a faster development
process shows up in a process that is in a sense messier. Different projects are organized differently, each to the needs of that particular project. People move around more in the organization as they shift from

project to project, each one with a different team and each located in a different part of the building. Decision making is more decentralized. This requires more management attention and higher caliber people, which implies higher recruiting, labor, and training expenses.

TIME-TO-MARKET IS NOT A UNIVERSAL SOLUTION

Over the past several years, many managers have climbed onto the rapid-development bandwagon. They know they need to do something differently, but they aren't sure just what. Faster and faster seems like a good way to beat the competition. Unfortunately, such fuzzy thinking about time to market is rather common. As a result, the whole subject has taken on many of the characteristics of a religion: it is a good thing to do, and more seems better than less. This might be acceptable if the gains to be made were free, but they aren't. They take work, if not money, just like the real gains to be made in a more conventional religion.

This subject begs for more rational decision making. We can estimate how much work a change will take, and we can calculate what the benefit to our business will be. Then we can decide whether the benefit is worth the cost involved. Depending on many factors, sometimes the price will be attractive, and sometimes it won't. Our objective in this book is to put the whole subject of rapid product development on a rational business basis, so that we can treat each decision in terms of whether it is worth the resources it will require.

One consequence of this approach is that faster time to market is not a universal solution. Depending on many factors, it is more advantageous for some projects, some companies, or some industries than others. Even the fastest-moving companies have some projects that they shouldn't be accelerating. Conversely, a quite mature company can usually apply some of these time-to-market tools to certain projects advantageously.

How do we know when to apply the tools? We look at the marketplace and the competitive situation. Will getting a certain product to market quicker give us a calculable economic advantage, or would it just be nice to have? The very common alternative is to look inward, judging our cycle time relative to our past performance. If our cycle time has been 22 months over the past two years, for example, we should be able to cut it to 16 months. Such reasoning often leads to benchmarking: "If other companies in similar businesses can get their

products to market in sixteen months, we should 'catch up' with them."
It may well be that these companies are already going faster than the
marketplace will support. Then our attempts to benchmark and catch
up will simply be efforts to follow a misguided leader.

Even the best-intentioned companies make the mistake of pursuing speed with no clear objective. For instance, one of our clients, a
major electronics company, conducted a corporate survey of their di-
visions' time-to-market practices. They found that virtually every division had a goal to cut development cycle time in half. Then they
asked why cycle time was being cut. They found that no division had
an identifiable reason; apparently, it just seemed like a good thing to
do, because everybody else was doing it.

In Some Cases, Urgency Is Not the Issue

Because managers often become frustrated with how long it takes to
bring a new product to market, time to market can become a convenient
excuse for what are basically other issues. For example, developers
may routinely misjudge customer needs, often developing products
that do not sell as well as expected. Or the demand may be there, but
not at a price that provides sufficient margins. Perhaps developers consistently and grossly underestimate the time or development expense
required.

In recent years DuPont has invested considerable corporate effort
in its development process and systems. But due to the variety of the
businesses in this large corporation, the process has been customized
for each one. In some businesses, the emphasis is on speed, in others
it may be quality or manufacturability.

The only reliable way we have found to objectively assess the relative importance of cycle time is to do the financial modeling described
in Chapter 2 to see just how important a month of delay is financially
and how its importance compares with that of other project objectives.
The financial modeling will lead you toward the major issues and indicate what their impact will be on your bottom line. Then you can
tackle the real issue.

To find specific opportunities for cutting cycle time, analyze a few
of your recently completed projects. Identify the common themes or issues that recur repeatedly. How important are these issues based on
their economic impact? How frequently do they occur? Do they really
relate to cycle time? What makes a difference to the customer? Guidance in conducting such process reviews is provided in Chapter 15.

Rapid Development Is Demanding, Must Be Applied Selectively

Even if rapid development is crucial to your business, you probably cannot afford to do it on every project. We said earlier that a project completed rapidly will probably have no higher expenses than a project run more traditionally. However, rapid development requires some of your most talented, enthusiastic individuals. After an accelerated project or two, these people may need time to rest or to get back up-to-date in their field. Accelerated projects require priorities in service areas, such as the test lab, that may be difficult to provide to all projects. Finally, fast projects require more management attention than other projects.

None of these limitations is insurmountable in the longer term for the organization that decides to invest in this capability. However, if you complete the financial modeling (Chapter 2) for all of your projects, you will probably find that there is a certain portion that justifies the investment and disruption involved. It may be 5 percent or it may be 80 percent, but it will not be 100 percent.

At Some Point, Another Focus May Bring Bigger Rewards

Accelerated development has proved that it is not just a fad, as some commentators were suggesting a few years ago. But its importance is likely to vary over time for a given company or industry. Today, it might be very important, just because it may have been neglected as other programs, such as quality programs or design-to-cost programs, took precedence. But after a few years of work on cycle time, it may be desirable to maintain the gains made and move on to a more fruitful area.

This is just what is being done by Black & Decker's Power Tool Group, which has worked hard at rapid product development over the past several years, having brought the average cycle time down by a factor of three on consumer products. The natural inclination would be for B&D to mount another major initiative in speed. However, B&D has looked at its marketplace and determined that it is well within the competitive range on speed to market. So B&D is turning its major efforts to product quality and cost initiatives that promise to pay bigger dividends now.

BUILDING A HOLISTIC APPROACH

In this book we strive to present a balanced, integrated view of rapid product development. This is not a marketing, engineering, or manufacturing book, though it goes into depth on practical issues in each of these areas. The greatest gains are to be made by integrating disciplines and considering their boundaries carefully.

Through applying these techniques in industry, we have learned that universal solutions are not effective, because each firm has different requirements and constraints. Furthermore, in order to create competitive advantage, each solution must draw upon that company's strengths. Our approach is therefore one of probing the pros and cons of various approaches, respecting the complexity of the problem, and providing enough guidance for you to make the final choice.

Although general techniques seem preferable, they carry the danger of seeming idealistic. Consequently, numerous examples, both positive and negative, from a broad range of products, show how the various techniques apply. These applications have purposely been chosen to span electronic and mechanical products, hardware and software, consumer and industrial goods, and both high- and low-volume production situations. Although the techniques presented usually apply across a range of company sizes from the small to the very large, we have purposely chosen most of our examples from more prominent companies, so that readers can appreciate the application in a familiar product and relate to it more easily.

Accelerated product development is primarily a certain management approach. At the outset, it may help to clarify our viewpoint by describing approaches we believe to be too restrictive, although they are popular in the literature. One such view is to ascribe rapid development to computerized aids, such as computer-aided design (CAD); Chapter 9 shows how such tools can *support* the management approach. Another type of shortsightedness is to equate accelerated product development with teamwork. There are in fact important elements of the solution that have more to do with the product than the team (see Chapters 4–6), and the team itself is largely a mechanism that enables the use of other techniques, such as overlapped activities (Chapter 9) and low-level decision making.

Finally, many people connect accelerated product development with project management. Here again, this perspective is too narrow, because it ignores the product-specific elements and the characteristics unique to product development projects. All too often "project management" fails because its key element is ignored: management does not provide its Project Manager with the authority or support necessary to reach the objective, an ambitious schedule in this case.

Doing the Right Product (versus Doing the Product Right)

When management decides to develop a new product, two basic issues arise. The first is deciding on the product to be developed (doing the right product), and the second is deciding on how development is to be executed (doing the product right). Because this is primarily a book on execution, we focus mostly on the second issue here, assuming that the first is handled adequately. However, there are important aspects of business objectives, product strategy, and product line planning that form the foundation of effective execution. The development team will be making trade-off decisions daily on such issues as cycle time, product cost, and serviceability. If management has not set the course clearly by elucidating the strategy, the developers will be navigating without a compass. The project will be slow if developers' decisions get reversed by management, and it will be slow if management has not clarified project priorities, so that the developers can limit the size of the job.

We provide some coverage of these more strategic issues in Chapters 3 and 4, but if you find that many of your difficulties stem from not doing the right product, please go beyond this book and consult other sources on product selection and product line planning, such as the Wheelwright and Clark book listed at the end of Chapter 3.

Development Acceleration Can Be a Good Leader for Other Organizational Changes

There are many approaches for improving product development. Some companies concentrate on defining and documenting the process. However, focusing on the process, as the starting point, can lead to a process that covers every contingency and is thus bureaucratic and slow. Others concentrate more on the scheduling and control aspects of project management.

Our experience suggests that time to market is an excellent focal point around which to build an improved development system. First, time has become an area of great opportunity for improvement, often driven by dynamic changes in technologies or markets. Companies that put effort into their development cycle are often able to shorten it by 50 percent in a couple of years, which provides the incentive to keep working at it. Compared with objectives such as productivity or quality, time is easier to understand and measure (provided that management can tie it to business success compellingly).

Perhaps the best reason for using time to market as the centerpiece of a change program is that it tends to drive the basic changes in desirable directions. In order to get to market quickly, everything else must be working well, too: people from different departments must communicate effectively, non-value-adding activities must be eradicated, customers must be involved intimately, and management must be supportive.

SUGGESTED READING

Crawford, C. Merle. 1992. The hidden costs of accelerated product development. *Journal of Product Innovation Management* 9 (3): 188–199. A few articles have been strongly concerned about accelerated development and allied areas, such as co-location, mostly authored by academics, not those actually executing rapid development in industry. This one is a good example, and it shows us where to be careful as we shorten cycle times; for example, don't just skip steps.

Griffin, Abbie. 1997. The effect of project and process characteristics on product development cycle time. *Journal of Marketing Research* 34: 24–35. Griffin's work is the most comprehensive we know of in actually measuring cycle time across companies. She reaches conclusions that an "average" project will shrink from 26 to 15 months when a cross-functional team and a formal development process are used, for example.

Stalk, Jr., George, and Thomas M. Hout. 1990. *Competing Against Time*. New York: The Free Press. A classic account of how time is used to gain competitive advantage in business today, in product development as well as other areas.

Stalk, Jr., George, and Alan M. Webber. 1993. Japan's dark side of time. *Harvard Business Review* 71 (4): 93–102. Time-based competition in Japan's consumer electronics industry has led to a mindless race toward commodities. These authors explain that this can be avoided by careful attention to a strategy that is tied to customer value.

CHAPTER 2

Putting a Price Tag on Time

Many companies believe that fast product development is good, and slow product development is evil. This is a dangerously sloppy way of thinking about rapid product development. It traps you into believing that any step to shorten cycles is automatically worthwhile, no matter how expensive it is or how it damages other important business objectives. We advocate a different view of cycle time. We believe that you should only shorten cycles when you will make money by doing so. *Speed is not the objective, it is a means to an end; the objective is making money.* Since our primary objective is to make money, we need a method to assess how a change in development cycle time will affect project profitability. Furthermore, because many other business parameters will affect profitability, we need a method to assess our management actions on the basis of everything that they affect, not just their cycle-time impact. Fortunately, there is a systematic and straightforward way of doing this.

Our guiding principle is that development cycle time is worth a quantifiable amount of money, and any steps that can buy us time for less than this price will improve our profits. This is the price tag that we put on time. The quantified value of cycle time is the touchstone that we use to evaluate all our management actions. To attempt to shorten cycles without knowing whether cycle time is worth $1,000 per month or $1,000,000 per month is a certain path to disaster. We can only make intelligent decisions to shorten development cycles if we know what cycle time is worth.

In this chapter we will discuss how to do this quantification and what we can do with the results. Throughout this book our business decisions are based on this quantified understanding of the value of cycle time. For example, consider the company wrestling a tough trade-off between unit cost and schedule. A key subassembly is not achieving its cost target due to the lack of a low-cost supplier. The high cost will reduce the product gross margin by 10 percentage points, a substantial figure. A new supplier can be brought into the project but it will delay product introduction by three months. On a typical team this would produce violent polarization between Manufacturing and Marketing. Manufacturing would insist that gross margin targets must be achieved. Marketing would insist on the strategic importance of time to market. The deadlock might have to be broken by the company President.

Provide this same team with the decision rules that we discuss in this chapter, and you will see an amazing transformation. Not only will we make a sound business decision, but this decision will be made quickly with buy-in from the entire team. When it comes to making progress on the tough trade-offs, there is no substitute for facts and analysis.

Curiously, some managers and developers will resist this quantification, claiming that many important factors cannot be quantified. While this is true, it is usually irrelevant. It is not necessary to achieve perfect quantification to improve management decisions. Our experience in helping many companies quantify these trade-offs suggest that even the crudest attempts at quantification can give extraordinary insight. We find that analytically based decisions achieve better outcomes, faster, and with greater reliability, than the intuitive judgments made by most managers and developers.

Let us give you a simple test to judge whether quantifying the cost of delay might be useful to you. Gather the members of a development team in a room. Ask them each to bring a piece of paper and a pencil. Ask each one independently to write down what they think is the cost of delaying their project by three months. Now take the numbers from this group and rank them from the highest to the lowest number. The smallest range we have ever seen doing this exercise has been a factor of 10 difference in cost of delays. At one Baldrige award winning company the team's intuitive feel for cost of delay differed by 200 to 1. Our goal in quantifying the cost of delay is to provide a better decision-making framework than the intuitive one generally used for making such decisions. Companies who do not quantify the cost of delay are unlikely to have any accurate sense of the value of cycle time. Since hundreds of management decisions on a development project will be based on this foundation, we need to ensure that it is properly laid.

THE FOUR KEY OBJECTIVES

The process of quantification is simply a sensitivity analysis to determine how sensitive profits are to changes in key project parameters. Once we know how sensitive profits are to these parameters, we can trade them off against each other to maximize profitability. In theory, you could do this sensitivity analysis based on almost any project parameter. In practice, we find that four key parameters are consistently useful. Managing new product development depends on balancing efforts toward these four key objectives, as shown in Figure 2-1.

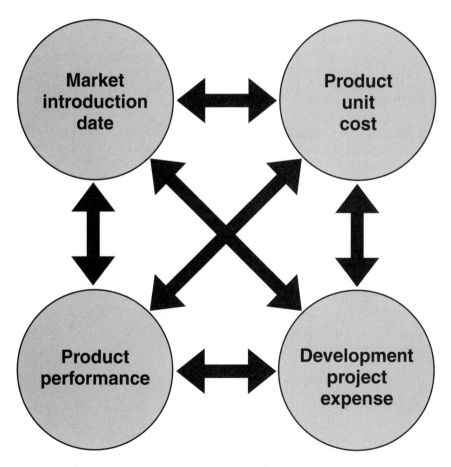

Four key product development objectives and six trade-offs.

FIGURE   2-1

The first objective is market introduction date. We measure this as when the final product is first available for sale to the customer. The second key objective is product's unit recurring cost. We normally use the manufactured cost of the product plus any variable costs that appear below the gross margin line.

The third key objective is product performance. The most useful way to measure performance is to look at the revenue stream of the product over its life. A change in this revenue stream can arise from either higher unit sales or higher sales prices. This is different than the way many companies think of performance. They think in terms of technical performance, or conformance to the product specification and believe that a design that exceeds its specification has achieved higher performance. However, changing a technical performance parameter of the product produces no benefit unless it can be translated into a change in revenue. For example, one instrumentation company produced a design that was 40 times more accurate than a competing instrument. Unfortunately, the competing instrument was accurate enough to meet the needs of the customers. The increase in technical performance produced no change in the revenue stream, and simply reduced the gross margin of the product.

The fourth key objective is development project expense. These are the one-time costs associated with the development project. We normally include costs that appear in Engineering, Marketing, and Manufacturing in this number.

What About Quality?

At this point, you may wonder how we could have neglected to include quality as an objective of a development project. Actually, we have already included it, but it is hidden within the four key objectives. Every aspect of quality that has economic significance is covered within the four key objectives. For example, rework in the development project will affect development project expense and market introduction date. Warranty costs and yield problems in manufacturing will show up in product unit costs. Performance problems with the product can reduce selling prices or market share. Because the model includes the entire product revenue stream and all the costs, both one-time and recurring, all effects on the profit and loss are automatically captured.

Trading-off Multiple Objectives

You will also note in Figure 2-1 that there are six trade-offs between the four key development objectives. This concept of trade-offs is important because development projects have multiple objectives which must be balanced. For example, an early introduction date may be useless if we cannot make any money on the product. A low unit cost may be useless if market share or sales price is too low. In practice, we usually cannot achieve the earliest possible introduction date and the lowest possible unit cost at the same time. This means that we need a fast, systematic way to make trade-offs between these objectives. We need to understand how sensitive profitability is to changes in each of the objectives. The tool for doing this is the decision rules produced by our financial model.

THE BASIC MODELING PROCESS

In this section we will present a simple modeling process. In the following section we will show you how to modify this simple approach for some of the more complex situations we have encountered on certain projects. These models are deliberately simple for some very important reasons that we will discuss later in this chapter. If you are concerned about the simplicity as we get into the modeling process, please refer to that section.

The modeling process, which is shown in Figure 2-2, is logical and straightforward. We find that both teams and managers can understand it quickly. We start by creating a baseline model that projects life-cycle profits if everything goes according to plan. Then, we create variations from this baseline. Next, we assess how profits will change due to these variations and transform these changes in profit into decision rules to guide our trade-offs.

Create the Baseline Model

The baseline model is simply a projection of product profits over its full expected life. This projection must be done as a cross-functional activ-

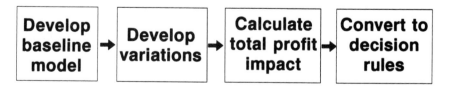

Four steps in the economic modeling process.

FIGURE 2-2

ity because it requires data from every function. While a financial analyst may be the custodian of the model, it is very important that the entire team participate in its construction. If they do not, they are unlikely to understand it and as a result will fail to use it to guide their decisions.

A typical baseline model is shown in Table 2-1. Let us review it line by line. First, we project the average sales price of a product over its expected life. These prices typically fall at a rate proportional to the rate of improvement in price-performance of a product's underlying technology. For example, semiconductor unit prices typically fall at a rate of 25 to 30 percent per year. Computer printers may decrease by 15 percent per year. Disk drives characteristically drop at about 25 percent per year, and mechanical systems may range from decreases of about 5 percent per year to increases in about the same range. Each market has its underlying long-term pricing trend. In this model we use a 10 percent rate of annual decrease. This drop in pricing will eventually cause us to discontinue the product because it can no longer be produced profitably.

Next, project the unit sales of the product. Unit sales are a function of both market size and market share. Typically, sales will grow until they reach a peak, then slowly trail off. A common exception to this is OEM (original equipment manufacturer) sales, which may remain low for a longer period of time in the beginning but rise rapidly once the OEM begins shipping its products. The baseline sales curve must be tailored to the specific product that you are analyzing. When in doubt, look at historical data from previous products and competitive data when it is available.

Now, calculate dollar sales, which are simply the units sold times the average sales price. After projecting dollar sales forecast the product's unit costs, which usually decrease because of the learning curves common in the industry. These costs almost always go down at a slower rate than prices drop. Typical learning curves might produce cost drops of 5 to 15 percent for every doubling of volume. The latter value would be called an 85 percent learning curve. The most sophisticated cost models will establish a combination of price trends and learning curves for material, labor, and overhead components of product cost, but we rarely find a need for this sophistication. Manufacturing should be involved in projecting these costs, since they will be most familiar with product cost behavior. For simplicity, the illustrated model shows unit costs dropping at 2 percent per year.

The factors mentioned so far allow us to calculate gross margin over the life of the product. You will note that the product begins shipping at a 50 percent gross margin, but that this constantly erodes until year five when the product is discontinued at a 23.5 percent gross margin. This constant margin erosion is typical.

TABLE 2-1

Baseline Product Profit Model

	Assumes	-2	-1	0	1	2	3	4	5
						Year			
Average sales price	-10 Percent/year								
Introduction price	$7,033			$7,033	$6,330	$5,697	$5,127	$4,614	$4,153
Market size (units)				10,000	20,000	40,000	60,000	40,000	20,000
Market share				10.0%	10.0%	10.0%	10.0%	10.0%	10.0%
Unit sales				1,000	2,000	4,000	6,000	4,000	2,000
Dollar sales				$7,033,000	$12,659,400	$22,786,920	$30,762,342	$18,457,405	$8,305,832
Unit cost	-2 Percent/year								
Introduction cost	$3,516			$3,516	$3,446	$3,377	$3,309	$3,243	$3,178
Cost of goods sold				$3,516,000	$6,891,360	$13,507,066	$19,855,386	$12,972,186	$6,356,371
Gross margin dollars				$3,517,000	$5,768,040	$9,279,854	$10,906,956	$5,485,219	$1,949,461
Gross margin percent				50.0%	45.6%	40.7%	35.5%	29.7%	23.5%
Engineering	16 Percent sales	$2,000,000	$2,000,000	$1,000,000	$100,000	$100,000	$100,000	$100,000	$100,000
Marketing	5 Percent sales			$1,125,280	$2,025,504	$3,645,907	$4,921,975	$2,953,185	$1,328,933
G&A				$351,650	$632,970	$1,139,346	$1,538,117	$922,870	$415,292
Operating expense		$2,000,000	$2,000,000	$2,476,930	$2,758,474	$4,885,253	$6,560,092	$3,976,055	$1,844,225
Profit before tax (PBT)		($2,000,000)	($2,000,000)	$1,040,070	$3,009,566	$4,394,601	$4,346,864	$1,509,164	$105,237
Cumulative PBT		($2,000,000)	($4,000,000)	($2,959,930)	$49,636	$4,444,237	$8,791,101	$10,300,265	$10,405,502
Return on sales (PBT/dollar sales)				14.8%	23.8%	19.3%	14.1%	8.2%	1.3%
Cumulative sales				$100,004,900					
Cumulative gross margin				$36,906,531					
Cumulative PBT				$10,405,502 Baseline					
Average percent gross margin				36.9%					
Average percent return on sales				10.4%					

Next, project operating expenses. Engineering expenses are direct estimates associated with the project. Marketing expenses may include one-time expenses associated with the specific project, as well as a portion of the selling and marketing overhead applied as a straight percentage of sales. General and administrative (G&A) expenses are normally applied as a straight percentage of sales. The percentages to use in each case are simply those that are customary for the business in question. These percentages are most easily obtained from the Finance Department.

After all operating expenses have been calculated, we can determine the profit before tax (PBT). We find it most useful to focus on cumulative profit before tax as a simple, easily understood measure of the development project. In our experience, more complicated measures add no additional insight but simply obscure understanding for team members less familiar with financial analysis.

We should note that in most cases the baseline financial model for a product already exists in the business plan used to make the decision to fund the project. It is usually a question of finding the baseline model and modifying it, rather than creating it from scratch.

Create Variations

Our next step is to create variations from the baseline model just developed by creating a new profit and loss statement for each of four scenarios: a development expense overrun, a unit cost overrun, a performance shortfall, and a schedule delay. In our first scenario, shown in Table 2-2, we raise development expenses. We normally raise these expenses both during the development of the product and after introduction. This is done to reflect the likely increases in support cost when product complexity increases.

In our second scenario, shown in Table 2-3, we raise product unit costs. The trick in this scenario is to recognize that if a product fails to reach its cost targets, this cost problem may not persist throughout the life of the product. Instead, it is much more likely that we will reduce the product cost within a year or two, to restore margins to the level that would have been reached if the original product cost target had been achieved. The critical assumption in this scenario is how long it will take to fix a unit cost overrun. To determine an appropriate period to use, look at how long it has taken you to cost reduce previous products. If you neglect the effect of cost reduction in analyzing this scenario, you will dramatically overstate the importance of product unit cost.

TABLE 2-2
Product Profit Model When Development Expense Overruns by 50 Percent

	Assumes	Year −2	Year −1	Year 0	Year 1	Year 2	Year 3	Year 4	Year 5
Average sales price									
Introduction price	−10 Percent/year $7,033			$7,033	$6,330	$5,697	$5,127	$4,614	$4,153
Market size (units)				10,000	20,000	40,000	60,000	40,000	20,000
Market share				10.0%	10.0%	10.0%	10.0%	10.0%	10.0%
Unit sales				1,000	2,000	4,000	6,000	4,000	2,000
Dollar sales				$7,033,000	$12,659,400	$22,786,920	$30,762,342	$18,457,405	$8,305,832
Unit cost									
Introduction cost	−2 Percent/year $3,516			$3,516	$3,446	$3,377	$3,309	$3,243	$3,178
Cost of goods sold				$3,516,000	$6,891,360	$13,507,066	$19,855,386	$12,972,186	$6,356,371
Gross margin dollars				$3,517,000	$5,768,040	$9,279,854	$10,906,956	$5,485,219	$1,949,461
Gross margin percent				50.0%	45.6%	40.7%	35.5%	29.7%	23.5%
Engineering		$3,000,000	$3,000,000	$1,500,000	$150,000	$150,000	$150,000	$150,000	$150,000
Marketing	16 Percent sales			$1,125,280	$2,025,504	$3,645,907	$4,921,975	$2,953,185	$1,328,933
G&A	5 Percent sales	$3,000,000	$3,000,000	$351,650	$632,970	$1,139,346	$1,538,117	$922,870	$415,292
Operating expense				$2,976,930	$2,808,474	$4,935,253	$6,610,092	$4,026,055	$1,894,225
Profit before tax (PBT)		($3,000,000)	($3,000,000)	$540,070	$2,959,566	$4,344,601	$4,296,864	$1,459,164	$55,237
Cumulative PBT		($3,000,000)	($6,000,000)	($5,459,930)	($2,500,364)	$1,844,237	$6,141,101	$7,600,265	$7,655,502
Return on sales (PBT/dollar sales)				7.7%	23.4%	19.1%	14.0%	7.9%	0.7%
Cumulative sales				$100,004,900					
Cumulative gross margin				$36,906,531					
Cumulative PBT				$7,655,502					
Average percent gross margin				36.9%					
Average percent return on sales				7.7%					

Higher development expense (annotation pointing to Engineering row, years −2 through 0)

Lower profit (annotation pointing to the Profit before tax / Cumulative PBT area)

TABLE 2-3

Product Profit Model When Product Cost Overruns by 10 Percent for Two Years

	Assumes	Year -2	-1	0	1	2	3	4	5
Average sales price	−10 Percent/year								
Introduction price	$7,033			$7,033	$6,330	$5,697	$5,127	$4,614	$4,153
Market size (units)				10,000	20,000	40,000	60,000	40,000	20,000
Market share				10.0%	10.0%	10.0%	10.0%	10.0%	10.0%
Unit sales				1,000	2,000	4,000	6,000	4,000	2,000
Dollar sales				$7,033,000	$12,659,400	$22,786,920	$30,762,342	$18,457,405	$8,305,832
Unit cost	−2 Percent/year		Two years						
Introduction cost	$3,868		of higher unit cost	$3,868	$3,790	$3,377	$3,309	$3,243	$3,178
Cost of goods sold				$3,867,600	$7,580,496	$13,508,000	$19,856,760	$12,973,083	$6,356,811
Gross margin dollars				$3,165,400	$5,078,904	$9,278,920	$10,905,582	$5,484,322	$1,949,022
Gross margin percent				45.0%	40.1%	40.7%	35.5%	29.7%	23.5%
Engineering		$2,000,000	$2,000,000	$1,000,000	$100,000	$100,000	$100,000	$100,000	$100,000
Marketing	16 Percent sales			$1,125,280	$2,025,504	$3,645,907	$4,921,975	$2,953,185	$1,328,933
G&A	5 Percent sales			$351,650	$632,970	$1,139,346	$1,538,117	$922,870	$415,292
Operating expense		$2,000,000	$2,000,000	$2,476,930	$2,758,474	$4,885,253	$6,560,092	$3,976,055	$1,844,225
Profit before tax (PBT)		($2,000,000)	($2,000,000)	$688,470	$2,320,430	$4,393,667	$4,345,490	$1,508,267	$104,797
Cumulative PBT		($2,000,000)	($4,000,000)	($3,311,530)	($991,100)	$3,402,567	$7,748,057	$9,256,324	$9,361,121
Return on sales (PBT/dollar sales)				9.8%	18.3%	19.3%	14.1%	8.2%	1.3%

Lower profit

Cumulative sales $100,004,900
Cumulative gross margin $35,862,150
Cumulative PBT $9,361,121
Average percent gross margin 35.9%
Average percent return on sales 9.4%

When modeling this cost reduction, you need to decide if it will come from internal sources or from suppliers. If the cost reduction comes from internal sources, you should include one-time engineering expenses in your calculation. If the cost reduction comes from suppliers, there may be no one-time expenses. In the case shown we have assumed that cost reduction is completed in two years with no one-time engineering expenses.

In our third scenario, shown in Table 2-4, we model a performance shortfall. Performance problems can be modeled either as a drop in sales price or as a drop in unit sales. The latter is by far the most common approach, because it reflects the most likely behavior of a company with a performance shortfall in its product. The typical company will usually walk away from market share before it will take a reduction in sales price. You should be very cautious when modeling a performance problem as a price drop because price decreases drop straight to the bottom line, so they will do great damage to profitability. The case shown reflects the common approach of dropping unit sales.

The fourth scenario, shown in Table 2-5, is a delay in product introduction. This is the most complex case to model. Generally most products fit into one of the following three cases shown in Figure 2-3. First, there are inelastic products with limited competition. For these products, total unit sales do not decrease. Instead, pent-up demand will cause the product's cumulative unit sales to remain constant even if it is introduced late. This can occur when loyal customers are locked into the product and relatively indifferent about its introduction date. In such a case the cost of schedule delay comes simply from price erosion because units are shipped during a relatively low-margin period in the product's life. This delay is generally the least severe of the possible schedule delays.

In the second case there is a somewhat smaller sales peak. Sales build at about the same rate as they would have with an earlier introduction, and the peak occurs in the same year as it would have under the baseline scenario. In this case the timing of the peak in market demand is determined by the marketplace rather than by the introduction date of our product. The result is a somewhat lower market share throughout the life of the product when compared to the baseline case. This causes a more severe decrease in profits than the previous case, but not as much as in the third and final case.

The third case reflects a severe and continuing reduction in sales. This decline can occur in products such as medical devices, where a six-month introduction delay may mean the difference between a 20 percent market share and a 2 percent share. The same effect occurs in many OEM markets where early introduction often results in design-in victories and the early winner cannot be dislodged by later competitors.

TABLE 2-4

Product Profit Model When Product Performance Problems Reduce Unit Sales by 10 Percent

	Assumes	-2	-1	0	1	2	3	4	5
						Year			
Average sales price	-10 Percent/year			$7,033	$6,330	$5,697	$5,127	$4,614	$4,153
Introduction price	$7,033								
Market size (units)	Unit sales			10,000	20,000	40,000	60,000	40,000	20,000
Market share	down by			9.0%	9.0%	9.0%	9.0%	9.0%	9.0%
Unit sales	10 Percent			900	1,800	3,600	5,400	3,600	1,800
Dollar sales				$6,329,700	$11,393,460	$20,508,228	$27,686,108	$16,611,665	$7,475,249
Unit cost	-2 Percent/year			$3,516	$3,446	$3,377	$3,309	$3,243	$3,178
Introduction cost	$3,516								
Cost of goods sold				$3,164,400	$6,202,224	$12,156,359	$17,869,848	$11,674,967	$5,720,734
Gross margin dollars				$3,165,300	$5,191,236	$8,351,869	$9,816,260	$4,936,697	$1,754,515
Gross margin percent				50.0%	45.6%	40.7%	35.5%	29.7%	23.5%
Engineering		$2,000,000	$2,000,000	$1,000,000	$100,000	$100,000	$100,000	$100,000	$100,000
Marketing	16 Percent sales			$1,012,752	$1,822,954	$3,281,316	$4,429,777	$2,657,866	$1,196,040
G&A	5 Percent sales			$316,485	$569,673	$1,025,411	$1,384,305	$830,583	$373,762
Operating expense		$2,000,000	$2,000,000	$2,329,237	$2,492,627	$4,406,728	$5,914,083	$3,588,450	$1,669,802
Profit before tax (PBT)		($2,000,000)	($2,000,000)	$836,063	$2,698,609	$3,945,141	$3,902,177	$1,348,248	$84,713
Cumulative PBT		($2,000,000)	($4,000,000)	($3,163,937)	($465,328)	$3,479,813	$7,381,991	$8,730,239	$8,814,952
Return on sales (PBT/dollar sales)				13.2%	23.7%	19.2%	14.1%	8.1%	1.1%
					Lower profit				
Cumulative sales				$90,004,410					
Cumulative gross margin				$33,215,878					
Cumulative PBT				$8,814,952					
Average percent gross margin				36.9%					
Average percent return on sales				9.8%					

TABLE 2-5

Product Profit Model When Product Introduction Is Delayed by Six Months

	Assumes	-2	-1	0	1	2	3	4	5
						Year			
Average sales price	-10 Percent/year								
Introduction price	$7,033			$7,033	$6,330	$5,697	$5,127	$4,614	$4,153
Market size (units)	Lower			10,000	20,000	40,000	60,000	40,000	20,000
Market share	unit sales			3.0%	8.0%	9.0%	9.0%	9.0%	9.0%
Unit sales				300	1,600	3,600	5,400	3,600	1,800
Dollar sales				$2,109,900	$10,127,520	$20,508,228	$27,686,108	$16,611,665	$7,475,249
Unit cost	-2 Percent/year			$3,516	$3,446	$3,377	$3,309	$3,243	$3,178
	$3,516								
Introduction cost	$3,516								
Cost of goods sold				$1,054,800	$5,513,088	$12,156,359	$17,869,848	$11,674,967	$5,720,734
Gross margin dollars				$1,055,100	$4,614,432	$8,351,869	$9,816,260	$4,936,697	$1,754,515
Gross margin percent				50.0%	45.6%	40.7%	35.5%	29.7%	23.5%
Engineering	$2,000,000	$2,000,000	$2,000,000	$1,000,000	$100,000	$100,000	$100,000	$100,000	$100,000
Marketing	16 Percent sales			$337,584	$1,620,403	$3,281,316	$4,429,777	$2,657,866	$1,196,040
G&A	5 Percent sales			$105,495	$506,376	$1,025,411	$1,384,305	$830,583	$373,762
Operating expense	$2,000,000		$2,000,000	$1,443,079	$2,226,779	$4,406,728	$5,914,083	$3,588,450	$1,669,802
Profit before tax (PBT)		($2,000,000)	($2,000,000)	($387,979)	$2,387,653	$3,945,141	$3,902,177	$1,348,248	$84,713
Cumulative PBT		($2,000,000)	($4,000,000)	($4,387,979)	($2,000,326)	$1,944,815	$5,846,992	$7,195,240	$7,279,953
Return on sales (PBT/dollar sales)				-18.4%	23.6%	19.2%	14.1%	8.1%	1.1%

Lower profit

Cumulative sales $84,518,670
Cumulative gross margin $30,528,874
Cumulative PBT $7,279,953
Average percent gross margin 36.1%
Average percent return on sales 8.6%

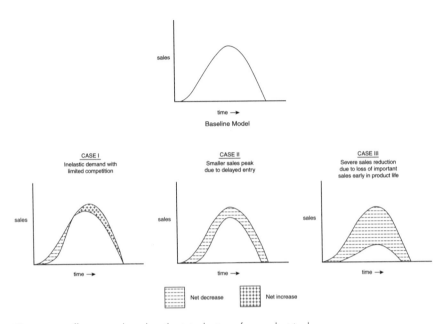

The various effects on sales when the introduction of a product is delayed.

FIGURE 2-3

Table 2-5 shows the profit impact calculations for a six-month delay. In this case we choose six months because it is usually large enough to have significant impact and small enough to remain within the linear range. In our experience, unless there are major discontinuities within the interval, you should choose a delay interval that is about 10 percent of the overall shipping life of the product.[1] Once the baseline case and variations have been prepared, we are ready to assess the profit impact.

Assess Profit Impact and Develop Decision Rules

The profit impact of each variation scenario can be assessed by comparing it to the baseline scenario. For the model just calculated, the profit variations are shown in Figure 2-4. While such data can be sur-

[1] If there are major discontinuities, the best approach is to break the cost of delay into a combination of piecewise linear segments and discontinuities which can be valued as step functions. This goes beyond the simple analysis we are illustrating in this book.

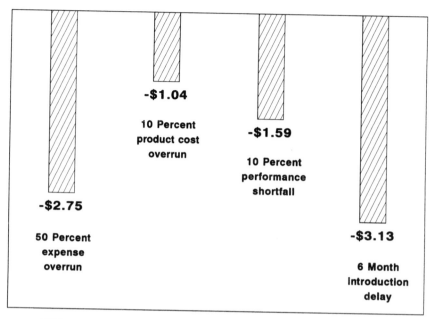

-$1.04

**10 Percent
product cost
overrun**

-$1.59

**10 Percent
performance
shortfall**

-$2.75

**50 Percent
expense
overrun**

-$3.13

**6 Month
introduction
delay**

Millions

The variation in life-cycle profits for the four scenarios.

FIGURE   2-4

prising to those who have never done such analysis, it is not partic-ularly useful. The true value of this analysis comes from converting the results into a set of decision rules for making tactical trade-offs on the project. These decision rules give us a way to convert a change in one or more of the four key objectives into the common denominator of life-cycle profit impact. The decision rules are created by scaling our profit changes to easily handled values such as changes of 1 per-cent or 1 month. For example, rather than saying that profits drop by $2.8 million because of a six-month delay, we express this as an av-erage profit decrease of about $470,000 per month.[2] If a 10 percent product cost overrun results in a $1 million profit impact, this can be expressed as approximately $100,000 per percent of product cost overrun. The decision rules for the case we have chosen are shown in Figure 2-5. In our experience, it is only when the model has been translated into these decision rules that it becomes a useful aid for decision making.

---

[2]Note that it is only time on the critical path that is worth the cost of delay.

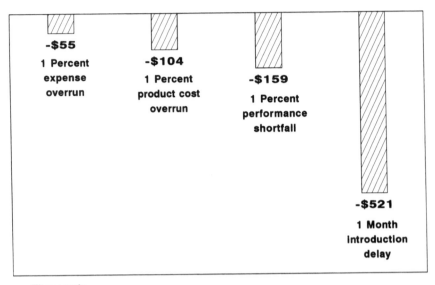

Thousands

The profit impact is converted into decision rules.

FIGURE   2-5

These decision rules are just the coefficients for an equation that states the changes in total life-cycle profits are a linear function of changes in introduction date, unit cost, product performance, and development expense. By determining these coefficients, we can make trade-offs between these parameters. The assumption that these four factors explain changes in profit is useful and accurate enough for most products. The assumption that these changes are linear is a good approximation when we are dealing with small variations from the baseline model. We can make this assumption even more accurate by choosing variation scenarios that do not include major discontinuities, such as trade shows.

These decision rules allow us to assess situations where more than one objective changes at the same time. For example, the development team may wish to delay the project to add a feature that is important to some of the customers. What should they do: make the customers happy or meet the schedule? Such questions can only be answered adequately by quantifying the effects of the decision. If it would add two months of delay that are valued at $521,000 per month, the cost of the delay is $1,042,000. The extra feature must therefore add at least this much to the product's life-cycle profits. Since each

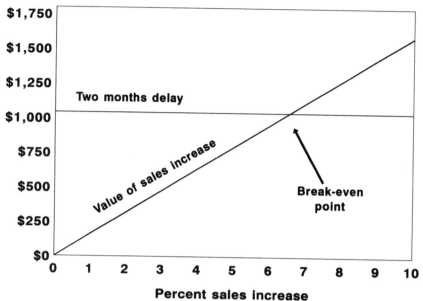

Using decision rules to trade-off delay versus the benefit of adding a feature.

FIGURE   2-6

percentage increase in sales revenue is worth $159,000, this means we need to achieve about 7 percent higher sales volume to counter-act the negative effects of delay. As shown in Figure 2-6, it would be a poor decision to add this feature if we could not expect such a sales increase. In fact, it is quite likely that the feature could be added dur-ing a model extension, or else saved for a future product (see Chap-ter 4).

ADVANCED MODELING

The previous section gave you a basic introduction to modeling for a single product. Certain cases are more complex to model, such as prod-ucts with long lives, interacting products, and products with high prices and low volume.

Long Product Lives

Some products have very long shipping lives, often in the range of 15 to 30 years. These are typically niche products in markets where the technology changes slowly. Since the economic analysis includes the entire life-cycle sales of the product, this means we need to forecast selling prices, unit costs, and unit sales 20 or 30 years into the future. Needless to say, people become uncomfortable making such forecasts.

In reality, errors in long-range forecasting have little effect on the decision rules, a fact that you can verify for yourself with some test calculations. As we explained earlier in this chapter, our sensitivity analysis is always comparing the baseline model with an alternative scenario. The further into the future we go the more these two cases will converge. While we may incorrectly forecast unit cost 20 years in the future, this error is embedded in both cases and it cancels out.

This points the way to a quick approximation of the cost of delay for a product with a long product life. Let us look at the extreme case, which is a product with an infinite shipping life. In such cases we often find, as you can see in Figure 2-7, the sales curve for the baseline scenario and the delayed scenario converge. In effect, at some point in the future the marketplace has no memory as to whether you introduced your product in January or June many years ago. In these cases the entire cost of delay is caused by the profit loss before this convergence point. The amount of lost revenue can be approximated as the area of a parallelogram. The height of this parallelogram is the peak sales and the base is amount of delay. This lost sales can be converted into lost profit before tax by using the average variable margin[3] during the period before convergence. This calculation illustrates why many developers approximate the cost of delay for a product by assuming they have lost an equivalent period of peak sales. Of course, this approximation is only true when you have convergence. If there is a permanent loss in market share due to later entry, then delay does much more damage and the lost profit is much higher.

This case also illustrates a more general principle: only a small portion of the financial impact of being late to market shows up during the period of delay. The true impact is caused by the fact that you have shifted the timing of the sales ramp. As you can see in Figure 2-7, only a small portion of the lost revenue occurs between the baseline introduction date and the delayed introduction date.

---

[3]Variable margin is the percent profit after all variable costs are paid. It is normally smaller than gross margin because it includes *variable operating expenses*. If you are unfamiliar with this term, just use *gross margin*, and you will still get a fairly accurate estimate of cost of delay.

Revenue

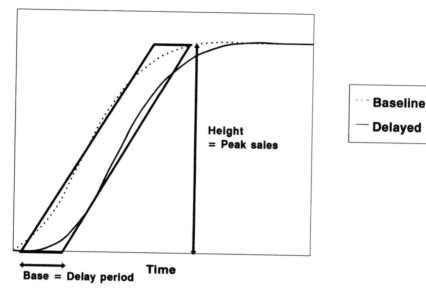

Approximating the cost of delay for long product lives.

FIGURE   2-7

Interacting Products

Another common complexity in modeling is the effect of interacting products. This can take place in the case of a product with an associated consumable or products that are replacing other products. The basic principle in these cases is to model all the revenue streams that change due to being late. For example, when a product has an associated consumable whose sales are influenced by the introduction of the product under development, we must add the revenue and gross margin of this consumable to the model. This means that both the baseline scenario and the variations will include the gross margin of the primary product and its consumables.

We use the same principle in modeling the effect of a product that replaces another product. Table 2-6 shows the baseline model for a product that replaces a another product which is beginning to lose margin. In this case, the newer product has a higher gross margin than the older product, because of its lower costs. Let us now consider the delayed scenario for this product, shown in Table 2-7. If the new product is introduced late, the sales of the old product will remain for a longer period of time and the sales of the new product will begin to build later. The net effect of a six-month delay is to is to cause a notch

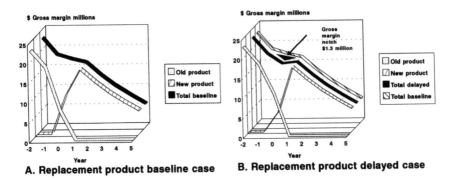

The gross margin notch caused by delaying a replacement product.

FIGURE 2-8

in the gross margin stream generated by the product, as shown in the right-hand chart in Figure 2-8.

Product with High Prices and Low Volume

A third situation that is challenging to model is that of products that have high prices and low volumes. For example, consider a system with a $10 million price tag. Over the life of this product only 10 such systems may be sold. In such cases the effect of delay must be calculated on the basis of how it affects individual orders, rather than by making simple adjustments in market share or sales revenue. This is done by creating a probability-weighted forecast of revenue and gross margin, which adds significant but necessary complexity to the model. For example, if the company has 50 percent market share, this means that there are 20 potential system sales that it could win. In the baseline model each of these sales has a timing, probability of win and an expected gross margin. In the delayed scenario each of these sales may have a different probability of win and expected gross margin because competitors will have a better chance of winning each order if you are late. Calculating the cost of delay and other decision rules is then a matter of determining the profit differences between scenarios and converting this into decision rules.

A Shortcut Method to Check the Model

Despite our counsel on simplifying models, many companies will develop elaborate models. How can you assess the reasonableness of such

TABLE 2-6

Baseline Product Profit Model for a Replacement Product

	Assumes	Year							
		-2	-1	0	1	2	3	4	5
Market size (units)	-10 Percent/year	60,000	60,000	60,000	60,000	60,000	60,000	60,000	60,000
Average sales price		$8,000	$7,200	$6,480	$5,832	$5,249	$4,724	$4,252	$3,826
Old product:									
Market share		10.0%	10.0%	5.0%	0.0%	0.0%	0.0%	0.0%	0.0%
Unit sales		6,000	6,000	3,000	0	0	0	0	0
Dollar sales		$48,000,000	$43,200,000	$19,440,000	$0	$0	$0	$0	$0
Unit cost	-2 Percent/year	$4,200	$4,116	$4,034	$3,953	$3,874	$3,796	$3,721	$3,646
Cost of goods sold		$25,200,000	$24,696,000	$12,101,040	$0	$0	$0	$0	$0
Gross margin dollars		$22,800,000	$18,504,000	$7,338,960	$0	$0	$0	$0	$0
New product:									
Market share		0.0%	0.0%	5.0%	10.0%	10.0%	10.0%	10.0%	10.0%
Unit sales		0	0	3,000	6,000	6,000	6,000	6,000	6,000
Dollar sales		$0	$0	$19,440,000	$34,992,000	$31,492,800	$28,343,520	$25,509,168	$22,958,251
Unit cost	-2 Percent/year	$3,300	$3,234	$3,169	$3,106	$3,044	$2,983	$2,923	$2,865
Cost of goods sold		$0	$0	$9,507,960	$18,635,602	$18,262,890	$17,897,632	$17,539,679	$17,188,886
Gross margin dollars		$0	$0	$9,932,040	$16,356,398	$13,229,910	$10,445,888	$7,969,489	$5,769,366
Total units		6,000	6,000	6,000	6,000	6,000	6,000	6,000	6,000
Total dollar sales		$48,000,000	$43,200,000	$38,880,000	$34,992,000	$31,492,800	$28,343,520	$25,509,168	$22,958,251
Total gross margin dollars		$22,800,000	$18,504,000	$17,271,000	$16,356,398	$13,229,910	$10,445,888	$7,969,489	$5,769,366
Engineering		$2,100,000	$2,100,000	$1,100,000	$100,000	$100,000	$100,000	$100,000	$100,000
Marketing	16 Percent sales	$7,680,000	$6,912,000	$6,220,800	$5,598,720	$5,038,848	$4,534,963	$4,081,467	$3,673,320
G&A	5 Percent sales	$2,400,000	$2,160,000	$1,944,000	$1,749,600	$1,574,640	$1,417,176	$1,275,458	$1,147,913
Operating expense		$12,180,000	$11,172,000	$9,264,800	$7,448,320	$6,713,488	$6,052,139	$5,456,925	$4,921,233
Profit before tax (PBT)		$10,620,000	$7,332,000	$8,006,200	$8,908,078	$6,516,422	$4,393,749	$2,512,564	$848,133
Cumulative PBT		$10,620,000	$17,952,000	$25,958,200	$34,866,278	$41,382,701	$45,776,450	$48,289,013	$49,137,146
Return on sales (PBT/dollar sales)		22.1%	17.0%	20.6%	25.5%	20.7%	15.5%	9.8%	3.7%
					Baseline				
Cumulative sales				$273,375,739					
Cumulative gross margin				$112,346,052					
Cumulative PBT				$49,137,146					
Average percent gross margin				41.1%					
Average percent return on sales				18.0%					

TABLE 2-7

Product Profit Model When a Replacement Product Is Delayed by Six Months

	Assumes				Year				
		-2	-1	0	1	2	3	4	5
Market size (units)	-10 Percent/year	60,000	60,000	60,000	60,000	60,000	60,000	60,000	60,000
Average sales price		$8,000	$7,200	$6,480	$5,832	$5,249	$4,724	$4,252	$3,826
Old product:				*More old product sales*					
Market share		10.0%	10.0%	7.5%	0.0%	0.0%	0.0%	0.0%	0.0%
Unit sales		6,000	6,000	4,500	0	0	0	0	0
Dollar sales		$48,000,000	$43,200,000	$29,160,000	$0	$0	$0	$0	$0
Unit cost	-2 Percent/year	$4,200	$4,116	$4,034	$3,953	$3,874	$3,796	$3,721	$3,646
Cost of goods sold		$25,200,000	$24,696,000	$18,151,560	$0	$0	$0	$0	$0
Gross margin dollars		$22,800,000	$18,504,000	$11,008,440	$0	$0	$0	$0	$0
New product:				*Less new product sales*					
Market share		0.0%	0.0%	2.5%	10.0%	10.0%	10.0%	10.0%	10.0%
Unit sales		0	0	1,500	6,000	6,000	6,000	6,000	6,000
Dollar sales		$0	$0	$9,720,000	$34,992,000	$31,492,800	$28,343,520	$25,509,168	$22,958,251
Unit cost	-2 Percent/year	$3,300	$3,234	$3,169	$3,106	$3,044	$2,983	$2,923	$2,865
Cost of goods sold		$0	$0	$4,753,980	$18,635,602	$18,262,890	$17,897,632	$17,539,679	$17,188,886
Gross margin dollars		$0	$0	$4,966,020	$16,356,398	$13,229,910	$10,445,888	$7,969,489	$5,769,366
Total units		6,000	6,000	6,000	6,000	6,000	6,000	6,000	6,000
Total dollar sales		$48,000,000	$43,200,000	$38,880,000	$34,992,000	$31,492,800	$28,343,520	$25,509,168	$22,958,251
Total gross margin dollars		$22,800,000	$18,504,000	$15,974,460	$16,356,398	$13,229,910	$10,445,888	$7,969,489	$5,769,366
Engineering		$2,100,000	$2,100,000	$1,100,000	$1,100,000	$100,000	$100,000	$100,000	$100,000
Marketing	16 Percent sales	$7,680,000	$6,912,000	$6,220,800	$5,598,720	$5,038,848	$4,534,963	$4,081,467	$3,673,320
G&A	5 Percent sales	$2,400,000	$2,160,000	$1,944,000	$1,749,600	$1,574,640	$1,417,176	$1,275,458	$1,147,913
Operating expense		$12,180,000	$11,172,000	$9,264,800	$7,448,320	$6,713,488	$6,052,139	$5,456,925	$4,921,233
Profit before tax (PBT)		$10,620,000	$7,332,000	$6,709,660	$8,908,078	$6,516,422	$4,393,749	$2,512,564	$848,133
Cumulative PBT		$10,620,000	$17,952,000	$24,661,660	$33,569,738	$40,086,161	$44,479,910	$46,992,473	$47,840,606
Return on sales (PBT/dollar sales)		22.1%	17.0%	17.3%	25.5%	20.7%	15.5%	9.8%	3.7%

Lower profit (Year 1)

Cumulative sales	$273,375,739
Cumulative gross margin	$111,049,512
Cumulative PBT	$47,840,606
Average percent gross margin	40.6%
Average percent return on sales	17.5%

a model without checking every calculation? There is a way to approximate the decision rules for a development project. We will introduce you to this shortcut method for one important reason. It allows you to do a "sanity check" on the output of the full financial model. You can quickly determine whether the decision rules are reasonable for the product. These quick calculations help you become a better user of financial models.

We must stress that these shortcut calculations should be used to check financial models, not as a substitute for them. While these calculations are fast, they contain some generic assumptions that will make them inaccurate in certain situations, such as when products have long lives or suffer a permanent loss of market share when they are delayed.

You can follow these calculations in Figure 2-9, where they are done using data from the original baseline model of Table 2-1. The first decision rule we calculate is the effect of an overrun of development expense. This is simply 1 percent of the total one-time costs of the project. This approximation will give us a decision rule of $55,000 per percent change in development expense, which is the same as the result of the spreadsheet calculation. Next, we approximate the effect of a unit cost overrun. This is 1 percent of the unit costs during the period that the cost overrun persists. For example, if you correct cost overruns within six months of product introduction, it would be 1 percent of the cost of goods sold during these six months. If you correct cost overruns within one year, it would be 1 percent of the cost of goods sold during the first year. This approximation gives us a decision rule of $104,000 per percent unit cost overrun, which is the same as the results of the spreadsheet calculation. Next, we approximate the effect of a product performance shortfall. This is 1 percent of life-cycle revenue times the variable margin[4] of the product. This calculation gives us a decision rule of $159,000 per percent performance shortfall, which is the same as the decision rule produced by the spreadsheet.

Finally, we can approximate the cost of delay. This approximation is the least accurate, but nonetheless it is dramatically more accurate than intuition. We take one-eighth[5] of the first-year unit shipments, multiply by the average selling price over the life of the product, multiply by the number of years of shipping life, and multiply by the

---

[4]Again, if you are unfamiliar with variable margin, just use the gross margin as an approximation.

[5]This factor comes from assuming a linear ramp that is shifted by six months. The geometry of such a shift reduces first-year unit sales by three-fourths. When this is scaled to months, the factor becomes one eighth. $(3/4 \times 1/6 = 1/8)$.

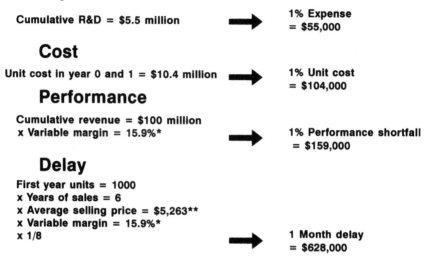

Shortcut calculations of decision rules for checking the financial model.

FIGURE 2-9

---

variable margin of the product.[6] This calculation gives us a decision rule of $628,000 per month of delay which is 34 percent higher than the decision rule produced by the spreadsheet. While this error may seem substantial, it is actually surprisingly accurate given the speed with which it can be calculated. Remember that our intuition is likely to produce an answer that is off by a minimum of 1,000 percent. This means that in one minute of effort we have improved the quality of the answer by at least 30-fold.

 Please don't use these approximate calculations as a substitute for the more detailed spreadsheet analysis since they can be misleading in certain specific situations, such as when products have long lives or suffer a permanent loss of market share when they are delayed. Instead, use them as a tool to quickly detect major flaws in your financial model. If the model passes the "sanity check" it is probably good enough. If it fails, check the numbers. We usually find that when a model fails the

---

[6]The shortcut calculation assumes that the delayed sales curve is the baseline shifted downward. We calculate lost units in year one, scale it up to lost units over life, convert units to revenue, convert revenue to profits, and we get an estimate of cost of delay.

"sanity check," there is a fundamental problem in either the design of the model or in the calculations. For example, at one company the model produced answers that didn't make sense. A careful review of the model revealed that all of the data were cut off beyond a certain date.

A financial model done correctly will always be more accurate than the shortcut calculations; however, the shortcut calculations can be very valuable to detect subtle problems in the model.

TIPS ON MODELING

There are a few things to watch out for as you use the financial models as part of your development process. First, we will discuss the biggest source of modeling errors. Second, we will explain why it is so important to keep models simple. Third, we will discuss why these models are best done as a team activity. Finally, we will cover what management can do to encourage the use of these models.

Sources of Error

Virtually none of the errors in models are caused by insufficiently detailed computational methods. Instead, accuracy is almost always controlled by the accuracy of the input data. This means that the leverage in improving the accuracy of the model lies in improving the accuracy of the input data, not in doing more elaborate financial computations. By the time your model fills more than one sheet of paper, your computations have probably gone beyond the accuracy of your input data.

Although we have at times used such sophisticated techniques as net present value, discounted cash flow analysis, and internal rate of return analysis, these techniques usually add unnecessary complexity. This is particularly true for products with sales lives of five years or less. As we shall explain later, the complexity of these techniques creates some very practical problems for development teams.

When we review models to determine which particular piece of input data was the biggest source of error, the answer is strikingly consistent. There is one single area where the input data can be off by a factor of 10: the forecast of unit sales. No other area causes as much difficulty, because accurate unit sales forecasts depend on both an accurate forecast of market size and market share. If you have an extra 10 hours to spend on the model, spend it on improving the accuracy of the sales forecast.

Keep it Simple

There is another very practical reason to avoid complex models: most people don't understand them. Simple models can be understood by 100 percent of the project team. The true measure of the value of a model is whether it actually influences behavior. If people do not understand a model, they are less likely to let it influence their behavior. Furthermore, a simple model is more transparent in the sense that you can perceive its inner workings and easily see when its assumptions are breaking down. Too often complex models become the domain of isolated experts. Their complexity either prevents the team from trusting them, or even worse, causes the team to trust a model long after it has ceased to accurately model reality. The real world requires simple models that are easily understood and easily maintained.

As you pursue this simplicity don't be surprised if the first few models you do are too complex. It takes a certain amount of experience to learn which factors are really important and which have a minor effect on the calculations. The best way to create simple models is to begin using these financial models. As you gain experience you will find yourself streamlining your models, a fact that will be appreciated by everyone who has to use them.

Cross-Functional Involvement

In our experience it is very important to do these financial models early in a project using the full cross-functional team. One obvious reason for doing this is because the data required to develop such a model come from Marketing, Engineering, Manufacturing, and Finance. You are unlikely to develop a accurate model if you leave the task to any one of these functions. Furthermore, even if the model was accurate you would miss an opportunity to create ownership in it. We consistently find that when team members participate in the construction and analysis of the model they develop a deeper understanding of the key economic success factors for the project, especially the connections between cycle time and profitability. Teams that create their own models believe the models and use them. Too often teams that have a model created for them simply ignore it.

For example, Keithley Instruments, Inc. is a leading supplier of electronic measurement systems. Charles Cimino, the Project Manager for a sophisticated instrument called the 2400 SourceMeter™, generated the decision rules for the project and kept them in front of everyone working on the project. He observed that the decision rules were useful every time there was a question of priorities, which at times was hourly. By making the trade-off rules visible, thousands of decisions were made both better and faster.

The Finance Department is an essential member of the modeling team for three reasons. First, it provides important data required to do the model and has the skills to set up the spreadsheets quickly. Second, it ensures that the modeling is done consistently between projects. Finally, it is an impartial group that is trusted by management. Whenever a model is done without the Finance Department involved, senior managers tend to view it with skepticism. Every development team should have a Financial Analyst assigned to it as a Financial Adviser (see Chapter 7).

Management Support

Up to now we have covered the technical aspects of financial modeling. We must also make some observations about the politics of this modeling. Too often we see teams develop decision rules which fall into disuse. When we search for the breakdown we invariably discover that management has been sending conflicting signals to the team. On one hand, managers insists that they want the team to make sound business decisions based on facts. On the other hand, they permit decisions to be proposed that have not been framed in economic terms, and appear to sanction decisions based solely on intuition. For example, at one company management forced the team to switch suppliers in the middle of the project because of a dispute with one of the suppliers. The change in suppliers cost several months of schedule, which was far more expensive than the disputed section of the contract. It became very difficult to get this team to adopt a decision-making approach based on economics when team members felt their managers ignored this in their own decisions.

Thus, it is extremely important for managers to role model rational decision making if this is how they desire teams to make decisions. When decisions are proposed without considering the economics, they should be sent back with the question, "How does this affect the economics of the project?" This does not mean that economics should be the only basis for decisions, but rather that they should always be considered. There is nothing wrong with choosing a course of action because you "feel" it is a lower risk approach; however, you should try to quantify the economics underlying this choice. Think of the low-risk approach as an insurance policy. You need to know whether you are paying $1,000 or $1 million for the insurance.

As organizations move to incorporate financial modeling in their development process, we have noticed that the easiest way to institutionalize it is to embed it in the business planning process. Since most business plans already include a baseline model to assess whether the project is worth investing in, it is simple to add the sensitivity analysis as a step in the business plan. This ensures that decision rules are automatically developed for every project that is funded. Furthermore, having the decision rules available at the time of funding is useful because they affect how heavily a company may wish to staff a particular project. In fact, at one company we discovered that the financial analyst was already doing all of the sensitivity analysis but had not been including it in the business plan because no one had ever asked for it.

In this chapter we have introduced you to what is probably the single most important tool contained in this book. You should retain three fundamental ideas. First, there is a knowable cost of delay for development projects that can be quantified systematically. Second, that this cost of delay can be used to balance development speed against other important economic objectives by using decision rules. Third, that unless management constantly forces decision makers to use these rational decision rules, they will fall into disuse. In our next chapter we will begin to apply this way of thinking to the beginning of the development process.

SUGGESTED READING

Reinertsen, Donald G. 1983. Whodunit? The search for the new-product killers. *Electric Business* 9 (8): 62ff–65. The earliest illustration of the modeling techniques covered here. This piece is often quoted as saying that a six-month delay cuts project profit by 33 percent, as though it were a universal constant. As this article makes clear, the "universal constant" is different for each project.

CHAPTER 3

The Fuzzy Front End

Time is an irreplaceable resource. When a month of potential development time is squandered, it can never be recovered. As we saw in the last chapter, each month of delay has a quantifiable cost of delay. Our goal as developers is to find opportunities to buy cycle time for less than this cost. These opportunities, large and small, appear throughout the development process. There is, however, one place that we could call the "bargain basement" of cycle-time reduction opportunities. It is the place that we consistently find the least expensive opportunities to achieve large improvements in time to market. We call this stage of development the Fuzzy Front End of the development program. It is the fuzzy zone between when the opportunity is known and when we mount a serious effort on the development project.

This chapter explains what causes delay in this early stage and what to do about it. As in much of the rest of this book, the approach here is different than is usual in other books on product development. Such books generally emphasize careful selection of the right opportunity rather than the speed of the selection process. The underlying logic of such conventional approaches is that the most expensive mistake in the Fuzzy Front End is the selection of an imperfect opportunity, and that this mistake is best avoided by adding more checks and balances to this stage. This logic is quite sound when markets are predictable and the cost of delay is low. However, it breaks down in fast-moving markets and when the cost of delay is high. In fast-moving markets, quick decision making shortens your planning horizon, which allows you to use more accurate shorter-term forecasts. On projects with a high cost of delay errors in opportunity selection may be much less expensive than starting a project late. Thus, speed can be a key driver of both the accuracy and cost of the Fuzzy Front End.

A simple test of your front-end processes is to ask how long it would take for you to begin work on a compelling product opportunity if it landed on your desk today. The sad answer in most companies is that it would take months and sometimes years before the first engineer would begin development work. You would be astonished at the systemic delays that have been built into your process. An IBM employee once pointed out that in the early 1980s, if you followed the accepted IBM product development process, it would take three years to ship an empty box.

WHY THE FUZZY FRONT END IS IMPORTANT

Three critical factors combine to make the Fuzzy Front End an area of extraordinary opportunity. First, it is a lengthy stage for most development projects. Second, it is full of cheap time-compression opportunities. Finally, it is an area in which the performance of individual companies varies dramatically. Let us look at each of these factors in turn.

It Lasts a Long Time

The first step to understanding the Fuzzy Front End is quantifying its duration. In Figure 3-1 we have drawn some project time lines from actual projects. Three events are listed on each time line: the time at which the product opportunity first became—or should have become— visible to the organization, the time at which a full development team started working on it, and the date when the first unit was shipped to a paying customer. Notice the extraordinary opportunity to save time at the front end. Roughly half the time to market has elapsed before the team is even assigned.

The time lines shown are not worst-case examples. In our consulting experience we have seen situations where as much as 90 percent of the development cycle elapsed before the team started work. In one case, a company sat on a new product idea for 15 years, then initiated a crash two-year development effort.

In doing this analysis it is extremely important to go back to factual data, because people's memories of the Fuzzy Front End tend to

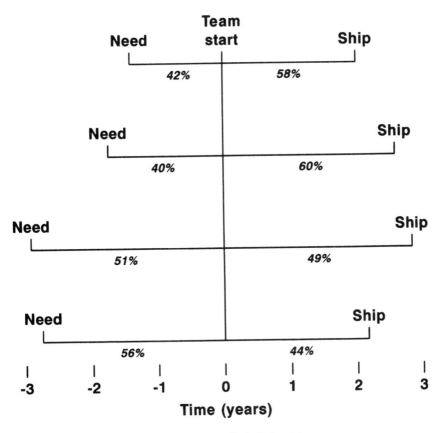

Time lines for four typical development projects, all of which exhibit a
long front-end period.

FIGURE   3-1

be especially fuzzy. People incorrectly remember both the time when
the opportunity was available and the time when a full development
team was started.

It Is a Cheap Place to Shop

The second striking thing we will notice about the Fuzzy Front End is
that it is an extremely cheap place to shop for cycle time. If we analyze the typical actions that we can take to buy a week of cycle time
at various stages of the development process, we discover enormous
differences in the price we have to pay. For example, one consumer
product company spent $750,000 to buy three weeks of cycle time near
the end of its development process by accelerating the shipment of

critical capital equipment. This was a sound business decision, because the cost of delay on the program was much higher than $250,000 per week. Yet the same three weeks could have been purchased for less than $100 a week during the Fuzzy Front End. This is 2,500 times cheaper! This is why we call it the "bargain basement" of cycle-time reduction opportunities.

Individual Companies Have Big Performance Differences

Another thing we will notice about the Fuzzy Front End is that companies differ extraordinarily in how they manage this phase. In one case, a well-managed *Fortune* 500 company saw a compelling opportunity at a trade show. The company did everything by the book, preparing a business plan, screening through their strategic planning process, and allocating R&D dollars for it in the budget. When qualified engineers became available to do the project, they began work. Unfortunately, it took 18 months before the first engineering hour was invested in the project. Meanwhile, a small start-up company had been to the same trade show and seen the same opportunity. The Chief Engineer of this company, who also happened to be the President, recognized the compelling nature of the opportunity and began designing a product to exploit it on the plane flight returning from the trade show. The start-up company had its entire product designed before the "well-managed" company had even begun development. The Fuzzy Front End at the start-up company was 500 times faster than it was at the Fortune 500 company where well-intentioned planning and budgeting processes guaranteed defeat.

What is striking about this example is that the Fortune 500 company had lost the race to market before it had even begun to develop the product. There was no way to recover from the front-end delays, even if the company had been able to complete the development program instantly.

DRAWING ATTENTION TO THE FUZZY FRONT END

To fix the Fuzzy Front End, you must think clearly about it. The economic analysis introduced in the last chapter is a good starting point. If we examined the economics of the Fuzzy Front End, we would observe that this stage usually consumes a small amount of the development budget, but it constitutes a large portion of available cycle time. The true cost of the Fuzzy Front End is much higher than managers suspect. The most important component of its cost is the cost of delay, not the cost of the people assigned to the project. The calculated cost of delay is often 500 to 5,000 times higher than the visible costs of assigned personnel. Because total front-end costs are dominated by the cost of delay, it follows that the economic parameter to measure and optimize is the duration of this front-end process. To measure time at the front end we use the concept of a market clock.

The Market Clock

The market clock measures the time it takes us to respond to opportunities in the marketplace. It starts ticking when a customer opportunity appears and continues inexorably until the customer's need is filled. The market clock is unforgiving. It keeps on ticking whether we are working on the project or not, and with each passing minute we pay the cost of delay. This cost keeps accumulating steadily even when nobody is working on the project.

When you view projects this way you will recognize that a week of delay in starting the project has the same economic cost as a week of delay at the end of a project. Thus, we should treat a week spent at the front end of a project with the same care that we would treat a week consumed at the very end. Such an attitude is sadly lacking in most companies. Instead, they have what we call a "burn rate" mindset. They worry about activities in proportion to the rate at which they consume, or "burn," money. Such a mindset assumes that there is no cost as long as no money is being spent. It treats cycle time as a free resource. This mindset is a natural consequence of failing to understand the true economics of product development. Once we calculate the cost of delay and attune our ear to the subtle but relentless ticking of the market clock, we can begin to focus on the true economic leverage points in the program.

The Urgency Paradox

Understanding the underlying economics also allows us to overcome the urgency paradox. This is the cruel tendency of the urgency of product development to be highest at the point in time when the market opportunity is lowest. Early in the life of a project there seems to be little urgency. Although the market opportunity is greatest at this time, the opportunity is not too apparent and there is little fear of competi-

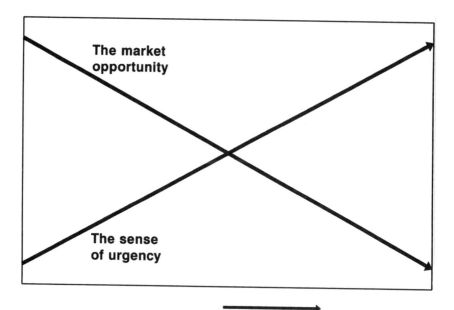

The urgency paradox: a sense of urgency and the market opportunity
behave oppositely.

FIGURE   3-2

tive product introductions. As the program progresses the opportunity
diminishes for your company as it becomes clearer to others and competitive activity heats up. Urgency rises. Once a competitor has introduced its first product, urgency rises to a feverish level, although the
market opportunity is waning. Unfortunately, this sense of urgency is
misaligned with the opportunities for leverage in the development
process, as we illustrate in Figure 3-2. It is exactly at the stage when
urgency is lowest that we have the greatest opportunity to cheaply influence the project.

IMPROVING FRONT-END PROCESSES

Let us now look at some specific actions you can take to shorten front-
end cycle time.

Institute Metrics

A first critical step in any attempt to shorten front-end cycle time is to measure it. Operating parameters that are not measured do not spontaneously improve. We begin by measuring the duration of the front end, because cycle time is the parameter of greatest economic importance here. To measure cycle time, we must agree on what marks the beginning and end of the Fuzzy Front End.

In theory the front end begins when a company could start working on an opportunity. Think of product development as a race. The Fuzzy Front End starts as soon as any competitor could start working on the opportunity, because you are falling behind after this point. From a practical point of view this is a difficult definition to use, because it requires detailed knowledge of competitor development activities. Instead, we normally use a less accurate but simpler definition. We consider the front end to have started when two conditions have been met. First, the idea must be documented as an opportunity, and thus visible to management. Second, the technology to implement the idea must exist somewhere in the world. The second criterion is important because it marks the critical distinction between product development and technology development. As we will explain in Chapter 4, we cannot consistently achieve rapid development by doing technology development on the critical path of programs.

The end of the front end can be defined in different ways. Some companies will use the opening of an accounting charge number for the project as the key marker that serious development has begun. This approach is easy to implement, but it has a serious deficiency. As we will see in Chapter 11, a major impediment to fast development in most companies is the inability to obtain adequate human resources once the project has been "approved." Approving a project or opening an account for it is free; the real test comes when substantial numbers of people start charging time to it. Thus, a more rigorous marker is when the team has been fully staffed, since little will actually happen without a team in place. In any case, develop a consistent definition and use it on all programs. When you do this you will suddenly be able to see how long the Fuzzy Front End is on your projects.

Calculate Cost of Delay

We must place a financial value on the front-end cycle time. We do this by using the cost of delay calculated as shown in Chapter 2. If we discover that the cost of delay is low, we don't need to invest a lot of effort in shortening the Fuzzy Front End. If it is high, we can justify spending effort and money to reduce it.

Assign Responsibilities

Make somebody responsible for this portion of the development cycle. By designating a specific individual responsible, you dramatically increase the chance that something will actually happen. The normal approach here is to assign the opportunity to the Marketing person who will later become a member of the development team. This is done because much of the work content in this stage is marketing activities. Using someone who will later be a team member will maintain continuity between planning activities and execution.

Assign Resources and Deadlines

Explicitly assign resources and deadlines to this stage of the process. When you analyze front-end processes, you will discover that they are composed of bursts of activity followed by long stretches of inactivity. These bursts of activity occur whenever a deadline is approaching. In 200 days of elapsed time 80 hours of work will be done on the business plan. You can cut the work in half and it will improve the cycle time by 5 days. In contrast, if you cut the inactivity in half you will improve the cycle time by 95 days. The primary way to shorten these periods of inactivity is to increase the percent of time that people working on front-end activities spend on these activities.

How do we increase the amount of time that people spend on front-end activities? First, we need to make it clear to people what percent of their time they are to spend on the project. If you want 80 hours of work done in 30 days you must be explicit that the people assigned will be working 50 percent of the time on this activity. This may require pulling them away from other duties, sequestering them in a hotel room off-site, and explaining to their boss that they are on a special assignment. If you fail to make the expectations of time commitment clear, you are likely to get less time than you expect.

The second step that we can take to increase the amount of time that people spend on front-end activities is to assign deadlines. This exploits the fact that most work actually takes place immediately before the deadline or, in some companies, right after it has been missed. For example, our 200-day front end could have been easily cut to 100 days simply be giving the team 100 days to accomplish it.

Underlying the lack of effort on Fuzzy Front End activities is often a set of values that suggests that these activities are less important than others that will bear fruit sooner. Consequently, be sure that corporate systems support the Fuzzy Front End, for example, by having adequate funds available for this phase and including it in job descriptions and performance appraisals. If the Fuzzy Front End is perpetually in a beggar mode it is unlikely to ever be very fast.

Capture Opportunities Frequently and Early

Capture new-product opportunities frequently and early. This is done by making it easy to submit an idea, and by collecting and reviewing these ideas frequently. This is a major shortcoming in the typical front-end process. Most companies require ideas to be substantiated with piles of data and analysis. Before any idea can be entered into the system, it must be justified with an elaborate business plan, then reviewed and approved by the entire management team. Because preparing and revising such a plan takes a lot of effort, the opportunity lies idle until Marketing finds time to complete it. A more effective approach is to make it very easy to enter an idea into the system. For example, one mechanical equipment company uses a simple one-page form that can be submitted by any employee. This project proposal form is reviewed to determine whether the idea justifies the investment of preparing a business plan. By making it very easy to enter an idea into the system, management has ensured that all ideas are visible to them very quickly. The objective of the idea-capture process is to achieve visibility, not to filter out bad ideas. The filtering activity should occur after the idea is visible to management.

In the typical company the idea-capture process is further crippled when management uses annual planning sessions to review new product opportunities. For example, consider what happens when a company does an annual new product planning session six months prior to the beginning of the next business year. The opportunities being reviewed will automatically be delayed by an average of 12 months. A much more effective approach is to look at new product ideas more frequently. For example, one small semiconductor company reviews new product opportunities once each month. This dramatically reduces the delay time in its front-end processes.

Subdivide the Planning

Subdivide initial planning activities and overlap them with design. Do we really need to complete all our planning activities before we begin any of our design activities? By overlapping these two processes, planning remains on the critical path of the project for the shortest time possible. In fact, it is possible to subdivide planning into pieces and overlap design activities with planning. This is illustrated in Figure 3-3.

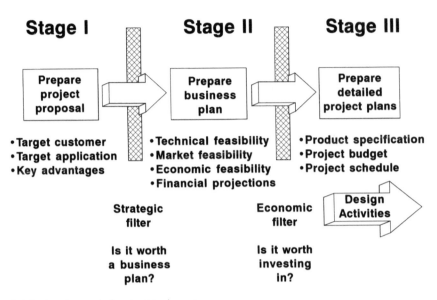

Subdividing front-end planning into three stages.

FIGURE   3-3

In the first stage of planning we determine the general nature of the opportunity. This is done by identifying the target customer, application, and the key advantage that the product will have over competing products and those currently offered in the portfolio. This information provides just enough data to assess the strategic fit of the opportunity. The key decision we will make at this point is whether we want to invest the time and effort to prepare a detailed business plan. If so, we can go on to the next stage. Note that at this point we have not defined a feature set for the product.

In the second stage of planning we will prepare a detailed business plan. At this stage we are creating an investment opportunity for the company. We need enough information to assess the economics of the project. To do this we have to assess technical, market, and economic feasibility of the opportunity. At this stage we create target costs and sales prices, profit projections, and an estimate of project duration and expense. We then decide whether to invest in the project.

Once the decision to invest has been made, we enter the third stage of planning. In this stage we prepare a detailed product specification, budget, and schedule. This is usually the most time-consuming stage of planning. We suggest doing this after the project team has been staffed and the project has started. The mistake that many companies make is to require this detailed planning to be done before they are willing to invest in the program. This creates three problems. First, this part of the planning is forced onto the critical path of the program, which means that we will incur the cost of delay while it is being done. Second, the future team members are precisely the ones who have the information needed to do this planning, so it is difficult to create realistic plans without them. Third, we miss the great opportunity of having the team members create *their* plan. This involvement in planning creates team ownership in the schedule, budget, and specification.

The essence of the approach just outlined is to displace the time-consuming third stage of planning into the design process. In practice, this means that these activities will take place faster, because project staffing is higher once the team has been staffed. The same 100 hours of work that would have taken six months to accomplish in a planning mode is accomplished in two weeks with a staffed team. Such an approach can produce a major reduction in cycle time without any significant increase in business risk.

Create Technology and Marketing Infrastructure

Too often technology development and market research are unnecessarily on the critical path of programs. This causes these activities to add enormous delay costs to the project.

Technology development is too often a source of project delays. Consider the example of a consumer electronics company with a line of high-tech products. Each product features some type of electronic technology that is new to the company. The company's policy is not to develop basic technologies or electronic components within the company. In a typical development program the company identifies a new product and writes a preliminary product specification using a product planning process that takes six to 12 months. Then the biggest delay starts. The company does not have the resources to develop the new technology called for in the product plans, nor does it know where to find it. Because no one in the organization has specific responsibility to find the needed technology, the project goes into a dormant state until the technology appears. Projects can sit in this state for years until the requisite technology appears, or a competitor's introduction triggers a panicked quest for the technology. In the next chapter we will discuss a superior approach, that of planning and managing technology development to support the product portfolio.

Some companies claim that their technology development must be done within development projects because they use cutting-edge technology. Often, we can avoid developing technology inside of a project by creating technology assessment activities. Compaq did this well in the early days of laptop computers. They were not the first to develop a laptop, but they did monitor the major components needed against their pre-established criteria. When displays, hard drives, etc. reached the threshold of maturity that Compaq thought necessary for success, they were prepared to jump into the market quickly.

Technology development proceeds according to a much less certain pace than product development. The management and scheduling approaches used for these two activities are much different. What this means for rapid product development is that including technology development within the project not only extends the schedule, it also provides excuses for delays in the portion of the project that could be scheduled more certainly. If new technology does have to be developed, it is wise to make this a separate phase of the project, then tighten up the controls when the technology is demonstrated.

We can use a similar approach for market research. Instead of viewing market research as an activity that occurs as an early step of product development, view it as an ongoing cost of business. To understand our customers, their preferences, our product applications, competitor products, and market trends should be an ongoing activity. We need to develop a base of market information independent of any specific new products. For example, one audio equipment maker does constant research on the product attributes that affect how the customer perceives the quality of the sound produced by its product. It has discovered that sound quality is a far more complex question than simple frequency response and distortion. It uses this research to accurately predict customer reaction to certain changes in the product. This means that the company can get instant answers on questions that used to require months of tailored market research.

Create a Strategy and a Master Plan

Create a strategy and a master plan for the entire product portfolio. The strategy defines which customers will be served, who we choose to compete with, and on what basis we will compete. The master plan for the product portfolio shows how products will be enhanced over time. For most businesses this can be fit onto a single sheet of paper. Figure 3-4 gives an example of such a master plan. In such a plan the horizontal axis is always time, while the vertical axis may vary depending on what is most useful for a particular business. A common choice is the selling price of the product, but it can also be organized by customer segments or applications.

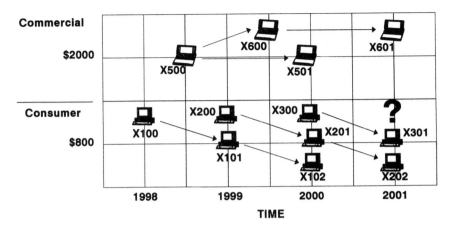

Sample product master plan.

FIGURE   3-4

A company gains enormous advantages when such a plan is widely understood and disseminated. It allows people to understand how their particular project fits into the overall plans of the company. Workers are always more motivated when they see how their activities relate to the "big picture." Furthermore, we find the existence of a plan prevents people from being distracted by other opportunities. One company we observed would only plan one product at a time. As development began on the product new ideas would become available. Since it was the only product that was scheduled to be developed it acted as a magnet for all these ideas. The team developing it was constantly fighting off new requirements being proposed by well-intentioned co-workers. When you have clearly identified follow-on products, the ideas can be deflected into these products.

Prevent Overloads

When too many ideas enter the planning process delays are inevitable. Eventually, the backlog can get so large that many of these ideas only get a cursory review. A better approach is to carefully assess how many ideas you can really evaluate in the course of a year. This is your process capacity. Then, monitor the number of ideas for which business plans are prepared. You need to keep the demand on the process less than its capacity or you will experience growing delays. We will discuss this issue of capacity management in more detail in Chapter 11.

Create a Quick-Reaction Plan

There is one more tool that can often be useful to overcome slow front-end processes. It does not address the root cause of the problem, but it can provide valuable temporary relief. It consists of creating a quick reaction plan for exploiting an unanticipated new product opportunity.

The military has long recognized that the time to plan for war is before war begins. They attempt to define likely military or political scenarios, then develop written plans to deal with these scenarios. If one of these scenarios should ever occur, they can implement the plan for it and have a large organization working in unison quickly. Though war plans are imperfect, they help to eliminate much of the confusion and consequent wasted motion that arise when an unexpected event occurs.

The same approach can be applied to preparing for an unexpected new product idea. When such an idea emerges, it often gets little attention because everyone is busy with their regular job. However, if a quick reaction plan is put into effect, everyone's duties and deadlines become much clearer and the new product idea can get a fast start.

The plan need not be an elaborate document. A task force of the pivotal interested parties—perhaps Marketing, Engineering, Manufacturing, and Finance—should write the plan and have top management approve it. The plan should have an aggressive but feasible timetable. On each day, specific activities of a marketing, technical, or financial nature should occur. At the end of the planned schedule a development project should be running, unless a decision was made along the way to abort it.

Just writing a plan and approving it accomplishes a lot. Writing it forces people to identify the important activities and put them in sequence. It implicitly says that other, unlisted, activities are not necessary to evaluate a new product idea. It alleviates the sense of indecision in which people wonder, "What do we do now?"

Approval of the plan is where top management "signs up" for a new style of handling new product decisions. The war plan usually differs from the normal process of dealing with new product ideas. Thus, everyone must make some changes to follow the plan without delaying the process. By signing the plan, management indicates its willingness to be the first to change in order to enjoy the benefits of getting a product to market faster.

In executing the plan, the key point—and the most difficult one, we have found—is for the general manager to extricate essential people from their regular duties to begin implementing the plan. Let us illustrate this with an actual example. A client of ours who serves the electronics industry normally took a couple of years to complete the Fuzzy Front End of a project. To improve this the client formed a task force to write a quick reaction plan. The General Manager assigned representatives from Marketing, Engineering, and Finance as well as an independent chair, and charged the group with writing a plan that could be executed in 60 days. The plan was submitted to and approved by the General Manager.

The plan was executed twice, each time with the same sad outcome. According to plan, the technical and marketing issues were in turn identified, addressed, and resolved. Unfortunately, it proved much more difficult to resolve the staffing issues. Since this company was a division of a large, diversified corporation with tight controls on headcount, it proved impossible to get new resources to start an unanticipated project and impossible to reserve capacity for an unidentified opportunity. The moral is to think carefully about where the resources will come from to exercise the quick reaction plan. Otherwise, you will be fooling yourself into thinking you have a capacity to react, which in reality is missing.

A SAMPLE FRONT-END PROCESS

Let us pull this all together by describing the sample front-end process shown in Figure 3-5. It integrates the steps that we have described previously. The project starts with a one-page project proposal form that can be submitted by any employee. This is reviewed at the monthly meeting of the New Product Steering Committee (NPSC). The committee determines if the idea appears to have business merit and whether it fits the stated strategy of the company. If it does, the NPSC assigns two people the task of preparing a business plan for the project. This assignment does four things. First, the NPSC identifies what key issues must be addressed in the business plan. Instead of requiring a standard one-size-fits-all business plan, the NPSC requests detail only on those factors that will make or break the investment decisions. Second, the NPSC states how much time it expects the people to spend working on the business plan. This allows the people working on the plan to assess whether they need relief from other duties to create it. Third, the NPSC establishes an appropriate budget for any technical feasibility studies or market research. Finally, the NPSC establishes a deadline for when the plan must be returned to them. The people who are chosen to prepare the plan are typically a senior marketing person and a senior engineer. They are usually key players on the team that

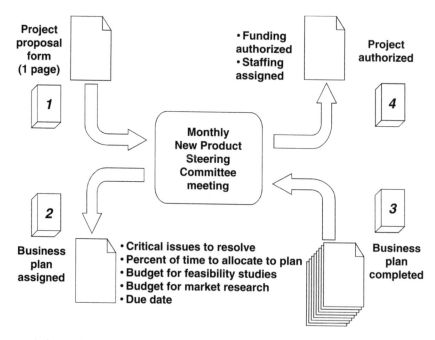

Sample front-end process.

FIGURE   3-5

will eventually be formed to start the project. This continuity is important to maintain momentum on the program.

By the designated deadline the business plan is submitted to the NPSC. The NPSC will then assess the economics of the proposed project to determine if it should be funded. It will also look at the existing portfolio of projects and determine when the project can be started. This may require shifting resources from an existing lower priority project. If this is done, the project losing resources must be rescheduled. Once the project is funded the team is staffed and begins work. As mentioned earlier, the initial activities of the team include preparing a detailed specification, budget, and schedule. This is a detailed version of information provided in the business plan. Because it is prepared by the people who will actually do the work, it will be more accurate and the workers will actually own it.

Other Process Alternatives

There are, of course, many other alternatives for structuring front-end processes. Let us review two common alternatives, starting with the new products group. Such a group can reside in Marketing, R&D, or another area, such as with a Vice President of New Products. Since this group has full-time responsibility for processing new product ideas, it tends to process ideas quickly. To make this group work, it must have the technical expertise needed, both in marketing and technology, to assess an idea adequately. There are two disadvantages with such a group. First, if the group lies in a particular functional area, such as Engineering or Marketing, it may conduct an imbalanced review of the idea. Second, it creates an inevitable hand-off to a development team. This hand-off can waste time, lose valuable unwritten product information, and undermine product ownership. All of these difficulties can be mastered.

A second common alternative is the ad hoc process. For example, the story is told of how Ken Olsen, the former CEO of Digital Equipment, once called a manager into his office and told him to put five people into a hotel room to plan a new product. In a week they had a well-thought-out idea that sailed through the development process with surprising smoothness, and was successful in the marketplace. Such an approach definitely works, but it can be disruptive to the rest of the product portfolio. It also does nothing to build a product development process that everyone understands. It should be reserved for the true emergencies that have very high costs of delay.

In this chapter we have given you a tour of a chronically undermanaged portion of the development process in most companies. The Fuzzy Front End is the "bargain basement" of cycle-time reduction opportunities. We will have to pay 100 to 1,000 times the price to buy the same amount of time later in the development cycle. As a result, smart managers pay careful attention to this stage of the development process.

SUGGESTED READING

Cooper, Robert G. 1993. *Winning at New Products.* Reading, Mass.: Addison-Wesley. Much of the marketing-oriented new products literature concentrates on screening in the front end of the development cycle to enhance the prospects for product success. This book is a good example of such literature. The trick is to accelerate such screening, taking the cost of delay into account.

Wheelwright, Steven C., and Kim B. Clark. 1992. *Revolutionizing Product Development: Quantum Leaps in Speed, Efficiency, and Quality.* New York: The Free Press. Rapid development requires a well-articulated product strategy as well as product line and technology plans. For additional coverage on these topics, see Chapters 2–4 of Wheelwright and Clark. However, note that it has little focus on development speed.

The Power and Pitfalls of Incremental Innovation

The rest of the book covers techniques that enable us to accomplish development tasks faster. We should warn you, however, that this is the hardest way to achieve rapid product development. *The easiest way to shorten development cycles is to minimize the work required to develop the product.* This is our first line of defense. When this first line of defense breaks down, we are forced to do damage control later in our development process. This chapter examines the technique of incremental innovation, an approach which breaks innovation into smaller, faster steps. We will examine the advantages and disadvantages of incremental innovation and explain what we need to do to use it as a tool.

ADVANTAGES OF INCREMENTAL INNOVATION

We are all drawn to tales of heroic success in product development. A development team steps up to the challenge of a seemingly impossible project and puts in superhuman efforts. This team is rewarded with exhilarating success as the spineless skeptics slink away with heads hung low. These projects are like the long touchdown passes that drive the fans wild. They are much more exciting than the running game that rolls down the field 10 yards at a time.

While these heroic projects make good news stories, they don't always make money. They can fail very dramatically and expensively. Since these failures do not make such good new stories, we hear less about them, and overestimate the success rate of megaprojects. We underestimate the importance and value of incremental programs and delude ourselves about the true risk of the megaproject. We need to look more carefully at these two approaches. We will argue that the incremental innovators are in fact the unsung heroes of product development. In examining the advantages of incremental innovation we will compare it to the opposite approach, the megaproject. The megaproject is just what its name implies. The tasks undertaken are formidable, the teams and budgets are large, and the schedule is long. Let us begin with an example from real life.

Keithley Instruments is a 50-year-old leading supplier of sophisticated electronic measurement systems. Several years ago they applied the incremental innovation approach described in an earlier edition of this book to the development of a voltmeter called the 2400 SourceMeter™. The Project Manager, Charles Cimino, having had experience with at least six major projects observed that the payoff of an incremental approach was extremely high. Using the traditional, technical emphasis, megaproject approach, they would have tried to produce the perfect instrument, talking to all possible users, and evaluating all competitors during the first development. This would normally result in a three-year project with lots of changes, high stress, overtime, reduced financial return and many burnt-out employees. In contrast, by shifting to an incremental approach, 80 percent of the market was addressed in a single product introduction that was completed in 12 months. This was followed by two other models, the 2410 and 2420, that targeted different customer segments but built upon the knowledge gained on the 2400, both technical and nontechnical. The incremental approach kept open options for change in the later introductions to be incorporated based on field experience with the first model. This proved critical when the 2400 began to be sold to a new set of customers with new and different needs. With two incremental follow-on projects in process, Keithley could quickly respond to these new opportunities, building confidence with their new customers.

Financial Advantages

The first thing we might notice about the incremental approach is its financial advantages. The relative investment in each product introduction is lower than it is for the megaproject and revenue and profits show up much faster. Cash flow is better because we don't have to invest for five years to see the first dollar of return. We would also note that we have avoided the risk of investing for five years in a project that bombs. We will get very strong feedback from the market after the first or second product increments if our product has missed the target.

Marketing Advantages

We would also notice some striking advantages from a marketing perspective. Because each incremental product would be developed within a relatively short horizon, we would be able to limit our detailed planning to the market that would exist at that time. It is much easier to forecast customer needs over shorter planning horizons. This means that we would be able to quickly create a more accurate specification, and get the entire team to buy into it. The further we look into the future the more our vision is based on pure speculation. For example, in a specification with only two degrees of freedom, uncertainty rises with the square of the time to the planning horizon. Since most product specifications have far more than two degrees of freedom, uncertainty rises exponentially with the time to the planning horizon.

And even if we made a mistake on the specification, we would be better off on the incremental program. We would get strong feedback from the customer as soon as we made our first product introduction. We would have four additional tries in which to adjust the product. This flexibility is a crucial advantage in fast-moving markets because we often don't know exactly what customers want, and sometimes the customers don't know either. Too often we faithfully write down exactly what the customers asked for, spend years developing it, and then come to the moment of truth when the customers finally begin using the fully functioning system. As they begin to use it in the real application they flood us with requests for modifications. We explain to them that we gave them *exactly* what they asked for and show them their signatures on the original specification document. "Well, now that I am using what I asked for," they say, "it's not what I want ... but you really helped me clarify my thinking." The flexibility offered by incremental innovation is vital in such situations.

Let us look at some examples of this. Black & Decker is a leader in eliminating cords from electric tools and appliances by replacing cords with rechargeable battery packs. Their Handy Mixer was among the first items in a line of kitchen appliances designed to capitalize on cordless operation. B&D's presumption in designing the Handy Mixer, even after introducing several cordless tools and vacuum cleaners, was that users expected the cordless product to be as powerful as the corded one. The primary emphasis was thus on developing a cordless mixer with performance nearly equal to a corded one, even though it became larger, heavier, and considerably more expensive than a corded mixer. After considerable discussion, Black & Decker decided to develop an "underpowered" version as well because a few people believed it might also have a small market. In the end, this minority was vindicated by the marketplace. Reports from people who bought the units indicated that convenience and light weight were its strong points, and they didn't expect the small model to be a heavy-duty mixer. The larger, more powerful unit, meanwhile, met with a poor reception in the market and was soon discontinued, because people saw little point in paying a premium for performance only equal to the corded unit they already had. In this case it proved wiser to listen to the market than it did to try to outguess it.

Lumonics, Inc., is the world's largest supplier of industrial laser equipment and developer of the LASERDYNE™ 140 Laser Welding System. This system was developed leveraging existing subassemblies and suppliers from three different sites on two continents. The new product was targeted at small-lot-size applications to assess manufacturing productivity improvements using precision laser welding. The project was completed in just over three months compared to the nine to ten months it would have taken without the incremental approach. Terry VanderWert, the Product Manager, commented that as soon as the LASERDYNE™ 140 went into use at customer sites the customers began to think of new uses for the product in higher volume applications. As Lumonics responded to these new needs, its activities were guided by real customers, with real applications, ready to buy the product today. This is a far more solid target than product planners speculating about possible new features.

Sometimes even when we listen to the market it misleads us. For example, consider the market for sports equipment. Customers will tell you that celebrity endorsements have no effect on their purchase decision. Yet sports equipment companies spend millions on getting these endorsements. Is this naive? It turns out that customers are misleading you when they say celebrity endorsements don't count. They will tell you that the most important buying criteria is how the equipment performs. "How do you determine which equipment performs best?" you ask. "Well, if the quarterback who won the Superbowl used this football it must be good!" People claim they want performance, but they buy on the basis of celebrity endorsements. Incremental innovation is a great way to spot these quirks. When you force the customer to make a purchase decision and you analyze it carefully, you learn things that don't come out in market research. Customers voting with their wallet are always the best indicator of what will really sell.

The ease of forecasting and flexibility are not the only marketing advantages of incremental innovation. When we have long intervals between products, our sales force and distribution channels get impatient. There is no better excuse to see customers than to introduce them to a new product. The steady flow of new products keeps the distribution channel happy and gives our sales force something to sell. It creates an accurate image of constant product improvement.

Furthermore, each product increment has the potential to lock in customers before the competition has a chance to sell to them. Intel has done this masterfully in the microprocessor market. Each generation of microprocessor offers a moderate improvement in performance. A clear upgrade path is provided, reaching back to the 8088 of the late 1970s. Instead of waiting five years to introduce a product with four times the performance, Intel improves it by 25 to 35 percent each year. This leaves little opportunity for anyone to snatch away leadership from them.

Engineering Advantages

There are also compelling advantages to incremental innovation from an engineering perspective. When we add product requirements we raise complexity dramatically. A mere handful of extra features can cripple a development project. We can see this effect in Figure 4-1. As each new element is added, it has to interact with both the existing elements and all the combinations of these elements. The number of potential interactions rises steeply as the number of elements increases. In this example it is useful to think of elements in two ways. We can treat them as functional modules within the project. They can be electronic subassemblies, mechanical subassemblies, and modules of software. Or we can think of them as individual features. The figure only indicates the potential for interactions, for the interactions between many elements can be weak or nonexistent. Nonetheless, the potential indicated for mushrooming complexity is clearly evident. Each new element roughly doubles the potential number of interactions. It adds as many potential interactions itself as existed among all the elements before it was added. For example, nine elements offer 502 potential interactions, and the 10th adds 511 more, for a total of 1,013.

As the system becomes more complex, the cost of adding each new feature increases. What is critical is that most of the complexity comes from the interfaces and interactions with the rest of the system. Doing the individual feature may be trivially easy, but getting it to work with the rest of the system can be very difficult. Adding a few elements can complicate a design to a much greater degree than is usually appreciated, which can ultimately have a great impact on the schedule.

A second engineering advantage of shorter incremental programs is that they are more effective at motivating team members. On a five-year

Potential interactions

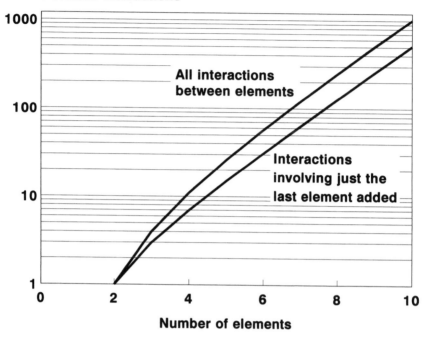

The potential number of interactions among elements approximately doubles as each new element is added, and the potential for complexity rises accordingly. (The equation for the upper curve is:

$$N = \sum_{i=2}^{n} \frac{n!}{[(n - i)!i!]}$$

where N is the number of potential interactions and n is the number of elements.)

FIGURE   4-1

program we find little urgency in the first year. Instead, we find people casually exploring potential technologies that may come to fruition in the next five years. Furthermore, it is hard to attract good engineers to these programs. A five-year program represents 25 percent of a 20-year career with a company. An aggressive young engineer will be quickly turned off by the idea of waiting five years to see the results of his or her efforts.

A third engineering advantage of incremental innovation is that we get the product out into the field early. This places it in the actual operating environment that we are designing for. This environment has a large impact on product performance, but it is extremely difficult to anticipate during development. For example, one maker of equipment for the restaurant industry put an infra-red sensor in its equipment to replace the less reliable mechanical sensor of an older model. When the equipment was installed in a restaurant they discovered that the sensor kept getting set off by spurious signals from the heat lamps that were used to keep food warm. This interaction was obvious once observed, but was very difficult to anticipate. The advantage of incremental programs is that you get this feedback much sooner.

A final engineering advantage of incremental innovation is that it permits technological commitments to be spread throughout the program. With foresight we can usually incorporate a year-four technology into the year-five product. In contrast, megaprojects almost always make their technology choices in year one and live with them for the duration of the program. It becomes very difficult to adapt these projects to emerging technology despite the best intentions of the project to stay flexible.

This ability to spread technology commitments makes it possible to accomplish more graceful adoptions of new technologies. A new technology goes through two stages when it is introduced into a product. First, we need to get it to work. Then, we need to learn the finer points, the potential trade-offs, and the techniques for increasing the leverage of the new technology. Incremental innovation allows us to separate these two steps. We can introduce a new technology in a low-volume product where the risk is low. In such products, problems with costs and performance do less financial damage. Once this is done we can scale up the technology in higher volume applications.

We must caution you that it takes a great deal of marketing and technical restraint to introduce a new technology in a minimal form. ⚠ The technologists and marketing people will all be aching to inject the new technology into a high-volume mainstream product. Resist this temptation. You will generally find it faster to adopt the technology using the two-step process because you waste little time optimizing it in the first increment. Instead, you do the optimization during the second step when you really know what the customer really needs to be optimized. Treat the first increment as market research that is being paid for by the customer buying the initial products. Sneak into the new technology with a product that is as similar as possible to an existing one. Don't promote the new features; instead, accept reduced margins if necessary on this transitional product. Then, use your experience with the first increment to guide the optimization of the new technology on its second application. Once you have proven it works in the first product you can market it heavily in the second one.

Rapid Learning

A final and more general advantage of incremental innovation is the way it accelerates the learning process in organizations. We learn a bit more about the marketplace, about the technology, and about our process of developing products with each additional development program. The more times we repeat this cycle in a given time period, the more chances we have to learn and to reinforce this learning.

Japanese companies tend to excel in incremental innovation. Despite marketing skills that typically lag behind those of their American competitors, Japanese competitors have rapidly captured strong positions in many consumer markets. They rely heavily on incremental innovation to do this. For example, the original Sony Walkman was introduced in 1979 at $200. It was not at first a very attractive buy, but Sony soon made it so by introducing dozens of small changes quickly and incrementally. These steps included manufacturing improvements aimed at cutting product cost and improving its performance. Many of these changes involved replacing mechanical components with lighter, more rugged, cheaper electronic items. As the product's price dropped, expanding its number of potential buyers, countless varieties were introduced to test the marketplace. The same approach continues today. If you walk into an electronics store in Tokyo's Akihabara district, you will typically find 150 models of MiniDisc systems or computerized rice cookers on sale, many of them varying in just color or controls arrangement. These are small lots used to test the marketplace before products are scaled up. This is learning by doing, not by planning and studying.

Think of incremental innovation as a way of doing cheap experiments in product development. Most companies, even slow ones, do a lot of experimenting. The critical difference is that most companies don't do their experimenting in the marketplace. Instead, they do it in what they perceive as the less risky environment of the development lab. Unfortunately, if you fail to experiment in the marketplace you get a small fraction of the learning that you could potentially achieve. When you experiment in the laboratory you only find out about the technical performance of the design. When you experiment in the marketplace you find out about customer requirements, decision making, and usage patterns, and you learn about the true operating environment of the product. Some of this information is priceless.

Thus, we can see that there are many compelling reasons to adopt a strategy of incremental innovation. Companies that rely upon megaprojects often find themselves locked into this self-reinforcing strategy, as shown in Figure 4-2. The size and duration of the megaproject means that it can only be done every few years. This means it must carry the burden of maintaining market superiority for several years in a future competitive environment that is hard to define. As a result we load it up with features. The large scope of the program makes it a big investment. Management likes to watch big investments carefully, so

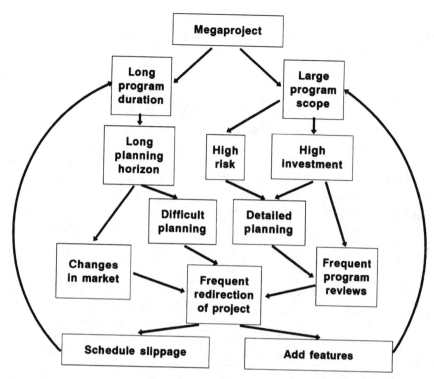

The self-reinforcing nature of megaprojects.

FIGURE 4-2

they require thorough planning and forecasts. Since these forecasts involve the distant future, they are hard to make, and go through many iterations. But the stakes are high, so this seems like the right thing to do. Management reviews the program frequently, and redirects it when the market shifts. Since the program is lengthy, it will experience more of these shifts than a shorter incremental program. These shifts often add features and cause the schedule to slip. The slippage and increased scope feed back and compound the problem. Furthermore, the deterioration of the program signals management that this project requires even more close supervision, which increases the counterproductive tendency to micromanage it.

The sad truth about the megaproject is that giant steps require us to take even bigger giant steps. We have often encountered managers who observed that they were pleasantly surprised by the unexpected advantages of incremental innovation. We have never encountered managers who said they were pleasantly surprised by the advantages of the megaproject. Yet this does not mean that megaprojects will always be a bad choice. Let us now look at the arguments against incremental innovation.

DISADVANTAGES OF INCREMENTAL INNOVATION

Incremental innovation is not an unalloyed blessing. It also has disadvantages. Most of these become prominent when the increments become too small. Let us now present these disadvantages.

Marketing Disadvantages

Perhaps the most important disadvantage of incremental innovation is that it overloads the distribution channel, sales force, and customer with a complex and constantly changing array of products. This forces us to train and retrain the sales force and distribution channel. It forces us to spend more money on advertising and promotion to communicate what is new about the products. Furthermore, this need to communicate comes at a time when we actually have less to tell the customer. Consider what would happen if our products had improved in performance at a rate of 20 percent every five years. If we shift to an incremental strategy, introducing a new product every year, the performance improvement will drop to 4 percent a year. It is very difficult to generate interest in the marketplace for a 4 percent performance change. This is exactly the situation that occurs with many consumer products, where the jaundiced consumer concludes that the only thing "new and improved" about the product is the color of the package.

One of the objections that is often raised to incremental products is that they steal sales from other existing products. This issue must be approached carefully. While you may steal sales from an existing project those future sales were not guaranteed to be yours. This issue was eloquently framed by Ted Levitt in his classic article "Marketing Myopia" (see Suggested Reading at the end of this chapter). Either you put your own products out of business or your competitors will do it for you. The best way to deal with this problem is to quantify it. Use the economic analysis tool in Chapter 2 and include both the cannibalized product and the new one in the analysis. But be careful. Don't treat the old product as happily shipping with high profits forever. Use a realistic baseline scenario with market share and margins eroding more every year, as competitors' incremental products cut into your market position. This gives a more accurate picture of the benefits of the new product.

The proliferation of product models can also create a headache for service and support staffs. Each model may require spare parts and training of the field service and customer support staff. It is difficult to support a flood of low-volume products. This disadvantage can be reduced by careful architectural choices (see Chapter 6).

Engineering Disadvantages

The most serious disadvantages of incremental innovation are the technical ones. Incremental innovation is beneficial because it emphasizes reuse of existing design work. The dark side of this reuse is that it makes it difficult to adopt a whole new technology. For example, the American railroad industry made the transition from steam to diesel technology during a 10-year period. At the beginning of this period the industry was 95 percent steam engines and at the end it was 95 percent diesel. During these 10 years the steam engine manufacturers innovated extensively, yet they all went bankrupt. The problem was that there was no incremental path between steam and diesel technology. Similarly, there was no incremental path between vacuum tubes and transistors. If you bet on incremental innovation in such situations, you will be left behind by the new technology. There is an ultimate danger to the company that relies exclusively on incremental innovation, because eventually a technology shift will put it out of business.

A second engineering disadvantage to taking small steps is the psychological effect that such small steps may have on design teams. Many engineers are more attracted to working on the grand breakthrough rather than on the incremental program. We must be very careful that the increments do not become so small that designers feel they are working on dull, boring products. Once a design team begins to believe that they are working on a boring product it is hard to get them to make an extra effort on the product. Anytime we can get the team excited about the product they are doing we increase the chance of success.

It helps when design teams are reminded that technical difficulty has little to do with business success. For example, Motorola achieved a great deal of market success with its colored pagers. These products did not require extensive design work, since they only changed the color of the pager housing. Yet the products were a brilliant market success. The pager market was shifting from doctors and lawyers to teenagers whose parents were trying to find them. These teenagers did

TABLE 4-1

Advantages and Disadvantages of Incremental Innovation

	Advantages	Disadvantages
Financial	Earlier profits Earlier cashflow Less investment risk	Duplicate fixed cost per introduction
Marketing	Shorter planning horizon Earlier feedback from customer More reliable feedback Flexibility Image of consistent product improvement Customer lock-in	Channel overload Sales force overload Customer overload Service and support overload
Engineering	Lower technical complexity More motivating to teams Early field experience with technology Spreads technological commitments	Hard to make technology breakthrough Boring products
Other	Accelerated learning	

not want to use the same old black pagers as their parents had. They wanted to express their unique identity with brilliantly colored pagers that were color-coordinated with the shade of their green hair.

Financial Disadvantages

There is also a financial disadvantage associated with incremental innovation. It forces you to duplicate the fixed cost per introduction with each product introduction. In some businesses this disadvantage can be avoided by making changes in the product introduction process to lower the cost of each introduction. In other businesses, it is impossible to reduce these one-time costs. For example, regulated products such as pharmaceuticals and aircraft may require a substantial one-time testing and approval cycle for each product introduction. It can be very expensive to have to continually submit these products for additional approvals. In fact, for some businesses such as aircraft parts you may have no chance to do incremental introductions. Once a part is type certified onboard an aircraft, it may be impossible to change it without extensive retesting. In such cases you must make all your change in a single increment, because you don't get another chance.

The advantages and disadvantages of incremental innovation are summarized in Table 4-1.

REQUIRED INFRASTRUCTURE

To be able to do incremental innovation well, we need five key elements of infrastructure. In the absence of these key elements we may get all the disadvantages of incremental innovation without capturing any of the advantages.

Technology Planning

The first key element of infrastructure is technology planning. Incremental programs do not have the luxury of developing technology as part of their project. This would add too much uncertainty and delay to the program. Furthermore, this uncertainty undercuts accountability for the schedule, causing further schedule problems for a program that needs to be tightly scheduled. Instead of including it as a part of the product development, the technology must be developed outside of the program. This means that we have to anticipate technology needs before they are required and start developing this technology early. This takes a plan backed up with adequate resources.

The most common way to accomplish this is by creating a technology road map, which focuses on the product attributes that are changing with time and the underlying technologies needed to support this change. For example, to improve the resolution of a laser printer requires advancements in the toners, the electronics, and the optical systems. Within each of these areas there are certain technologies available. Each technology has achieved a certain level of performance and is improving at a certain rate. With some simple forecasting one can anticipate which candidate technologies are available to advance particular subsystems. These technologies can then be evaluated to determine when investment in them must begin to support the product plans.

Not all technologies must be developed internally. In many cases it is more attractive to work with an external partner, particularly when the partner can achieve scale economies by developing this technology for many markets simultaneously. For example, it would rarely make sense for a company to invest scarce technology resources in microprocessor development because companies like Intel can amortize their investments in this area over a much larger customer base.

The most common defect in technology planning in the companies we work with is not in the plan itself, but rather in consistently applying resources to the plan. Unfortunately, the resources allocated for advanced technology development are commonly viewed as expendable. Technology development has uncertain payoff and is sometimes not directly tied to this year's revenue. It becomes an attractive place to steal resources from. In one case, we observed that two-thirds of the planned investment in technology development was being diverted into handling customer crises and manufacturing problems. The consequence of this diversion was that development programs were starting without adequate advance technology development and invention was taking place on the critical path of programs. We need to put adequate resources behind the technology plan and to resist diverting this resource every time a short-term crisis appears.

Technology Transfer

When we were inventing on the critical path of programs, we didn't have to worry about technology transfer. The technology was delaying the program and the team was waiting impatiently to get it. Once we do technology development off-line we need to worry about technology transfer. The most effective way to transfer technology into a program is to use a human carrier. One of the technologists who developed the new technology becomes a member of the first development team to use the technology.

For example, consider the infamous case of PARC, Xerox's Palo Alto Research Center. It has been a hotbed of great technology that never seemed to get transferred into any of Xerox's products. Observers report that one of the primary reasons technology transfer out of PARC has been ineffective is that the scientists were never transferred along with the technology. In fact, the scientists at PARC were sometimes told that they would be able to devote themselves purely to new ideas in the beautiful Californian setting in Palo Alto. When it came time to get technology transfer you had to convince them to move to the business units in Rochester, New York, in the middle of the snow belt of upstate New York. Needless to say, almost nobody wanted to move.

Moving people with the technology has fringe benefits when technologists eventually depart the team and return to the advanced technology laboratory. They return with a deeper understanding of how certain product attributes are valued by the customer and what the design engineer really needs to know about the technology. This in turn influences the future focus of their efforts to improve the technology. This constant bi-directional flow of people between the product development teams and the advanced technology centers is very important to achieving effective, well-linked technology development.

Empowered Teams

Empowered teams allow us to exploit the power of incremental innovation. This is a key cultural difference between organizations that are biased toward megaprojects and those that are oriented toward incremental innovation. When a company does megaprojects the stakes are high, and when the stakes are high senior management wants to review and approve many management decisions. This review and approval lengthens the program, which turns it into even more of a megaproject.

In contrast, incremental programs can take a fundamentally different approach to controlling risk. Instead of controlling individual program decisions, the risk of an incremental program is controlled by the size of the increment incorporated into the program. The basic scope of the program limits the risk, and therefore eliminates the need to micromanage the program.

This is exactly the method that venture capitalists use to control the risk of their projects. Rather than trying to second-guess every decision made by a management team, they provide the team with increments of funding. The start-up company has a great deal of autonomy to make detailed decisions, but if the progress on an individual increment is insufficient the money for the next increment will either be unavailable, or it will be priced at terms which are less favorable to the start-up.

This empowerment does not arise automatically just because the program is incremental. Moving to empowered teams is a cultural issue that will demand explicit effort (see Chapters 7 and 8). Yet if you do not empower teams, you will be in the worst situation: small steps of incremental innovation with the overhead and delays of the megaproject.

Product Line Planning

The product needs a coherent plan, such as the master plan described in the previous chapter. This master plan identifies the incremental enhancements that will occur in each version of the product and when these products will be introduced. This is often called a product road map and it has important benefits for the developer. When you know what enhancements are to appear in future products it is easier to plan ahead for these enhancements in the current design. Furthermore, the existence of a plan will prevent the current product from acting as a magnet for everybody's great ideas. The plan gives Marketing more than one chance to get its brilliant ideas into a product.

This sort of product line planning is challenging for the company that is used to megaprojects. Megaprojects allow a product planner to load a product with every idea he or she can possibly think of. No choices are required. In contrast, the incremental program can only carry a handful of new features. We must know which features are most important to choose the ones to introduce first. In general, companies that do incremental innovation will be more involved with their customers than companies that do megaprojects, both because they need customer information to make the choices and because the fast feedback incremental innovation provides is so valuable for taking the next step.

Sometimes managers and developers fall into the trap of thinking that incremental innovation can only be done by introducing a platform project representing a major innovation followed by derivative products. While this is certainly the most common strategy, it is not the only one. In fact, there are many opportunities to make incremental changes before the larger platform project. These early increments can be used to test out technology and validate market requirements. For example, consider the 1991 model Buick Park Avenue, which was being planned by the end of 1986. This car was to be a major facelift, including a new body, significant engine and transmission enhancements, and a whole group of suspension and steering improvements. The program planners also wanted to minimize design complexity, because they needed a short development cycle to meet a March 1990 target for starting production. Their solution is interesting because it is so counterintuitive. The planners pulled ahead many of the suspension and steering improvements for introduction during the 1989 and 1990 model years as their Dynaride package. With a few adjustments to struts and engine mounts, Dynaride was then available as an existing element in the 1991 model. This allowed some of the risk of the platform change to be pulled forward into earlier introduction years.

Product Architecture

Finally, we need a product architecture that supports incremental innovation. The first increment of the product must have enough "legs" to it to permit it to be the base for further increments. If it does not, we may have to redo that portion of the design later on. We will discuss this issue of architecture in Chapter 6.

One of the most important causes of megaprojects is that we don't understand the customer well enough. This is at the heart of the product specification activity that we cover in the next chapter.

SUGGESTED READING

Foster, Richard N. 1986. *Innovation: The Attacker's Advantage.* New York: Summit Books. This is an excellent treatment of technological substitution. It illustrates the importance of planning for technological shifts and provides a useful framework for doing this planning.

Hagel III, John. 1988. Managing complexity. *The McKinsey Quarterly* (Spring): 2–23. An illuminating discussion of the impact of product complexity on development difficulty, particularly as reflected in development expense. Includes examples from the electronics industry.

Levitt, Theodore. 1960. Marketing myopia. *Harvard Business Review* 38 (4): 45–56. A popular piece illustrating how companies dry up because they view their businesses too narrowly. It argues that incremental innovation can help companies remain in touch with change by continually offering customers a fresh assortment of products.

Levitt, Theodore. 1966. Innovative imitation. *Harvard Business Review* 44 (5): 63–70. Levitt argues that breakthrough innovation receives more attention in the press than it deserves. The greatest flow of newness comes from imitation, not innovation, and most progress results from imitating something that already exists. This being the case, the wise company will concentrate on being able to imitate quickly.

Capturing Customer Needs

At the start of development we attempt to capture customer needs in a document often called a product specification. This sounds simple enough but is actually a stumbling point for many product developers, and the consequences of a poorly written specification show up as lost time later in the project. Specifications provide input that is critical to both the product and the development process. The techniques covered in this chapter will help you to avoid writing specifications slowly or producing ones that are slow to win approval, yield overly complex products, or waste resources, thus impeding project execution.

Specifications also offer powerful opportunities to fundamentally redesign the product delivery process. When Boeing specified its 777, the company looked beyond delivering the product to delivering value. That aircraft's mission is intercontinental flights which, for the proposed twin-engine design, requires compliance with so-called ETOPS (extended twin-engine operations) safety regulations. A three-hour ETOPS allows the plane to fly as far as three hours from the nearest airport, which means that it can fly nearly anywhere in the world. Thus, ETOPS certification is the key to intercontinental travel, the value behind the 777.

Before the 777, the only way to obtain three-hour ETOPS was to fly the plane for about two years in revenue service to demonstrate the plane's reliability. Boeing turned this situation on its head—cutting two years out of customers' "time to value"—by *specifying* that the 777 would be three-hour ETOPS certified upon delivery to the first customer. Boeing then proceeded to develop the 777, working with government regulatory authorities as they went, to establish a whole new route to ETOPS certification and a new basis of competition in their industry.

PRODUCT SPECIFICATIONS: A VITAL COMMUNICATION LINK

Later, in Chapter 8, we emphasize the fundamental role of effective communication in rapid product development, and we suggest some powerful techniques to enhance communication within the development team. An early test of that communication occurs when the specification is written.

The Many Views of a Product

Figure 5-1 illustrates the two types of communication breakdowns that a good specification aims to overcome. One is differences in understanding among the various constituencies within the company: for example, Marketing presumes that the product will be usable straight out of the box while Engineering supposes that some assembly and software setup are normal. The other potential breakdown is between the customer and the company as a whole; for instance, the customer taking the product to the beach but no one at the company considering its use in such a hostile environment. The basic job of the specification is to help these groups within the company to acquire a customer-centered, common vision of the product so that such differences in viewpoint, if not eliminated, will at least be questioned so that they can be checked out.

Such differences in viewpoint result in wasted effort and redesign as the product's vision shifts. These shifts, especially if they recur often, undermine development team morale, which in turn destroys the very confidence the team will need to put in the extra hours needed to get the project back on track. A reasonable person would wait for the product vision to settle out before working strenuously just to find that yet another change had occurred.

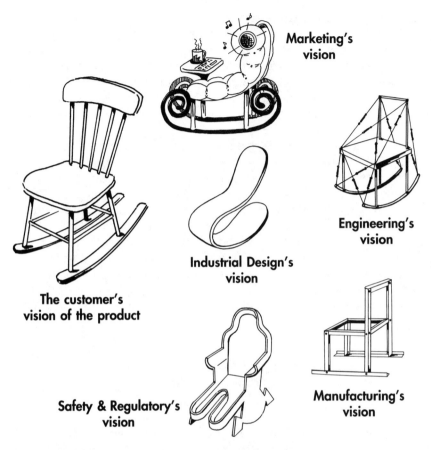

Marketing's vision

Engineering's vision

Industrial Design's vision

The customer's vision of the product

Safety & Regulatory's vision

Manufacturing's vision

The two crucial issues that specifications seek to overcome are getting common agreement within the organization on the product vision and aligning this vision with the customer's need. Illustrated by M. Viktorin

FIGURE   5-1

Communicating What the Product Will Not Do

We usually think of specifications as outlines of what the product will do, but the omissions can be just as important to cycle time, as this example of a medical computer shows. In this client company Marketing, being in closer contact with the customer, was supposed to write specifications, but on one project Engineering went ahead and did it, because the engineers were anxious to get started and Marketing was unavailable. However, the Engineering leader of this project was astute and had observed how the firm's specifications had failed in the past. So he wrote the specification in three sections. The first one covered what the product would do. The second outlined features that would not be included in the initial model but could be added later if Marketing so chose. The third section described features that effectively would be precluded by the architecture that Engineering was proposing.

This engineer took his specification to the Vice President of Engineering for approval. He obtained approval for the first two sections, but the vice president objected to the third one. He believed that it represented "negative thinking," which the company discouraged. So the Engineering leader deleted the third section and proceeded with design.

Today, this company is paying dearly to add the features that were in that third list, the undiscussibles. We have related this story to many of our clients, and some of them have taken it to heart, adding a "third list" to their specifications. This allows them to explicitly consider growth options for the future, speeding up future generations of their products.

DIFFICULTIES IN WRITING SPECIFICATIONS

One complication in writing specifications is that many types of knowledge—engineering, marketing, manufacturing, and others—are needed to define the product, just as they are to develop it. This means that many specialists must interact to share information and reach a mutually satisfactory solution.

At its heart, the design process requires the common solution of conflicting requirements by making trade-offs, as depicted in Figure 5-2. For instance, an automobile will be more fuel efficient if it is smaller, but then crashworthiness is likely to suffer. The best design is therefore probably not the single point suggested in the specification but rather some other combination of values that suits the user better. The designer needs information beyond what is written in the specification in order to make appropriate trade-off decisions.

Some of the most crucial elements in a specification are often hard to put into meaningful words or to quantify. Qualities such as "user friendly," "easy to clean," or "solid feel" can have a great influence on product sales, but they resist accurate description. Quality standards, such as ISO 9001, and governmental regulations, such as

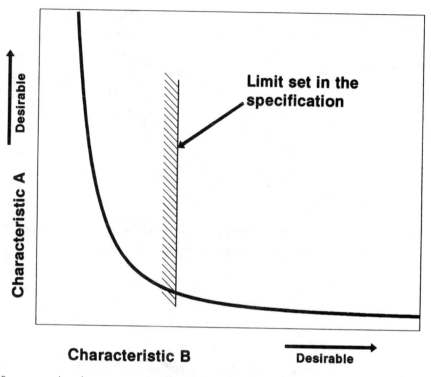

Because product characteristics interact in perhaps unknown ways, limiting Characteristic B in a specification may force Characteristic A into a region that provides poor customer value.

FIGURE   5-2

Truth in Advertising in the United States, push us toward defining the undefinable by suggesting, if not requiring, that any attribute mentioned in the specification be measurable against some standard.

The Information Isn't All Available When We Write the Specification

Some design relationships that come to light only after design starts determine the basic value of the product. We illustrate this point in Figure 5-3 using a photocopier as an example, but the principle applies broadly to other products. Many models and brands fill the photocopier market, and their value—thus their price—is determined basically by their speed, in copies per minute. It is tempting to specify this basic variable initially. However, this speed arises from several technologies

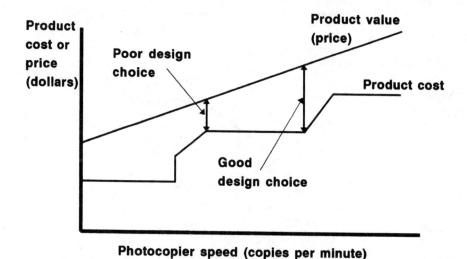

The value curve is known in advance, but the cost curve depends on design work that must be done first. Thus, the high-margin opportunities appear only after completing some design work.

FIGURE 5-3

applied in diverse ways, and these variations drive product cost, as illustrated in Figure 5-3. The detailed shape of this cost curve becomes apparent only after the technologies are fit into a specific design, but the shape of this curve can have a great impact on product margins, as shown. Thus, it is unwise to specify speed beforehand, because this may adversely limit profit potential. Xerox, in fact, recognizes this point and specifies a speed range, not a certain point, leaving the exact value for the developers to determine later.

Marketing Specifications versus Engineering Specifications

Before we leave the difficulties in writing specifications and proceed to the solutions, there is one more point to cover. Some organizations recognize that Marketing and Engineering write specifications for different purposes, a disparity they deal with simply by having two specifications. This practice is especially prevalent in the electronics, particularly the computer, industry. There, Marketing writes its specification from a sales and business perspective. Then Engineering writes a specification that describes how the product is to work in considerable detail.

Having separate Marketing and Engineering specifications is dangerous in two respects. First, it cleverly skirts the essential step of having Marketing and Engineering work out their differences and reach a common view of the product. Engineering thus never has to understand rather subjective market research suggesting why customers want certain features, and Marketing avoids having to work through engineering parlance and logic to figure out the pros and cons of a technical approach. The organization thus never gains the benefit of making sound trade-offs between features and technology.

Second, we have consistently found that when there are two specifications they describe two different products, even if one originally derives from the other. As each specification evolves, it changes and takes on a life of its own. Engineering forgets that there is a Marketing specification and regards its own as the only guidebook. Marketing frequently can't understand Engineering's specification and thus ignores it.

Our advice is to call only one document in the organization the specification, and it should be the joint product of all departments. Any engineering documents needed to initiate design should be called engineering design documents, and they should be ultimately traceable to the specification, including changes in the specification.

KEEPING THE CUSTOMER IN THE FOREGROUND

A specification is an attempt to capture customer needs, which must start with the customer:

- Who is the target customer?
- What is that customer's problem?
- How will the product solve this problem?
- Which customer needs will this product not satisfy?
- What benefits will it offer compared with other solutions that are available to the customer?
- How will the customer value these benefits?
- On what basis will the customer judge the product?

Everyone involved with a development project must understand who the customer is and especially what needs will be satisfied. Most specifications provide merely a perfunctory one- or two-sentence statement of the raison d'être for the product. A much more detailed discussion is needed, though, to help those who will be doing the designing later so that they can make fast decisions consistent with customer needs. A solid statement of the product's mission guides developers toward answers for all the questions not covered explicitly in the remainder of the specification.

Another advantage of a clear customer and mission statement for the product is that it keeps the specification relatively short, which in turn helps insure that it is read and understood. The last thing we want is a watertight specification that attempts to close every loophole legalistically. Because the customer defies being packaged so neatly, this approach is bound to fail.

A needs-centered specification keeps developers open to opportunities to satisfy customer needs while saving time.

As we suggested in our medical computer example earlier, the specification should also circumscribe the scope of the project by delineating what the product will not do. This apparently "negative thinking" serves two purposes, both related to cycle time. First, it clarifies explicitly what has been omitted, so that the developers will not be blindsided later by items for which they could have provided, thereby making their jobs easier and faster in the future. All projects have things they unconsciously omit, some of which have major implications later. We simply want to make this process open and up-front so that we reduce the risk of schedule surprises later.

The second reason for being clear about what is not being done is to control project growth. Projects have a tendency to grow on their own, so we must counter this inclination by being quite clear about what will not be done. A key message of Chapter 2 is that every portion of a development project has a cost and a benefit. Rather than including any attribute that has some benefit, our approach is to include only attributes for which the benefit outweighs the cost.

We check on this tendency in a given company by asking a sales executive in the company about the adequacy of the feature set in the company's last few products. Being quite knowledgeable of sales opportunities lost, this individual will be quick to point out any missing features. If he or she thinks the feature set is adequate, we suspect that the firm has erred on the side of providing extra safety features at the expense of cycle time.

Involve Customers

The specification is only a pointer toward the customer. It is customers, not specifications, who will buy our products. Although the specification is a valuable tool for doing this pointing, it remains only a pointer. We cannot hide behind the specification if it proves to be wrong. Thus, customer involvement is an essential subject, both to construct an accurate specification, and to continually provide a sanity check on what we are developing.

In some cases the buyers and the users of the product will be the same, but when they are different both groups should be understood. Consider, for instance, a supermarket checkout system. A person who operates this system 40 hours a week will be in the best position to judge weaknesses or opportunities. Others in the buying chain, such as the employer who paid for it or the dealer who installed it, will have different—but normally less valuable—information on the product's attributes. The best approach usually is to work closely with users, then check with other buying-decision makers and those in the distribution channel to make sure you have not erected any obstacles for them.

Besides actually visiting customers and users, there are many other ways of getting customer input. Boeing, when developing its 777 airliner, invited the first customer to order the plane, United Airlines, to become heavily involved in defining the product, and later invited United to provide resident customers as part of the development team. This unrestricted exposure to Boeing's "dirty laundry" created some problems, but it uncovered and solved critical design issues much faster. Other nonvisit options for involving customers include observing focus groups, including your customer service representatives on development teams, organizing customer councils, and attending trade shows. These all have their value in understanding customer needs better, but none is a substitute for actually experiencing the customer environment firsthand.

Two principles guide customer involvement in a development project. One is that the bulk of the contact should occur before design starts. The reason for this is simply that most critical product decisions will occur early in the project. If the customer is not involved before these decisions are made, momentum is going to make it unlikely that the decisions are reversed later as a result of customer input. Customer input is soft enough that it is easy to rationalize away later.

The other principle is that those actually making the design decisions daily—the design engineers—must be in direct contact with customers. This is critical because in making the countless daily decisions that go into a new product, the context in which it will be used is crucial to quickly getting it designed right. Taking time to debate how the product will be used, in the absence of direct experience, will simply delay the project. And if the product isn't designed to fit customer conditions initially, it will have to be redesigned to suit them later.

When we suggest that designers spend more early time in the user environment, we often hear objections:

- Engineers are too valuable to have traveling around doing market research. Response: they are not primarily doing market research, and without giving them this "calibration," the project is likely to be delayed even longer, due to poor engineering decisions.
- Engineers are too honest with our customers. Response: this may be true, but some initial training will overcome the potential problem of spoiling a sale.
- Engineers will overgeneralize from the few visits they are able to make. Response: it is their Marketing counterparts' job to make sure that the engineers put their observations into the proper context.
- Travel is expensive. Response: how expensive compared with the cost of delay? (see Chapter 2).

Walk in the User's Shoes

An example from *Harvard Business Review* (September–October 1994, p. 136) illustrates why engineers must get out of the lab. Hewlett-Packard was about to develop the initial model of its successful DeskJet printer line, and their Marketing people recognized that a major change in product vision was needed. Over the years HP had operated largely by using its "next bench" check, in which the engineer at the next lab bench was a good surrogate for the customer. This worked well initially, because early HP products were engineering lab instruments. However, the DeskJet was targeted at households and priced accordingly.

Due to their next-bench style, HP engineers typically made up their own minds as to what the customer really needed. So when Marketing did mall-intercept research of the targeted market and brought back 24 suggested changes, the engineers rejected all but five. Marketing could see that the designers were not close enough to the targeted customers yet, so they repeated the mall research, this time taking the engineers with them. When the engineers saw for themselves how customers fumbled with their design, they then accepted 17 of the suggestions.

New software products are no different, as Dave Olson explains in his book, *Exploiting Chaos: Cashing In on the Realities of Software Development* (International Thomson Computer Press, 1993):

> Every software developer builds products for someone. The label for this "someone" is the customer surrogate who lives in the developer's head. This customer surrogate whispers requirements more compelling than any found in requirements documents. This customer surrogate colors every development decision made.
>
> But what does this customer surrogate look like? In the absence of any other influence, the customer surrogate looks just

like the developer. You've probably heard statements like, "Our customers won't want to do that; I never do."

The best software developers have customer surrogates in their heads who look just like real, knowledgeable customers. But these customer surrogates don't grow there by accident. They grow out of contact with real application users, out of knowledge of the business associated with the application, and out of an understanding of the differing perceptions and desires of many people.

Sometimes, customers look at our products much differently than we do. One company that makes sophisticated medical diagnostic computers and prides itself in miniaturization discovered a way to make a pocket-sized, scaled-down model of their desktop unit. The engineers were proud of their accomplishment, and they took it out to hospitals to get feedback from customers. Hospital administrators looked at the unit and said, "Can you make it a little bigger? Such small items tend to walk out of our hospital." This clearly was not the perspective of the designers.

Similarly, Sentrol, Inc., a Tualatin, Oregon, producer of building security sensors, learned about smallness from its customers. Sentrol also valued miniaturization, thinking that a smaller unit was less obtrusive. The customer Sentrol focused on was the installer, and visits with installers showed just how difficult it was to mount and wire a miniature device on the ceiling of a room. Consequently, Sentrol made its new design more forgiving for the installers in their difficult environment.

Not only did Sentrol's customer visits pay off in launching the development with a clear vision of customer requirements, it also saved time later on. At one point in the project, the circuit board layout depended on just where the screws mounting the case to the ceiling were located. The best circuit board layout for the electrical engineer would not be best for the installer. So the team "borrowed" some wallboard from a company remodeling job, took it to the lab, and started making holes in it as they had seen the installers do: using a screwdriver and a hammer. They measured the tolerance on their bashed holes, and quickly reached a team conclusion as to acceptable case-mounting hole locations and circuit board layout options.

Each product has a variety of customers, and often their conflicting needs are discovered in customer visits. In Sentrol's case, interior designers probably would not be pleased with a sensor package that suited the installers. Had the medical computer engineers talked only to nurses and doctors, they would have reached different conclusions than they discovered from administrators. The best customer involvement integrates many types of customers and applications. Black & Decker accomplishes this quite well by sending its engineers out with mobile customer sales and support technicians for their professional line of DeWALT® tools as the technicians make their rounds of home centers and construction sites.

There is just no substitute for seeing the product in typical daily use to appreciate the product attributes that really matter to customers and users. We once sat through an all-day software walkthrough (design review) for a medical computer. A major design decision that stymied these software engineers was the relative prevalence of situations where the computer would have to be cold-started, as opposed to warm-start situations. Because none of the engineers in the room had spent time in an emergency room or critical care unit, they had no idea of how often the computer would be moved.

Another client makes vessels used in medical laboratories. Their marketing and sales people had spent enough time in medical labs to recognize that cleanup and sterilization were important issues in the lab. So they insisted that the next new design have a lid seal that was removable and autoclavable. This turned out to be a brilliant sales feature, but since the engineers who had to design and specify the seal had not gained an appreciation for how things get cleaned in a medical laboratory, they did not recognize that any seal that is removable is likely to get not only autoclaved but also dunked in laboratory solvents that are not good for rubber. It was back to the drawing board for that seal late in the project.

Let Customers Tell You When You Have It Right

When we do not know the customer well, we have to make assumptions about how the product will be used. If in doubt, we usually err on the side of including the feature or providing plenty of performance, just to be sure. It is like the baker who throws in an extra muffin for every dozen you buy, just to be sure that the count isn't short. This philosophy would be fine if the extras we give away with the product were free, but they aren't. In particular, they consume extra development effort, thus time.

Fortunately, there is an effective alternative to overdesigning. It is to provide what we are most sure the user wants, and plan to follow it up quickly with what is clearly missing when the product is in service. This way, we are putting development effort into only what we know will be used and valued.

Let's see how a client, a power tool manufacturer, handled such a situation. The Market Manager enthusiastically uncovered an unmet need. But extending the capability of this tool could cost the development team three to six months. Higher sales volume and more satisfied customers wouldn't offset the critical timing of being first to market in this segment (this client is a firm believer in the financial analysis covered in Chapter 2). So the team pushed forward, knowing they would have some disappointed users. In this case, the risk paid off in huge dividends: the company gained 10 points of market share and achieved more than a 70 percent return on investment. Now the company is adding the improved feature to further entrench itself in this segment.

FOCUSING ON WHAT COUNTS

Concentrate on Product Benefits, Not Features

Too often, specification writers work with features rather than benefits—but customers buy benefits, not features. For example, in writing a specification for a fax machine it may be tempting to specify a stepper motor or servo drive to move the paper or print head. But is that a benefit? Can the customer perceive it directly? If not, then we should specify what the customer will actually notice, such as speed, print quality, or noise level.

Certain features may be unnecessary to achieve product benefits, and imposing them only adds unnecessary design constraints, as in the fax machine example. In this case the final choice of motor technology should depend on size, cost, or power restrictions that appear as the design materializes. When designers concentrate on benefits, they can select from a richer, more value-driven set of features and may even be able to eliminate the need for a particular feature. For example, early FM tuners had an AFC (automatic frequency control) switch that was a valued feature because it kept the tuner from drifting off-station. Then as designs shifted to more stable phase-locked loop circuits that provided the benefit, this feature became superfluous.

Because customers buy benefits, not features, an effective way to test that your specification is operating at the benefits level is to ask yourself whether the customer would pay more for the product if it included the item in question. If not, you are likely to be specifying a feature. Say you are writing the specification for a refrigerator and you specify a certain type of liner. Will the customer pay more for this liner? Perhaps it just has an elegant look to it or it has a high-tech connotation; for instance, graphite-epoxy. If this is not a solid reason for the customer to be paying extra for your liner, probe deeper: will your liner provide more uniform lighting, making food look more attractive, or will it be more resistant to damage or less apt to absorb odors? If so, you have your benefit; specify that instead. If you are having difficulty coming up with a connection between your "benefit" and price, consider not specifying it at all. This will remove one constraint from the design, thereby cutting development time.

Use a Benefits Focus to Open Up Design Options

There are often several technical options available to designers to achieve the stated design objectives. Designers should be left free to choose among the various implementation options as the design materializes. This flexibility allows them to make choices that save time. For example, one design avenue might entail a long lead time in tooling, but another might use an available part instead.

We have mentioned the original Hewlett-Packard DeskJet printer before as an example of good practice. The specifications for that unit were quite simple and benefits-oriented: (1) plain paper printing, (2) laser-printer print quality, and (3) a price under $1,000. More recent models have had similar goals, with the addition of color printing and a trend toward much more aggressive pricing.

Involve All Functions in the Trade-Offs

At a minimum, Engineering, Marketing, and Manufacturing should be involved as a team in writing the specification. Depending on the product and industry requirements, other functions such as Purchasing, Quality Assurance, Testing, or Customer Service may be brought in as well.

It is natural to ask whether time spent in wrestling with the trade-offs inherent in a product and ensuring individuals' involvement simply delays the project. In fact, many companies seem to try to get the specification stage over with quickly by avoiding as much controversy and involvement as possible. This simply delays the controversy until a time when it consumes more time, both because time will have already been spent on items that may have to be redesigned, and because positions will then be more entrenched, thus slower to change.

To us, involvement means joint participation in actually creating the specification on an equal basis, not playing Ping-Pong by sending the specification back and forth between departments. In many companies one particular department, usually either Engineering or Marketing, creates the specification, then passes it on to other functions for review, comment, or approval. When there is little response, they assume that everyone agrees with their view of the product and they can proceed. More likely than not, however, no response means that people have yet to read it seriously. Then the issues remain dormant, waiting for the next design review to erupt. This is not a fast way to run a project.

An important outgrowth of involving all key players in writing the specification is that in the process of contributing to it they in effect "sign up" for the project. This commitment or buy-in is essential to getting the project completed quickly. Without it, people brought in later will spend time learning about the project, wondering why it is not being done differently, and generally just picking it apart to see if they like it. When a person actually contributes to writing the specification, though, he or she says, "This can be done. I agree with this approach, and I will find a way to make it work." Because it is embarrassing to the writer when a specification turns out to be infeasible, the writer is likely to put effort into making it successful.

Highlight the Time-Critical Factors

Specification writers must force themselves to identify and describe the crucial elements of the product, because the easy ones will take care of themselves. Most specifications are too long, but even with all their verbiage still do not describe the most important aspects of a product. People tend to write about what they can describe, things they understand. The factors most likely to delay a product are the ones nobody understands, which seldom get mentioned or written into the specification.

Avoid putting trivia in a specification, by not using a standard boilerplate product specification template. An engineer in a company that makes household appliances once told us, obviously feeling insulted, "They [Marketing] specify that the product has to be UL listed. I *know* that; it's company policy." If you feel that you must include the boilerplate, consider putting it in a backup company standards document to which the specification can refer, to keep the specification short and focused on what is really important.

One way to focus on the critical factors that will affect the schedule is to build a custom checklist to concentrate attention on areas where your specifications have failed before. Do not, for instance, use a checklist supplied by 3M or Hewlett-Packard, as enviable as their innovation records may be. Using other companies' checklists will just add irrelevant, time-wasting steps. The objective of this checklist is to ensure that you really understand the product concept and its schedule implications, not to add even more steps.

Review some of your recently completed projects to identify product-definition problems that have snared your staff before. Try to generalize these problems a bit and use them to create a checklist that is customized to your product line. It may be helpful to consider yourself the General Manager: someone gives you a specification for your signature, so you reach for your checklist to be sure that the developers haven't skipped anything critical.

Here are some broad categories to get you started thinking, but do not use these as your checklist:

✓ Interactions with associated products, past, present, or contemplated
✓ The potential for design growth or modification
✓ The physical environment in which the product will be used
✓ Patent infringement/protection
✓ Safety or liability
✓ Quality or reliability
✓ Ergonomics
✓ The users' abilities
✓ Sourcing and assembly
✓ Packaging or distribution
✓ Documentation, training, servicing, or maintenance
✓ Unusual equipment or facilities needed

Another way to develop a checklist is to put yourself in the place of the customer or user. Ask yourself a variety of questions designed to illuminate issues that have held up previous projects: What other alternatives are available to customers? Why might they choose another product instead of this one? Is this product going to save customers time, money, or aggravation? If so, how? What difficulties might customers encounter in adding this product to the setup they already have?

WRITING SPECIFICATIONS JOINTLY

There is a way to write specifications so that they achieve the beneficial objectives discussed above. Again, these objectives are to write and approve a specification quickly while enabling the principal participants in the development effort to buy into the project. It is also essential to expose key trade-off issues by including users and various company disciplines as equal partners in the process.

In our experience these goals can all be achieved most easily by using an off-site workshop in which the developers create the specification jointly, starting from a broad statement of the need for the product. It is important that the workshop begin with a fresh start on the specification. No function should arrive with an initial product definition, expecting that the other participants will use it as a starting point. Everything about the product is to be decided in the workshop, and everyone is to leave committed to what has been decided by the group. The purpose of the workshop is not only to produce a specification but also to build support for, and an understanding about, the product among those who will have to bring it into being.

Workshop participants should be chosen carefully to ensure that there is appropriate representation among those who will have to execute the resulting specification. This is a powerful opportunity to build project buy-in, and it should not be wasted. Remember to include users or user representatives also. The workshop is for doers, not top management. Managers should participate only if they can attend the entire workshop and only if they will be involved in the project on a daily basis. Otherwise, they may attend as silent observers. There is, however, one exception: one senior manager should kick off the workshop as a keynote speaker, indicating in broad terms how the product fits into management's vision of the company's future. Workshop participants then assimilate this vision as a context for defining the product.

The workshop should be led by an individual with no stake in its outcome. Most often this will be an independent, outside facilitator. The principal project participants, such as the project leader, head engineer, or marketing product manager, are particularly inappropriate to serve as workshop leader because of their vested interest in its outcome. They must play a role by advocating specific viewpoints, which undermines their ability to be an objective moderator. Furthermore, their contribution to the content of the specification is too important for them to be distracted by trying to keep the meeting running smoothly.

The facilitator is responsible only for the process of the meeting, which becomes a demanding, full-time job when conflicting interests arise, as they will when alternatives and trade-offs are exposed. The content of the specification is the responsibility of the participants, not the meeting's facilitator. A neutral facilitator can often be obtained from a department having little to do with product development, such as Human Resources. Training and development people are likely to be trained in how to lead meetings and deal with conflict.

A workshop should be held off-site, to minimize distractions. It typically takes about three days. The participants should be briefed beforehand to explain the objective and the rules. Start the workshop by discussing broadly the need for the product and the benefits it should provide. Work down to details like product features, functions, performance, and cost. Recording the proceedings on old-fashioned flip charts that then can be taped on the walls makes it possible to see what has been decided in the workshop and to transform this into a document later.

Can Quality Function Deployment Accelerate the Process?

A popular technique called quality function deployment (QFD) is closely allied with much of the material in this chapter, so the question naturally arises: what is the role of QFD in rapid product development?

QFD is a highly structured, analytical technique developed in Japan in the 1960s. It is built around a sequence of matrices that relate, in turn, customer needs, design attributes, and ultimately manufacturing process variables, thus in principle providing a clear linkage from the customer, through design, to the factory floor. The first of the matrices, often called the House of Quality, is the most popular and the most directly applicable to defining new products.

As its name suggests, QFD is primarily a quality tool, and many companies have adopted it as such. Because our focus is on speed, we restrict ourselves here to the relationship between QFD and speed. There are three ways in which QFD can potentially speed up product development:

- It helps to catch product definition oversights, which can avoid redesign later.
- It acts to focus attention and force decisions on what will add the most customer value to the product, thus helping the team to reduce the scope of the project effectively, which leads to speed.
- It helps the team to distinguish customer needs from customer wants, the former being more pertinent and less numerous than the latter. This too improves focus and thus saves time.

 For us, the shortcoming of QFD is that it can take a great deal of time to construct all of the matrices. Worse, any attempt to be compulsive about filling in all of the boxes in the matrices can be a time trap. Consequently, QFD should be regarded more as an aid, and a complete analysis should not be a required deliverable for fast-cycle-time projects.

The trick is to take the structure that is the hallmark of QFD and use it as an asset rather than a time sink. The structure aids us in three ways. It helps us keep the voice of the customer, as they call it in QFD, in mind; it focuses cross-functional team communication on the important product definition issues; and it acts as a check that we have not overlooked a product requirements issue.

Consequently, most practitioners who emphasize cycle time use an abbreviated form of QFD, variously known as simplified QFD, turbo QFD, or blitz QFD. Such abbreviated forms commonly

- use only the first (House of Quality) matrix;
- focus only on portions of the product where critical trade-offs occur;
- restrict the number of variables (rows and columns in the matrix) to 20, ideally fewer than 10;
- include self-checking mechanisms to terminate the process when it has answered the critical questions.

Finally, QFD, like many other market research tools, works best for products to which customers can relate, ones for which they can articulate preferences. If you are working on an upgrade, changes in size, color, or the like of something familiar, QFD is appropriate. Its power to capture the pivotal value drivers for really new products is much less certain.

The Alternative to Frozen Specifications

The specification is by nature an imperfect representation of an imperfect product. As a team learns how to get off to a faster start, it will be starting with less information, so the specification will be more likely to have shortcomings. This is why it is so important for everyone on the team to have a broad view of the product, its goals, and its benefits. Good development team members can usually fill in missing details or make adjustments if they have the big picture, customers, and users clearly in mind.

Many developers advocate "frozen" specifications, which would certainly make their job easier. Unfortunately, frozen specifications do not fit with reality, which is that the initial specification is quite unlikely to be correct, and even if it were, the marketplace would most likely change before the company can deliver the product. (The faster you are to market, the less likely this shift is.) Thus, freezing the specification is usually foolhardy.

Fortunately, there is an alternative to frozen specifications. It is a knowledgeable, empowered, cross-functional development team. This team, described in detail in Chapters 7 and 8, has all of the information, resources, and authority needed to make fast decisions on most proposed specification changes quickly. An important piece of this information is the financial analysis covered in Chapter 2, which enables the team to judge quickly whether the extra time needed to accommodate the change more than outweighs the value of making it.

SUGGESTED READING

Clausing, Don P. 1994. *Total Quality Development*. New York: ASME Press. Includes a thorough treatment of QFD, but being a mainline book on the subject, it is not oriented toward speed.

Fisher, Roger, and William Ury. 1991. *Getting to Yes*. New York: Penguin. Reaching agreement on a specification by several parties is essentially a process of negotiation, and skill in negotiating win-win agreements speeds up the process. Fisher and Ury's approach supports our suggestion of concentrating on benefits. These authors emphasize that it is more productive to understand each party's underlying interests than just to state positions, which then tend to become inflexible.

Hauser, John R., and Don Clausing. 1988. The house of quality. *Harvard Business Review* 66 (3): 63–73. Probably the most readable description of QFD generally available. Examples show, through a sequence of matrices, how customer needs influence design characteristics and lead to production requirements.

Herstatt, Cornelius, and Eric von Hippel. 1992. From experience: developing new product concepts via the lead user method: a case study in a "low-tech" field. *Journal of Product Innovation Management* 9 (3): 213–21. The lead-user method is one of the few that applies to really new products, and it can be a fast means of identifying customer needs. This is a good example by von Hippel, a leader in this method.

McQuarrie, Edward F. 1993. *Customer Visits*. Newbury Park, Calif.: Sage Publications. An excellent, compact book on this important subject. It stems from the customer visit training he has conducted at Hewlett-Packard. However, McQuarrie has a traditional market research tendency that needs to be turbocharged a bit to accelerate the process.

C H A P T E R 6

Using System Design to Compress Schedules

As we are completing the product specification we are often beginning the most critical stage of design activities, that of product architecture or high-level system design. In our experience, few managers understand the critical importance of this stage to accelerating the development process. Yet this is where so many products seal their fates. It is almost impossible for a subsystem designer to compensate for a major defect in architecture. In contrast, a good architecture can easily compensate for major defects in subsystem design.

From a practical perspective we classify decisions as "architectural" based on two properties. First, they must impact many other design decisions. Second, they must be difficult to change later in the design. If a decision has these two properties it requires management attention, or it could lengthen our development cycles. Let us use the analogy of building a house. Architectural decisions include whether it will have a basement, where the load-bearing walls will be, and how high to make the ceilings. Such decisions have a fundamental impact on many other design choices and they are hard to reverse. In contrast, decisions about wall coverings and the size of the cabinets are rarely architectural.

Architectural decisions are critical to rapid development for two reasons. First, good architectural choices enable us to do more development tasks concurrently, thereby shortening development cycles. Second, good architectural choices permit us to use other tools such as incre-

105

mental innovation, discussed in Chapter 4, and small teams, discussed in Chapter 8. Good architectural decisions shorten our cycle time.

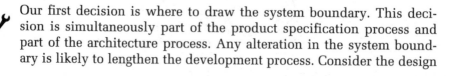

Let us illustrate this with an example. Lumonics, Inc., is the world's largest supplier of industrial laser systems and developer of the LASERDYNE™ 140 Laser Welding System, mentioned in Chapter 4. The Product Manager, Terry VanderWert, estimated that it would have taken nine to ten months to design the LASERDYNE™ 140 if they had done a completely new design. Instead, they chose an architectural approach that emphasized reuse. The motion system, enclosure, control system, software, optics, and laser were reused from a variety of existing systems. They limited themselves to minor changes of these subsystems, concentrating on sections that were critical to achieving cost and performance targets. This had a dramatic effect on the schedule of the project, which was completed in just over three months. Furthermore, despite the speed of the project, the design's reliability was outstanding. The use of well-characterized, tested subsystems dramatically reduced the technical risk of the project.

This chapter describes the principles of structuring a product for rapid development. We will begin by discussing the key architectural decisions and how each of these is likely to affect development speed. Then we will discuss the impact of architecture on risk. Finally, we will examine the process of architecture and who should be involved in making architectural decisions.

THE KEY ARCHITECTURAL DECISIONS

Certain decisions have a much greater tendency to be architectural than others. We will focus on five of these decisions. First, we must decide on where to draw the boundary between the system and the rest of the world. Second, we must decide how modular to make the product. Third, we must decide where to locate functions within the system. Fourth, we must define the interfaces between subsystems. Finally, we must decide how we will maintain flexibility within the system. We will examine each of the decisions in turn.

Setting the System Boundary

Our first decision is where to draw the system boundary. This decision is simultaneously part of the product specification process and part of the architecture process. Any alteration in the system boundary is likely to lengthen the development process. Consider the design of a cordless shaver. This product has a different system boundary than a plug-in shaver, because it obtains power from the product's internal power source. When we shift this boundary we partially invalidate our previous knowledge of the customer. The user of a self-powered product has different needs than the user of one dependent on external power. For example, early cordless shavers designed by Braun had an on/off switch similar to those of a plug-in model. Such shavers could accidentally be activated inside a traveler's luggage. This new problem did not exist in the plug-in model. Later generations of the same razor solved the problem by adding a switch that could be locked in the off position. By redefining the system boundary, the use of the product changed, which required a reevaluation of the requirements. This means that whenever the system boundary changes, prepare to spend more time with your customers. If you want to save this time, focus on a known customer with a well-understood application.

The Degree of Modularity

The second architectural decision is how modular to make the system. The product's functions can be broadly distributed throughout the system or they can be concentrated into modules. Modularity is a powerful tool to shorten development cycles, but it must be used carefully because it has a price.

The primary advantage of modularity is that it permits more concurrent development and greater flexibility to adjust the scheduling of modules. Consider a cable TV decoder design which placed the power supply in a separate box with a cable leading to the unit on top of the TV set. This added extra cost but it divided development into two separate tasks. For example, the power supply module may be simple to design and test, but it is on the critical path due to its need for (in the United States) Underwriters Laboratory approval. By getting the potentially dangerous voltage out of the set-top box, this more complex unit is not burdened by UL approval time. By dividing the system into well-defined chunks we can work on those chunks independently, which permits overlapping activities and reduces the length of the design process.

The cycle-time benefit does not come free. Modularity is likely to impose two basic disadvantages: it adds cost and reduces performance. Modularity adds cost because modules must be interfaced with one another. They may require mechanical interfaces such as fasteners to connect the modules. If the two parts could have been produced as a single piece, no interface would have been required, no holes made, and no fasteners or fastening operation required. Similarly, modularity may require electronic interfaces such as cables and connectors. These extra parts add both material and labor costs to the product.

The performance disadvantage of modularity arises from that fact that interfaces are frequently the weak links of a system. In electronic circuits the interfaces create limitations on speed and reliability. In mechanical systems the interfaces are the frequent source of failures. Think of the loose legs on an old wooden chair or the annoying drip from a leaky pipe fitting.

The financial effect of these cost and performance penalties can be assessed using the economic model discussed in Chapter 2. We usually find that the cost and performance disadvantages are small compared to the cycle-time impact. Often these cost and performance penalties can turn out to be surprisingly small because of another interesting side benefit of modularity. Modularity makes it possible to upgrade overall functionality without completely redoing a design. A classic example of this is the modular oscilloscopes designed by Tektronix. Their designs could be enhanced by simply improving their input modules.

Locating Functions

The third architectural decision is where to locate functions. Fast development programs locate functions so that they do not cross module boundaries. A great example of creative design was Hewlett-Packard's first low-cost plotter. Most plotter designs of the time used a mechanism to move the plotter pen in both the x and y directions. Because this mechanism was fairly massive, it required large motors to move it quickly over the paper. Hewlett-Packard recognized, however, that the function of movement did not necessarily have to be concentrated in the pen assembly. Instead, the design moved the paper in one axis and the pen in the other. Now the pen only had to move from left to right, while the paper moved up and down. Since the paper was light in weight, it required smaller motors to move it, and it could move quickly. The overall result was a quick, inexpensive plotter.

Unfortunately, such creative design is usually at odds with the need for speed. Shifting functionality from one module to another creates additional interface problems to solve, and this lengthens the design cycle. To keep the development cycle as short as possible, keep functionality in roughly the same module from one design to the next, and minimize movement of functionality between modules.

Designing Interfaces

The fourth architectural decision is the design of interfaces. If modules are the bricks of design, then interfaces are the mortar that holds them together. Just as mortar provides a buffer that isolates irregularities in one brick from those in its neighbor, a good interface isolates design decisions in one module from those in others. This allows modules to proceed largely independently of each other. This independence is maximized when interfaces are stable, robust, and standard.

The first principle of interface design for rapid development is to keep the interfaces stable. Having stable interfaces is vital because interfaces are the key external constraint of the module designer. If an interface changes, the module designer may need to redesign the module. Such a redesign could range from a relatively minor task to one in which the entire current design would have to be discarded.

Since the objective is to design as many modules concurrently as possible, interfaces must be defined early in the design process and prevented from changing. Doing so allows the module designer to work with a fixed set of rules. For example, on one complex system design more capability was added to a key instrumentation module partway through the design. This functionality caused every other piece of the system which communicated with this module to change. This meant massive changes in the system software which forced retesting a large portion of the system. This situation could have easily been avoided if the original interface to the instrumentation module had been defined to allow the easy addition of functionality. That way the interface would not have had to be changed during the design process.

Stable interfaces have the added benefit of improving development team morale. People will often give 110 percent when they are properly motivated. However, nothing destroys the motivation to give extra effort as much as seeing work that is almost completed made totally useless because the requirements have been changed. This is like trying to run a 100-yard dash, only to be stopped 90 yards down the track and told that you are running in the wrong direction. It should be no surprise if after several such episodes designers simply slow down the pace. They will have learned that there is less wasted effort by waiting for everybody else to finish before completing their module. Unfortunately, if no one wants to finish first no races will be won.

The second principle of interface design for rapid product development is to make the interfaces robust. An interface with generous margins is unlikely to need changing and therefore likely to stay stable throughout the design process. For example, many electronic systems have a collection of electrical conductors carrying power and signals, called a bus, connecting modules. In some cases a bus will be designed to work at a particular speed or frequency. Busses can be designed to work over a narrow range of frequencies or, with more difficulty, over a wide range. The wider the range of frequencies, the more robust the bus and the more flexible it is for the designer. Busses can also be designed to have extra, unused conductors in them that can be used later if someone forgets to allow a path for a particular signal, or plans change. This flexibility is what helps keep an interface stable as the design progresses.

Mechanical interfaces can also be designed to be robust using the same principles. If, for instance, a part is mounted to the frame with larger bolts than required, then if the part becomes heavier it may be unnecessary to change the bolts. The more robust the interface, the less likely the need to have to change it.

Robust interfaces are generally more expensive. They amount to buying insurance against design changes or mistakes. Chapter 2's tools will help you decide how much of this insurance to buy.

The third principle of interface design for rapid development is to use standard interfaces whenever possible. Standard interfaces have a number of important advantages: designers and suppliers already understand them, and their quirks will have already been discovered. However, they will not be perfectly suited for a given design. In fact, there is no standard interface which an engineer of even average competence cannot improve on. The advantage of the standard interface is that it is stable, tested, and understood. This minimizes communications between modules and allows each module to move at its own optimal pace without much dependence on other modules.

Maintaining Flexibility

The fifth architectural decision is how to maintain flexibility within the system. Flexibility in the architecture can accelerate development. For example, the original IBM Personal Computer was introduced into a market being served by the Apple II and a Radio Shack computer called the TRS-80. The Apple II used a floppy drive for storage while the TRS-80 used a cassette recorder. It was probably unclear to the IBM product planners which of these approaches would become dominant. Instead of trying to choose one interface they wisely decided to offer both and let the market sort it out. The customer preference for the floppy drive was overwhelming, and the follow-on product, the IBM PC XT, eliminated the cassette port.

The key lesson here is that you don't always have to know exactly what customers want as long as the architecture is flexible enough to meet their needs. Such flexibility has a cost impact, but this cost may be far lower than the cost of the cycle time required to resolve the uncertainty.

Flexibility is also dramatically improved with a modular structure because it bounds change into a smaller area of the product design. For

example, one manufacturer of electronic equipment designed the upper housing of its product in two pieces. One piece was the main body,
which required a large tool with a long lead time. This part of the design was frozen first. The second piece was the insert for the control
panel. This was a small part which could be made quickly. Such a
structure permitted the long lead time tool to be started before Marketing resolved the front panel design. It also permitted Marketing to stay
flexible on the layout of the front panel without delaying the product.
It illustrates a very fundamental principle underlying modular design,
which is to put the variability in as few modules as possible.

When we make these five key architectural decisions well, we reduce the rework which normally delays the design process. Such rework often occurs because a change in the design of one module forces
a change in the design of an adjacent module. Such propagating changes
can show up at the worst possible time for a designer, right near the
end of the design process when there is no time available to work on
it and there is no time left to test whether the new design works. We
protect ourselves from these changes with good interface design.

MANAGING RISK

A particularly important decision in the management of architecture
is how we will manage risk in the system. Architecture can be a powerful tool to reduce both technical and market risk, terms we will define in more detail in Chapter 12. There are three important issues we
must consider. The first is whether the risk in the system should be
concentrated or distributed. The second is our approach to controlling
system integration risk. This is the risk that modules which individu-
ally work will not function when combined into a system. The third
issue is how we will control the risk of individual modules. Let us
look at each of these issues in turn.

Risk Concentration

In our experience, projects that concentrate risk in a certain area of the
system achieve faster development times than those that distribute
these risks broadly throughout the system. Most developers underestimate the overall risk in a program with distributed risk. The multi-
plicative effect of distributed risk makes the overall system's risk level
surprisingly high. Figure 6-1 illustrates the essence of this problem.

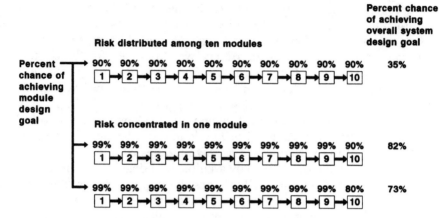

If risk can be concentrated in a few modules, it will become easier to achieve system objectives.

FIGURE   6-1

If there are 10 modules in a system, each with a 90 percent chance of achieving its design goal, there is only about a one-third chance that the overall system will achieve its design goal. (The goal is a target cost, target performance, and a delivery date.)

Contrast this with the situation where the risk is concentrated in a single module. If nine modules each have a 99 percent chance of achieving their design goal and the 10th has a 90 percent chance, the overall probability of success would be over 80 percent. Thus, restricting the risky technology to a single subsystem more than doubles the probability of success, or looking at it the other way, it cuts the probability of failure to nearly one fourth of what it was.

In fact, by concentrating risky technology in a single subsystem we could use technology with an 80 percent chance of meeting its design goal and still more than double the chance of success from that in the first case with all modules at 90 percent.

There are several other benefits in employing proven technology for the majority of modules and concentrating risky technology within a few modules. Modules with risky technology tend to be communication intensive. Concentrating the risk in a single area minimizes the total amount of external communication, reduces the risk of miscommunication, and forces communication to take place within a smaller, more cohesive work group. All these factors facilitate faster development.

The concentration of risky technology within a few modules also simplifies management. The most talented people can be assigned to these modules. Furthermore, management can monitor these modules more closely and detect and react to problems quicker. In contrast, when risk is broadly distributed we have almost no ability to antici-pate where the project's problems will come from.

Another big advantage of concentrating risk is that we can iden-tify it, plan how to deal with it, and monitor these plans (see Chapter 12). These management plans should employ the financial model dis-cussed in Chapter 2 for deciding whether to switch to backup tech-nology. This is done simply by evaluating the financial consequences of delivering a product late by sticking with a current plan, compared to delivering a product with lower performance or higher cost by us-ing a backup plan. In most cases this analysis, which can be done in minutes, will point to staying on schedule by using the more expen-sive technology. The economics usually tend to work out this way be-cause high cost in an individual subsystem is a rather small portion of overall costs, whereas schedule delays and performance shortfalls tend to have great impact on life-cycle profits.

Low risk in the remaining system modules is usually achieved by using proven technology, which is the essence of the incremental in-novation approach described in Chapter 4. In fact, companies that achieve rapid development cycles typically use proven technology in as many modules as possible.

Controlling System Integration Risk

System integration risk is the risk that correctly functioning individ-ual modules will not work together when combined into a system. Whenever you have loaded a software program into your personal com-puter and discovered it did not work, you have experienced system integration risk. The computer worked before and the manufacturer verified that the program worked. Yet when the program was combined with your particular computer configuration, things stopped working.

System integration risk is disastrous for the schedule because system integration occurs on the critical path near the end of the de-velopment process. This is the worst possible place to experience an unpredictable activity, since it will cost us an unpredictable amount of cycle time.

System integration risk is increasingly important for almost all developers because it is rapidly becoming the dominant technical risk in most product development projects. This occurs because system in-tegration risk rises exponentially as the number of design elements in-creases, as shown in Figure 4-1 (page 72). Designers who did not have to worry about system integration risk 10 years ago are now learning about it, painfully, today.

System integration risk can be reduced by using two techniques already highlighted. First, it will be reduced greatly when we concentrate risk within the system, because this allows us to use high-confidence modules in most of the system. Such high-confidence modules have well-characterized interfaces that have been thoroughly tested in other systems. This means that most of our system integration problems will arise from interfacing with the single risky module.

Robust interface design is another route to managing integration risk. By placing generous margins around critical system components we can reduce the risk of integration problems. In contrast, inadequate margins raise the likelihood of interactions between system elements that will lead to problems during system integration.

Individual Module Risk

In general, individual modules are not the dominant source of technical risk. Usually, one can establish that there is at least one technically feasible way to achieve the module's function, then leave it to the module designer to either implement this approach or find a better one.

However, be careful about asking for functionality in a module that requires magical powers to implement. For example, on one telecommunications product the system design required an individual module design to transmit data faster than permitted by a fundamental theorem of communications theory, called Shannon's Theorem. Needless to say, this became a challenge for the design team, who eventually requested relief from this requirement. One project manager at Hewlett-Packard labels such design tasks with the acronym TAMO, which stands for "Then a miracle occurred." Module designs that require miracles to occur tend to delay entire projects.

WHO SHOULD DO ARCHITECTURE?

The final architectural issue is an organizational one. Who should make these decisions about product architecture? The sad truth is that many companies do not even highlight these decisions as being fundamentally different from other design decisions. For them, architecture is something that happens by accident as the design engineers encounter it.

Effective product developers take a very different approach. Most companies that undertake large systems design designate an explicit organization position called the system architect. In some cases architecture is done by an entire department, which is further supported by systems engineering effort.

Unfortunately, even in these sophisticated companies architecture is too often seen as an engineering issue. It becomes a technical decision made to maximize product performance or minimize product cost. In reality, this fails to exploit the true potential of good architecture to accelerate development. Managers must see architecture as one of their primary management tools. It is an enormously important tool to shorten cycle times by permitting parallel effort.

This chapter ends with two classic examples. The first illustrates how architectural choices can get products to market quickly. The second, how architecture can interact with organization. They should remove any doubt about whether top management should be concerned about product architecture.

Consider the architecture of the original IBM Personal Computer. No individual component of its design was beyond the technical capability of IBM. Yet the microprocessor was sourced from Intel, the floppy disk drive from ALPS, and the operating system from Microsoft. The system design was deliberately "open" to attract third-party application software suppliers. These decisions had a great impact on the time to market for the product. But time to market was not the only thing that was affected. The architectural choices also had enormous impact on who would control the strategic portions of the system. In retrospect, it appears that IBM underestimated the importance of controlling the operating system layer of the system architecture. The company that controls this layer has control of the interface between the hardware and the application software. Microsoft gained control of this layer with the original version of MS-DOS/PC-DOS and has maintained control ever since.

Another example of the broad-reaching effect of architecture lies in the contrast between unibody construction and frame and panel construction in the automotive industry. The United States automotive industry traditionally focused on frame and panel construction. This permitted the frame to remain relatively unchanged while the body panels could be restyled every year. The new look of the next year's model would make American consumers want to replace their cars. Frame and panel construction uses the frame to carry structural loads while the panels are used for styling. This architecture leads to an organizational separation between the people who worry about the structural loads and the people who worry about styling. The organizational separation then preserves the architecture.

European firms took a very different approach to automobile design. They adopted unibody construction, in which the body panels act as structural members. This ability to use the panels to do two jobs resulted in lower costs, and lower weight cars with better fuel economy. It meant that the styling could not be changed every year on the car. Interestingly, the lack of constant style change was not a problem in the European market where car owners did not like their cars to go out of style within 12 months.

It proved very hard for United States automotive manufacturers to accept the advantages of unibody construction. Despite their successful inroads into the United States market, foreign designs were at first ignored, then ridiculed. Yet it is possible that unibody construction presented more of an organizational challenge than a technical one. The clear separation of styling and structural design would have to be dissolved. People who had power to control certain decisions would lose it.

This example illustrates two key points about architecture. First, that there is a very important linkage between architecture and organization which creates momentum behind a particular architectural approach. Once such momentum is established it is hard to change direction. Managers should establish this initial direction carefully and recognize that their influence may be essential should a change of direction become necessary. Second, it illustrates the critical interaction between architecture and non-engineering functions. The inability to change styling with unibody construction has to be an integral part of the overall marketing strategy of such products. They need to be positioned on the basis of enduring value to customers who care about value. We cannot make architectural decisions independent of marketing decisions. Furthermore, the architectural choices also had impact on manufacturing technologies and costs. Thus, we need to get Marketing and Manufacturing management involved in our architectural choices.

The paramount message of this chapter is that architectural decisions are not simply technical decisions that should be left to Engineering. They have enormous impact on cycle time and penetrate to the very essence of the business. As strategic decisions, they must be made by management drawing on the full expertise of Engineering, Manufacturing, and Marketing. When architecture is viewed as a technical issue alone, its potential will not be exploited.

As we are beginning to make our architectural choices, we are starting to grow our development team. In the next chapter we will examine the issues of staffing and motivating this team.

SUGGESTED READING

Eppinger, Steven D., and Karl T. Ulrich. 1995. *Product Design and Development*. New York: McGraw-Hill, Inc. Chapter 7 of this book makes it one of the few books on product design to give a good treatment of product architecture. It has a strong focus on mechanical hardware and emphasizes physical structure rather than logical structure. Consistent with the engineering background of the authors, it also treats architecture primarily as an engineering problem.

Rechtin, Eberhardt. 1991. *Systems Architecting: Creating and Building Complex Systems*. Englewood Cliffs, NJ: Prentice Hall. This is perhaps the best book we are aware of on the subject of systems architecture. It is full of real-world examples and has an interesting collection of practical heuristics.

CHAPTER 7

Forming and Energizing the Team

During specification definition and system design we begin to staff our team. In some cases we may start with a skeleton team of experienced people preparing the specification and doing system design. In other cases, we will be able to staff the entire team at the very beginning of the project. The latter approach is preferred for most projects since it will both accelerate these initial activities and increase the commitment of team members to the project's objectives.

We can distinguish a team from other groups of people, such as committees, crowds, or clubs, by the cohesiveness of its purpose. Members of a team are strongly aligned to a common goal and are willing to place attaining this goal above many of their personal objectives. If members are not aligned or do not attach importance to the goal, we will not get the essential behaviors that we need on rapid development teams.

In this chapter we will discuss choosing and motivating team members. In the following chapter we will discuss organizing teams to facilitate communication and rapid decision making.

In our look at forming and motivating teams we will consider four distinct issues. First, we will consider the problem of selecting leaders for the team. Then we will look at the problem of selecting team members. Next, we will look at the activities that allow a team to become productive quickly. Finally, we will consider how teams can be motivated.

THE TEAM LEADER

Of all the decisions management makes in doing accelerated new product development, none may be more crucial to success than choosing a team leader. A strong leader will be able to overcome many other shortcomings and imperfect decisions, but a mediocre one will be stymied even by small obstacles. The leader is often the buffer insulating the team from inappropriate management practices that run rampant in the rest of the company.

It is important to pick a leader carefully and announce the choice publicly. Everyone should know exactly who is responsible for successful completion of the project and what authority he or she has been granted by management. Diffuse responsibility may work in many management situations, but it rarely works in the fast-moving world of rapid product development. Successful projects typically designate a clear leader and maximize the continuity of leadership.

Upon occasion management does not designate a specific leader. For example, in one telecommunications company the team leader changed every week at the weekly team meeting. We rarely see successful projects using such an approach. Another company believed in letting the natural leader emerge. We asked all the members of several teams to name the person who was leading their project. A wide variety of responses included two Vice Presidents of a $500 million operation. In one

of the projects that ran into many last-minute manufacturing problems, the largest number of votes went to the manager of the manufacturing plant, which was halfway around the world. Such free-for-alls may be the breeding ground for leaders, but the confusion in this natural selection process lacks the focus needed to develop a product quickly.

Maintaining continuity of leadership is as important as giving clear authority to the leader. Too often a new leader completely redirects the product. This leads to delays and frustration on the part of team members. Based on our experience we recommend making a thoughtful choice in leadership and sticking with it.

Selecting the Leader

There are three basic success factors in selecting a leader:

- Ask the leader to volunteer rather than being assigned.
- Use the leader in a management role rather than as a technical contributor.
- Give the leader the power to influence the organization.

Using a volunteer rather than an assigned team leader is important because of the psychological effect it has on the team. The team leader more than any other individual on the team becomes a role model for team behavior. He or she becomes a symbol of the team. Any team leader will be far more committed to the objective of the team if that person has volunteered for the job. This higher level of commitment flows through to other team members.

In practice, these "volunteers" are solicited very carefully by management. Management will first assess what skills are necessary for the success of the project, then draw up a list of candidates who meet these criteria. Then management will sit down with individual candidates to discuss the opportunities and potential challenges represented by the project and why they think the individual should take advantage of it. Usually, the rate of volunteerism is high.

The volunteers that are sought are not simply the strongest technical contributors in the organization, because the team leader position is not primarily a technical role. Instead team leaders are really the future general managers of the organization. They are people who can view the development project as a business proposition, not simply as a technical or marketing problem.

However, this does not mean that we can totally ignore technical skills. In general we find the best leaders for technically oriented teams have a technical background themselves. This background gives them credibility with engineering members of the team and allows them to more accurately make judgments regarding the risk of certain courses of action. This technical background need not be world-class expertise. It simply needs to be strong enough to communicate effectively with the experts. In fact, it is often quite risky to have a world-class expert as a team leader because of that person's tendency to be drawn into technical problem solving, leaving a vacuum in team management. One of our clients explicitly avoids using technical powerhouses as team leaders.

Occasionally we are asked if the team leader should come from Engineering. Many, including respected professors in business schools, say the leader of a technical product-development project must come from Engineering. Others argue that only a marketing- or business-oriented person will have the breadth of vision needed to keep the project headed in the right direction for the company. Another group suggests persuasively that if the product is going to get into manufacturing quickly and at low cost, the project leader must come from there to provide an orientation toward manufacturability.

Each viewpoint is valid, but they all miss the point. What they are saying is like asking, "Should the quarterback come from Chicago?" The quarterback must come from wherever you can find the best quarterback. Team leader skills are scarce in any company and different projects have different success factors. The team leader should be chosen on the basis of how well his or her skills fit the needs of the project, not on the basis of functional background. We have seen good team leaders come from Engineering, Marketing, Manufacturing, and even Finance.

Wherever they come from, the team leaders must be capable of influencing both fellow team members and people in the company who are not direct members of the team. This means that they have to understand the workings of the company and politics of the company well enough to obtain resources and get things done. They also need credibility within the team. Usually, this means that the team leader will not be an individual who is brand new to the company. Such people rarely have the influence that has been acquired by an equally competent leader who has been around the company for a few years.

One of the primary sources of influence for the team leader is his or her clear vision of what the product will do for the company. This vision should be based on a deep understanding of customer requirements and competitor product offerings. The team leader is often the keeper of the vision for a team, who preserves the overall integrity of the product. Teams that lack such leadership often produce products that look like they were designed by a committee. These products lack a clear thrust in the market and seem to fail to make any customer happy. Furthermore, a lack of leadership and vision can cause the project to vacillate or drift away from its objectives.

Tom West, the team leader in *The Soul of a New Machine* (see Suggested Reading at the end of this chapter), provides an excellent example of how a clear vision helps guide the team. It was not clear to the younger members of the team what West did, but without his constant reassessments, his backstage arrangements to keep the Eagle project moving forward, and the directives he passed down to the team at critical points, the project would surely have foundered and possibly died.

Empowering the Leader

Once the team leader has been selected it is important to give him or her unambiguous authority for the job of running the team. This is best done in a meeting in which management transfers specific authority to the team leader. It is important that this transfer of authority be witnessed by both team members and the functional departments that are losing the authority, otherwise the team leader will have future problems in accessing functional resources.

The transfer of authority should be more than ceremonial. Teams need to know specifically what authority they have to do things like select suppliers and change product requirements. The best method we have found to clarify these roles is to have the team leader and the functional managers discuss the specific decisions that will remain within functional authority and those that are delegated to the team.

This helps set clear expectations for all parties at the beginning of the project. Such expectations prevent demotivating surprises.

There is no one right answer to the amount of authority transferred to the team leader. The solution is specific to the company, the project, and the specific skills of the people on the team. The decision is complex because the desire for authority by a team leader may be a symptom of deeper problems in the company. For example, when procuring parts is a bottleneck, the team leader will want authority to perform this task. Granting this authority is a good short-term solution but it may fail to address a deeper problem—poor capacity management in procurement. In some cases it will be better to attack the deeper problem rather than simply circumventing it on a single project.

In practice, this empowerment of team leaders does not only flow from the top of the organization downward. Many of the most successful team leaders we have encountered are very willing to test the limits of their authority. They often find it is easier to ask for forgiveness than permission.

THE TEAM MEMBERS

Once the team leader has been selected, the leader should recruit the team members. This is most commonly done by preparing a list of desired team members and negotiating with the functional owners of these resources for their time. Such negotiations go much faster when the team leader has the clout of the General Manager behind her or him. Once these team member candidates have been identified, and the function is willing to release them, then the team leader goes to them and tries to "sign them up."

The importance of having team members volunteer for the project is often underestimated. This can be a major change in viewpoint for an organization long used to simply assigning employees to jobs that must be done. In one such company we recently met with a client team leader six months after he had started a team. He said that, even though he had understood—from a previous edition of this book—the difference between assigning and recruiting, assigning team members was one of the biggest mistakes he had made. Now the people on the team wanted off of it, and those off of it wanted on.

In such a volunteering process the team leader tries to honestly present the opportunity and challenges represented by the project to a prospective team member. The prospective member then has an opportunity to articulate concerns and to identify personal goals that the project could help him or her achieve. For example, a new engineer might want to learn more about the manufacturing process and therefore would desire the opportunity to work on tasks involving this function. Once the deal is struck we have made a subtle psychological breakthrough. When team members volunteer, they are psychologically more committed to the success of the team than when they have simply been assigned. Furthermore, the team leader is more committed to working with the team member when the leader has selected them than when they have simply been assigned.

 We must reemphasize that the product development team is cross-functional and requires, as a minimum, strong and continuous participation from marketing and manufacturing functions. Companies frequently fail on both these counts by either not putting these functions on the team or trying to control their participation to avoid having marketing and manufacturing specialists spend too much time with the team. This is very dangerous, as we shall see when we discuss choices of organization form in the next chapter.

We should also mention that team membership is a job, not an opportunity to criticize the work of other employees. We often see "team" meetings full of people who come into the room, offer some sage advice, point out some deficiencies, and then head for their next meeting. A good rule of thumb is that everybody who attends team meetings must leave with some action items. If you have no action items you are not doing anything to move the project forward, which means you are just deadweight on the project.

The Fallacy of Fragmented Teams

One of the biggest problems we see in team design is the fragmentation of team member time among too many projects. Team members who are dedicated to a single project a high percentage of their time are much more productive than those who are part-time members (see the text associated with Figure 11-1 on page 207 for further discussion). Yet it remains very difficult for companies to dedicate resources to specific projects. Managers appear to fall into two traps in organizing their teams. First, they focus too much attention on full-time team members. Ironically, though full-time members do most of the work, this does not mean that they are the most likely source of delay on a project. Second, managers underestimate the difficulty of making a fragmented team work. It is natural for managers to focus attention on full-time team members. After all, it is logical to think that the development activities that contribute the most value to the project are those that need to be optimized. This thinking invariably leads us to think that engineering activities are the heart of product development.

Managers who understand development speed have a different perspective. They realize that the activities that are most likely to delay the project are those of the part-time players supporting multiple projects. It follows that these are the people who are most important to manage, because they are likely to create the delays on the critical path of projects. As a rough rule of thumb, assume that the less work someone has to do on your project, the more likely they are to be a delay on the critical path. When you are interested in cycle time, you focus on the part-time players, not the full-time ones.

Furthermore, managers frequently underestimate the difficulty of making a fragmented team work. We have been so indoctrinated in Adam Smith's division of labor that we fail to realize that higher levels of dedication create two important advantages. First, they will produce a smaller team size, which in turn reduces communications overhead, as we shall see in a moment. Second, people will naturally have a higher level of commitment to tasks that occupy a larger portion of their time. Part-time players will constantly be diverted from the project by other intervening priorities. Such diversion is precisely where schedule slippage comes from.

A warning to managers is in order here. It will not be easy to keep some people on the team full-time if the organization has not been used to having full-time commitments. Consider an example of a software engineer on a team we helped set up. He was very talented and highly specialized in developing computer code for the machines his company produced. After a few months of working full-time on the team for just one machine, he told us he disliked the arrangement, because he was used to working on several machines simultaneously. When he ran into a tough spot on one, he would put it aside and work on another for a while. This specialist was unconsciously dictating the schedule of several new products according to the tough spots that happened to arise in writing their code. He disliked the full-time team concept because it forced him to confront a problem and deal with it until he had licked it. Full-time team members have nowhere to hide; they have to work on whatever problem is on the critical path of the project.

The Specialist Problem

One of the primary causes of fragmentation is the use of specialists. We can significantly reduce fragmentation by adding generalists to the team. Such generalists help the team in two ways. First, they keep the project work under the control of team members who are spending a large portion of their time on the project. Such team members have the strongest motivation to ensure the work is completed on time. Second, the generalists are resources that can be shifted to whichever activity is on the critical path. This flexibility is important because the location and duration of critical path activities can be hard to predict.

Unfortunately, the creation of generalists within most companies is obstructed by most of their personnel policies. Instead of rewarding team members for their breadth, they are rewarded for their functional expertise. Engineers are given golden badges when they obtain 10 patents. One can certainly defend this practice as a way of encouraging technical expertise, but it is a strong disincentive for the engineer who wishes to develop generalist skills. We often find that the most useful engineers on the team are not the Ph.D.s who are near the state-of-the-art in their fields, but the ex-technician who became an engineer and can run a machine tool, set up a test, or complete a few drawings on the CAD system.

Leading developers in industry recognize the importance of generalist skills. For example, Don Caudy is Vice President of Battelle's Product Development Group, an organization that provides contract development services to many companies with striking success. His organization must constantly meet challenging goals on cost, quality, and cycle time. He observes that one of the keys to Battelle's success has been the way the company develops its people. Most engineers that join his organization from industry or academia are what he calls "I" shaped individuals are deep in their discipline and perform well as individuals (I's). Battelle must turn them into "T" shaped individuals, people who can not only do one thing well, but who also know a number of other things at an adequate level to understand how their work integrates with the other stakeholders on the team. Developing such a staff is crucial to success in this demanding business.

If some generalists will help a team, we might be tempted to think that an all-generalist team will be even better. Unfortunately, the problem of using specialists is more complex than this. All-generalist teams typically work only for very simple products. For most development projects, specialists are needed because they already know the answers to many problems that a generalist would have to solve on the critical path of the project. For example, the IBM Proprinter owed much of its success to astute use of materials. Plastics on this design substituted for both simple metal parts like fasteners and complex ones like lead-screws and frames. The materials had to be carefully formulated to achieve attributes like conductivity, acoustic damping, durability, and cost. Without access to the materials specialists, the project would never have succeeded. In a similar manner, the design had to overcome challenges to be sufficiently quiet. Without acoustic expertise from outside the team, it would have been impossible to overcome these challenges in time. Rapid product development without specialists is unlikely.

The challenge is to use specialists without letting them slow down the project. If you can do this, you can accelerate development projects

Dedication to project (%)

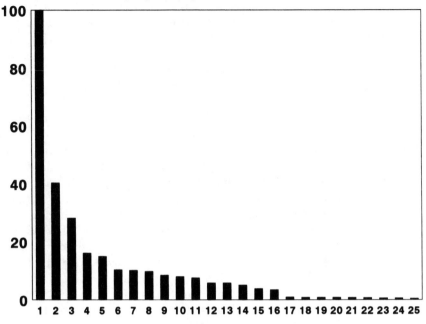

Individuals on the team

In functionally organized companies, teams tend to be staffed with many specialists, most having only low levels of dedication to the project. This illustration is the result of actual project data.

FIGURE   7-1

by taking advantage of the superior knowledge and speed of the specialist. To use specialists in this way we must understand why specialists so often slow us down. The danger in using specialists lies in their low involvement in individual projects and the multitude of tasks competing for their time. When these specialists support multiple projects their loyalty is equally fragmented. No single project is at the top of their work list for long. The specialist almost always has a queue of work waiting for his or her attention. Figure 7-1 shows the team dedication breakdown for a relatively straightforward product with about 30 parts. Of the 25 people on the team, only one was working on the project full-time. Eighty percent of the people on the team were specialists with a 10 percent or lower level of dedication. When such specialists are heavily loaded they appear to be efficient, but in reality contribute large delays to a project.

This kind of fragmentation, which has been the operating mode in North American industry for years, is deeply ingrained. The first breakthroughs away from this mentality came in the place we would least expect them: manufacturing. World-class manufacturers recognize that this kind of specialized efficiency is not really efficient in a broader context. As a result they are emphasizing flexibility in their workers and their production equipment. This thinking has been slow to migrate into product development. As product developers we need to recognize the importance of valuing breadth as much as we value specialized expertise.

Of course, this requires an attitude change on the part of team members. We need to choose team members partly on the basis of their flexibility. On one of our consulting projects we heard many complaints from engineers that certain people in Marketing were aloof and really did not care how the product worked. We asked team members, in a questionnaire, if they thought the Marketing representative on their team could disassemble and reassemble their relatively simple consumer product, given a few tools. All the engineers could do was chuckle at this question. They could not picture their Marketing member handling a screwdriver or a pair of pliers. The point is that not only should the Marketing member be comfortable with a soldering iron, but the scientist on the team should also be able to demonstrate the product to a group of visiting customers or create a first draft of advertising copy if need be. Flexibility leads to speed.

The Core Team

Often the workload of a project is larger than can be accomplished by a group of 10 or fewer people (see Chapter 8 on team size). In such cases, it is customary to designate a core team that functions as a management group for the activities of other team members. This allows you to avoid the large, unproductive meetings that might be caused by having all team members involved. Instead, lead managers for each group can work together and communicate with their subordinates.

The trick in organizing such a core team lies in choosing the fundamental theme that we will use to organize subteams. In general, we find most companies inclined to organize these subteams around functional skills. The mechanical engineers are grouped together, as are the electrical engineers and the software engineers. This is simply implementing a functional organization within our cross-functional team.

Our experience suggests that there is a much better way to organize such teams. If we organize around physical or logical subsystems of the product, we tend to get much faster development. For example, it is common at Microsoft to pair off programmers and their associated testers. This enables close interaction between the two groups, which find problems faster and fix them earlier. Another example is the design-build teams that Boeing used to develop the Boeing 777. Instead of splitting the design by functional skills, the Manufacturing and Engineering representatives were grouped together for each of 240 subsystems. This dramatically decreased the difficulty of the hand-off between Engineering and Manufacturing as we shall see later in Chapter 13.

One risk in using such a core team is the tendency to create two classes of project members. If the core team members attain higher status we will have a problem keeping non-core team members fully involved in the project. This problem will usually not show up with the extended members who are assigned full-time to the project. It can show up when the extended team includes members who are part-time or located away from the primary work site of the project. Problems can also occur when the core team is really a group of managers working part-time on the project, delegating the work to other members who are working full-time on the project.

There are three primary ways to keep the extended team involved. First, they must be granted equal access to important project information. A common technique for doing this is project-wide communications meetings. For example, Boeing used a large airplane hangar to gather the 10,000 team members on the Boeing 777 team to communicate to them all at once. Second, we need to show the extended team member how they fit into the overall project. Team members are always better motivated when they understand the relationship between their work and the success of the project. Third, we can use periodic attendance at core-team meetings as a method to keep them engaged. This can be done when a particular technical issue needs to be reviewed or recognition should be given for a particular success. The core-team meeting should not be viewed as a meeting for the core team only. One company we work with made it a policy to tell all team members that they can come to a core-team meeting whenever they wish. This open-door policy made it easy for people to voice concerns or simply to get recalibrated on the current status of the project.

Suppliers and Customers on the Team

Involving suppliers and customers on the team is another challenging problem. Many companies are reluctant to incorporate suppliers and customers as members because they are afraid that knowledge of their development project will leak out to competitors and customers. In our experience the risk of this happening is small, compared with the advantage of having early inputs from customers and suppliers.

If you are going to use suppliers on your team, involve them during the process of preparing the specification. For example, it is not unusual to find 80 percent of a product's value to be purchased from suppliers. From a schedule perspective, we frequently observe long delays for custom materials purchased from suppliers. These can be items such as injection-molded plastics, specialized integrated circuits, castings, and forgings. These long-lead-time items can have an enormous impact on development schedules. For example, it is hard to be certain if a molded part will be satisfactory before inspecting the first ones coming off a tool. Because of flow patterns and cooling effects that depend on the molding process, the part's shape and strength remain in question until the first parts are molded. So we must go through the time-consuming process of building the mold and actually making some parts before being able to tell if the parts will work. If they don't work, much of the lengthy cycle must be repeated. For some innovative products that stretch materials knowledge to its limits, it may be necessary to repeat this cycle several times. Not only does doing so add a lot of time to the schedule, but it also adds uncertainty, because it is impossible to determine beforehand how many times this loop will have to be repeated. Computerized tools help address this problem, but often they encourage us to push the limits of the technology even harder. The earlier we can involve the supplier in the project the more we can shorten these cycles and take them off the critical path of the project.

Suppliers should also be included as team members when the new product involves critical technologies in which the company is not expert. With product technologies becoming more complex and cross-functional, it becomes infeasible for even a large company to fund research in all potential product technologies. In a fast development project there simply is no time for the team to get up to speed on a new technology. The limitations and pitfalls of a new technology can be subtle, and must be recognized quite early in a rapid development project. The best way to gain this knowledge rapidly is to work closely with suppliers from the outset.

This close supplier relationship is even helpful when the company is as knowledgeable as its suppliers. For example, in 1980 it would have been difficult to think of a company that knew more about making computers than IBM. But when IBM decided to develop the PC on a crash schedule, it opted to source the two key parts of this computer, the central processing unit (from Intel) and the operating system (from Microsoft). The Intel 8088 microprocessor was already available and Microsoft, by working closely with the IBM team, could develop the DOS operating system faster than could internal groups. IBM's desire for rapid development dictated the use of outside suppliers (but see Chapter 6 for other implications of this choice).

If a product's schedule is highly dependent on a particular supplier's ability to supply parts that meet demanding requirements, consider requiring a supplier representative on site with the development team. In less demanding conditions, we can have the supplier visit the team for a few days each month, have a supplier representative attend team meetings, or arrange for team members to visit the supplier regularly. The key is to get the supplier deeply enough involved in the project to feel some ownership in its outcome and become keenly aware of how delay will affect the product's success.

Don Caudy, mentioned earlier in this chapter, is Vice President of Product Development at Battelle, which supplies product development services to many well-known companies. His very business depends on successful relationships with clients, so he does not leave this to chance. His observations are relevant to anyone who wishes to work well with suppliers. He suggests the following:

- Use a detailed plan with clear deliverables and intermediate milestones.
- Define what must be delivered to the supplier when it must be delivered.
- Have the supplier list all assumptions and known risks and discuss them with you.
- Never assume you are using the same vocabulary (a concept model can mean different things to different organizations). Instead, agree on the meaning of specific terms.
- Use concrete samples of typical deliverables to test whether you have achieved this common understanding.
- Use common information systems and software whenever possible.
- Achieve face-to-face communication as early as possible.
- Prepare interface specifications and drawings when the design work on a product or system is split between two or more organizations.
- Have an on-site presence whenever this is practical.
- Create robust communications channels by promoting contact at many levels between the two organizations.
- Use every communications tool available.
- Have on-site meetings with all the organizations involved in the project. This reduces the impersonality of subsequent long-distance communications.
- Capture your experience in checklists so that you don't repeat the same mistake twice.
- Assume that misunderstandings can occur and work to resolve them quickly.

It is striking how many of these tools are focused at the problem of getting good communications. Organizational boundaries and distance can play a large role in creating communications problems. We will cover this issue more in the next chapter.

Like suppliers, customers can also play a significant role on development projects. Some companies are so convinced that customer involvement is crucial that they will not even fund a development project without a target customer. Other teams complain that the customer sometimes sees this involvement as an opportunity to play design engineer, as he or she gladly encumbers the product with every personal whim that had been rejected in previous projects. One solution is to make sure that the customer requirements are truly representative of the market as a whole, not the dreams of one user. Another is to help customers understand your trade-off rules (Chapter 2), so that they will recognize the cost of their suggestions. Customer team members seem to work best on products that are sold to a handful of large customers. In such cases, to miss the needs of a single customer can be very expensive, and satisfying this customer can justify the entire business. In contrast, products being designed for highly fragmented markets benefit from more filtering of customer requirements. In such cases, we can still put customers on the team, but we must be very careful to assure that these customers are reliable indicators of true market needs. The issue of confidentiality has rarely been a problem that can't be solved by a combination of confidentiality agreements and careful preselection.

TEAM FORMATION

Once we have selected our leader and our team members, we enter a critical stage of team formation in which the team transitions from being a group of people to a team. Again, we stress that a team is a group sharing a common objective. This common objective causes team members to behave in a mutually supporting way, i.e., teamwork.

The activities that are accomplished early in team life are key predictors of whether the group will ever become what is popularly called a high-performance team. Before we cover these activities we should say a word about when to staff a team.

When to Staff

We have never run into a company that assigned its people to teams too early. Invariably the opposite mistake is made, which results in dramatic increases in project duration. Many times we have found that the total project effort in person-hours is exactly as forecast but the project is months late. In such cases it is common to see staffing taking place too late.

Most companies fail to realize the critical importance of having team members present for early team activities. They try to save a little money by not assigning people before they are needed. This is the most expensive savings they will ever find. As we have mentioned earlier and will cover again in Chapter 13, most of the project's ultimate results are determined early in its life. If members from functions other than Engineering and Marketing do not participate early, they lose 90 percent of the available leverage.

Furthermore, it is psychologically important to join a group early in its life. It is very difficult for an individual who joins a group late to attain the same status as early joiners. This difference in status can lead to less participation by the late joiner. In addition, the late joiner will not have the same degree of ownership in critical work products, such as the schedule and specification, which are the "glue" of the team and are developed early in the group's existence.

All critical team members should be assigned at the beginning of the project, even when it appears this is wasteful. There is always plenty of work to be done on a rapid development project.

Early Team Activities

Certain early activities help the team to gel quickly (see Figure 7-2). Begin by giving them a clear, challenging, and important objective. Teams will come together much faster under these conditions. This objective is generally communicated to the complete team by a representative of senior management. If the President thinks it is important enough to attend the kickoff meeting then the project is obviously important. This also allows management to clearly communicate the objective of the project. In one case, we encountered a team that did not have such contact with its Division President. They were six months into their project and totally confused about whether low cost or rapid development was the key mission. This problem could have easily been avoided if the President has been present at the kickoff—or at any team meeting after the kickoff.

Second, the team should devote some time to discussing their work process. Teams that discuss how they will do business will clear the air on many unspoken issues. This will allow them to come to productivity faster. In contrast, teams that devote no time to discussing group process are often at each other's throats much later in the project because important issues were not confronted early.

☐   **Set a clear, challenging, important objective.**

☐   **Discuss and agree upon team work process.**

☐   **Plan layout of work area.**

☐   **Build financial model for project.**

☐   **Create product specification and project schedule.**

☐   **Assess risk areas on the project.**

Checklist for forming teams.

FIGURE   7-2

Third, the team should decide on the layout of the work area. This is an early opportunity for the team to work together "designing" something. It can be good practice for resolving product-design issues later. The mere fact that the team has input on this decision gives them a sense of control and a commitment to making the chosen layout work. It is an easy place to start building teamwork.

Fourth, the team should build the financial model for the project if one does not exist, and refine it if it already does. This will make all team members aware of the project's cost of delay and give them a consistent way of viewing project trade-offs. Again, a shared view of the economics is likely to align the actions of individual team members.

Fifth, the team should create or refine the specification and schedule for the project. This may take more than one meeting because many of the team members may need to be exposed to customer visits, as described in Chapter 5. Depending on the background and experience of team members, and the depth of market research data, this can take from several days to several weeks. It is an important investment of time because participation in these activities causes the team to own the schedule and the specification.

Finally, the team should assess the risk areas on the project (see Chapter 12 for techniques).

You may notice that we have not included barbecues, volleyball parties, and mountain-climbing on this list. Such activities are low-risk ways for team members to get to know each other on a personal basis, useful when the team members come from radically different backgrounds and are working together for the first time. But this is rarely the case on a rapid development project where team members should have had some previous contact with each other. In such cases, jumping straight to productive project work enables team members to learn to work together at the same time as they complete important tasks.

MOTIVATING THE TEAM

For managers putting together rapid development teams, the subject of team motivation and rewards invariably comes up. There are few clear answers here, but we can provide guidance, especially on what to be wary of.

What Motivates Developers?

In 1996 the Product Development and Management Association held a conference session specifically on rewarding product development teams. Most of the participants were line managers overseeing development teams, so they had direct experience with and a strong interest in the topic. They had done some work beforehand and brought the standard questions with them. Should the team be paid extra? How should we handle those who support the team? How about overtime? What if the team misses its targets?

They struggled with these issues for two days in small groups of peers, then formed conclusions and action plans. Amazingly, these plans had very little to do with pay or bonuses at all. When they got into the heart of the question of motivation, they realized that developers foremost want to do a successful job of developing the product so that they feel good about what they have done. Consequently, these managers' action plans supported the developers in achieving success by

- giving the developers more control over specification changes so that they didn't feel that the specification was being jerked around on them;
- providing consistent team staffing, rather than pulling people on and off of the team as priorities shifted;

- furnishing prototyping and testing resources that amply supported the team's plans.

The shift in thinking these managers made over those two days was away from rewards and toward eliminating obstacles to the success of projects. One of the blessings of product development is that developers derive great intrinsic satisfaction from their work. Motivating them has less to do with adding additional rewards than it does with removing the obstacles that prevent them from succeeding.

Financial Rewards

Using financial rewards to incentivize development teams is a dangerous business. Occasionally we see people succeed using such an approach, but more often the rewards backfire. As Alfie Kohn (see Suggested Reading at the end of this chapter) puts it: Do rewards motivate people? Yes, they motivate people to get rewards.

 Kohn gives many reasons why rewards may not produce the effect desired. Among these is the fact that the reward becomes expected, and then when withheld takes on the character of punishment. For example, one software team was promised a trip to Hawaii if the project succeeded. The scheduled date came and went. Management generously readjusted the schedule. Spouses began purchasing beachwear to enjoy their vacation. When the project missed its second schedule, management felt it could not give the reward, which created serious discontent on the team as well as in their households.

One of the biggest problems with financial rewards is that we have to draw the line on who will be part of the participating group. Unfortunately, this usually means that part-time team members are exactly the people who get left out. Yet these part-time team members are likely to be the source of huge delays on the critical path. In this case team-based financial rewards can demotivate exactly the people who need the most motivation, making it that much harder for the team to get the support it needs from the rest of the organization.

Recognition

In contrast to the problems with rewards, genuine recognition is less troublesome. Few team members would resent a part-time player being recognized. Such recognition should come from people who are respected by the team. Often this is the senior technological leadership of the company rather than the managerial elite.

Recognition is often more valuable because it is more visible to other employees. It motivates both the team and other members of the company. Thus a culture is built to support fast product development. For example, individuals who have been especially effective in some aspect of cycle-time reduction can give a seminar in which they describe their technique to others. This provides recognition at the same time as it transfers know-how.

The firm of Carrier Transicold gives us an excellent example of providing this visibility. They used a fast development team for their Phoenix semitrailer refrigeration unit. The team was highly successful, developing in six months a product that would normally have taken two years, with a product that won a prestigious design award in addition. Carrier wrote up the project not just in its own company newspaper but helped get it into a national engineering magazine. The parent company, United Technologies, then went further by including a full-page photo of the three team leaders in its annual report. Beyond this, United Technologies placed full-page ads with a photograph of the team leaders in national publications, including *The Wall Street Journal.* This is priceless recognition for a job well done. The company's main objective was undoubtedly to publicize its new product, but at the same time it sent powerful messages to its employees about what it valued. However, notice that excluding the rest of the team from the photo could alienate other team members. Even recognition can raise issues of fairness.

A client created effective recognition for his team. He wanted to make sure his team focused on the proper end point, so he called upon a former engineer from the organization who was exceptionally talented and greatly admired by the employees. This engineer had risen quickly through the corporate hierarchy to become a Group President of the *Fortune* 500 parent company. Our client simply announced to the development team that he had invited this Group President, the team members' former colleague, to visit the plant on the scheduled completion date to watch the product operate. The date was on the executive's calendar, and he was too savvy to have been buffaloed by an incomplete product. Besides, the team would gain sincere recognition by being able to demonstrate their creation to an executive fully capable of appreciating its performance.

One last caution about rewards and recognition. We sometimes notice that excessive concern over rewards indicates something more basic is missing in the motivation equation. Perhaps basic pay is poorly distributed or the team is not given enough autonomy to be intrinsically motivated. In such cases rewards do not address the more fundamental problems.

Once we have our team selected we must take a deeper look at how to organize them. We cover this issue in the next chapter where we look at which organizational forms will accelerate communications and decision making.

SUGGESTED READING

Kidder, Tracy. 1981. *The Soul of a New Machine.* New York: Avon Books. This story of the development of a new computer illustrates many of the points discussed here on staffing a development team. One shortcoming, though, is its suggestion that engineers develop a product without interacting with other functions. *Must read* for anyone who has never been on the inside of a development team.

Kohn, Alfie. 1993. *Punished by Rewards: The Trouble with Gold Stars, Incentive Plans, A's, Praise, and Other Bribes.* Boston, Mass.: Houghton Mifflin. This book provides some well-documented arguments for why reward systems often fail to motivate workers. It makes a careful distinction between short-term effects and more insidious long-term impacts.

Meyer, Chris. 1993. *Fast Cycle Time: How to Align Purpose, Strategy, and Structure for Speed.* New York: The Free Press. Chapter 6 of this book has useful ideas on designing and implementing cross-functional teams. The author has extensive practical experience in this arena.

CHAPTER 8

Organizing for Communication

The last chapter and this one are central to the book, simply because it is groups of motivated developers who turn all of the other tools in the book into action; high-performance groups are the key to fast action. Following the pattern of a recipe, Chapter 7 described the ingredients needed for such groups and this one explains how to combine them effectively.

Not surprisingly, the topic here is team building. However, "teams" and "team building" are overused terms in the current management lexicon, so they have lost their meaning. For example, one of our clients calls all employees "team members," so the employee entrance at the back of the building becomes the "Team Member Entrance." This may improve employee morale and "team spirit," but it means that we will have to be especially careful to describe the characteristics that set rapid development teams apart.

Example: Core Teams

Many companies use so-called core teams to develop their new products. Some of these teams are effective and some aren't, so let's see if we can spot the differences. Figure 8-1 is a typical diagram of a core team. It comprises a team leader in the center, core team members from the disciplines critical to the project, and extended team members in

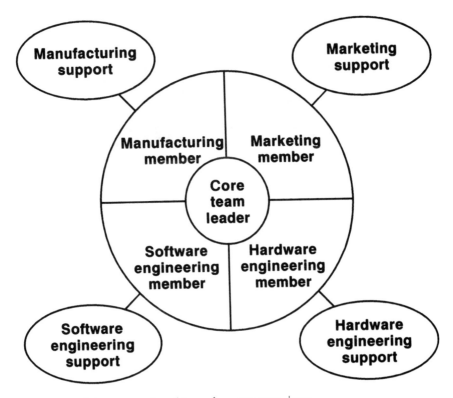

Organizational diagrams, such as this one for a core team, leave many questions about team effectiveness unanswered.

FIGURE 8-1

the associated departments. Does this chart depict an organization that can bring new products to market quickly? The answer is that we do not have enough information to decide, because it depends on many factors that, at best, are only suggested on this appealing diagram. How much authority does the team leader have? Do core team members report to the team leader, are they assigned to this project full-time, do they do real work on the project or just delegate it to the extended team, and are they all co-located with the team leader? Are extended team members working on the project full-time, are they co-located with the team, and who controls their assignments, the core team or the functional manager? Who writes annual reviews for members of the core and extended teams? These are the factors that will determine how quickly this group can bring a new product to market, so they are the issues addressed in this chapter.

Communication: The Central Capability

Developing a new product entails making thousands of decisions, and weak communication can delay these decisions or yield poor decisions that result in unnecessary design rework. The delay may seem minor, perhaps a day or a few hours, but the aggregate effect of delaying thousands of decisions is staggering. If project decisions are not made by the people working on the project daily, the project can be delayed every time such a decision is needed. Consequently, our team-design strategy is to minimize the need for external communication by giving the team the resources and authority to make the vast majority of project decisions itself. Appropriate organization and delegation of decisions avoids many of these delays.

ORGANIZATIONAL OPTIONS

Managers always seem to be searching for a better organizational design. This search is frustrating, because each organizational form has its strengths and limitations. Fortunately in our case, decision-making speed provides us with a good criterion for making organizational choices. Consider the organization diagrams in Figures 8-2 through 8-6. We will explore these in detail soon, but first just consider the ease of making horizontal (cross-functional) decisions in each diagram. As we progress from Figure 8-2 toward 8-6, the horizontal communication channel opens up more, and cross-functional decisions become more direct and faster. At the same time, the vertical channel, strong communication within a functional department, weakens.

In the functional form of organization, illustrated in Figure 8-2, a project is divided into its functional components, with each component assigned to its own appropriate functional manager. Coordination is handled either by functional managers or by upper management. Because all projects are managed by the same management group, they all tend to get standardized treatment. Standardization is an advantage if the organization wants to use uniform components and methods, but it can also dangerously mix urgent and routine projects to the point that it becomes impossible to speed up anything. The financial analysis tools in Chapter 2 will help you to decide which is really driving your business, speed or standardization.

Functional organization can be effective for stable activities that take place within a single functional area without needing extensive

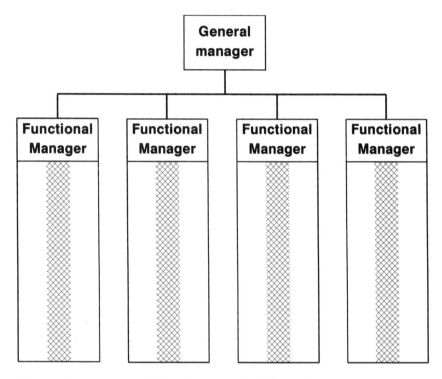

A functional organization, in which authority rests with the functional managers.

FIGURE 8-2

communication with other functional areas, such as the manufacturing of established products. Functional organization also has great strengths for an R&D organization that is working on fundamental technology advances, because it keeps technical specialists close together where they can support each other. Although some development projects fit into these categories, our experience in consulting to many companies suggests that the bigger problem, by far, is the communication gaps that occur between Marketing and R&D on product requirements and customer orientation, and the breakdowns between R&D and Manufacturing on manufacturability and cost issues.

As we move progressively from the functional organizational form to the more cross-functional ones, there is one characteristic that separates them: the relative authority of the team leader and functional manager over the project's resources and design decisions.

The next form of organization, and probably the most dangerous one, is the lightweight team leader form. As shown in Figure 8-3, there

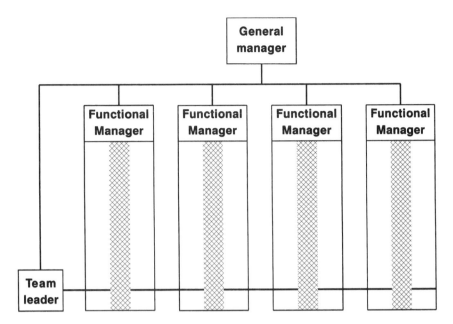

In the lightweight team leader form, team leaders exist but have little authority relative to that of functional managers.

FIGURE 8-3

is a nominal team leader in this case, who is devoted to the project. The problem is that this person has no real power and just oversees plans created by others. He or she usually knows just how much the project is late or over budget, or just who isn't pulling their share of the load, but they have no authority to take action. In this person responsibility and authority are poorly matched. Functional managers, from their experience, seniority, or political acumen, retain real authority over the project. Communication in this form of organization is as circuitous and decision making as slow as in the functional form, because any real decisions must involve the functional managers as well as the "team leader."

The danger in the lightweight team leader form is that the companies using it usually believe they are using a more powerful team approach than they actually are. They moved from the functional form to the lightweight team leader form and now think they have a project team. Actually, they have taken only one step out of the three or four they could take. Nor do they realize that the effect of what they have done is to add one more layer to their bureaucracy.

We call our next organizational form the balanced one because it makes an attempt to balance the power of the functional managers and

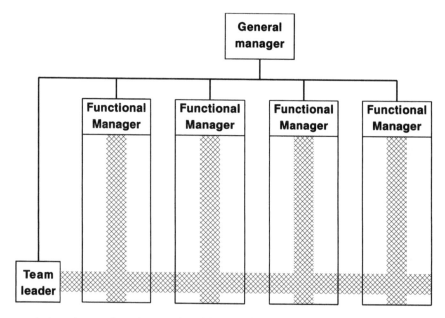

In a balanced matrix the authority is shared between functional
managers and the team leader, but the division of power is unclear.

FIGURE 8-4

the team leader. This arrangement is often called the matrix form (see
Figure 8-4).

One way to divide up authority between functional managers and
the team leader is to give the team leader control over how an individual's time is to be spent and have the functional manager be responsible for the individual's professional growth and development within the
company. (Observe that this works best when individuals are assigned
full-time to a single project, because otherwise the functional manager
gets drawn into project resource management issues.) Another approach
is to give the team leader control over project-related matters and assign functional managers control over functional expertise.

 Unfortunately, within the project team it is difficult to establish
appropriate boundaries between functional technical guidance and design freedom. Consider a case where the functional manager wants to
use an electrical connector used by many other of the company's products, but design trade-offs on this particular product suggest using instead a special connector to accommodate certain automated assembly
machinery the team plans to procure. In a case like this the functional
manager gets involved in the team's product design decisions, which
enlarges and slows down the decision-making process.

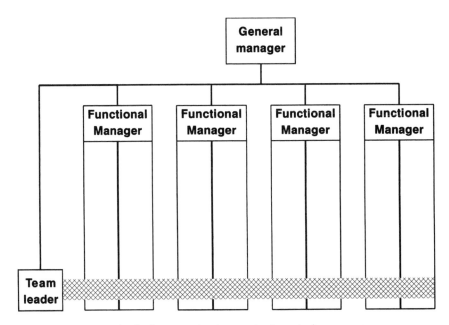

The heavyweight team leader form provides the team leader with clear authority over the team members on the project.

FIGURE 8-5

In principle, the balanced form seems to offer the best of both extremes. In practice, though, it is a difficult form to manage because it is hard to separate the areas of authority. Much time can be wasted in working out the turf issues.

The next organizational form, illustrated in Figure 8-5, has a heavyweight team leader. Here the leader controls all the project-related issues, including design trade-offs, but the functional manager retains title to the people. The functional manager normally continues to write their reviews while they are on the project. When the project is over, these people return to their managers.

This form, by definition, gives the team leader the authority needed to get products developed quickly. It avoids the type of ambiguity just described over who has authority to specify fasteners, for instance, by clearly assigning all such decisions to the team leader. This form can also provide professional coherence and assure that there will be a home for team members when a project is over.

The last form of organization, the separate project, is shown in Figure 8-6. Here the project team is truly an independent unit within the organization. Relative to the heavyweight team leader approach,

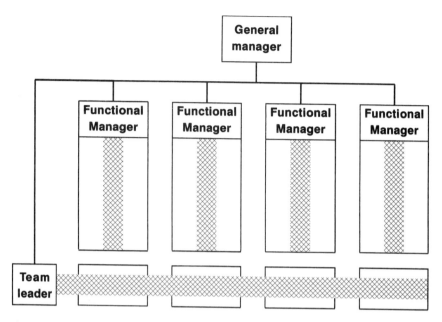

The separate project form severs ties to the functional departments.

FIGURE 8-6

this one can foster a more independent, entrepreneurial environment in which time to market can be a do-or-die concern.

Venture groups are an example of separate projects, but they tend to be more than just projects, because they carry their own full business and administrative responsibility. Developing a business structure takes energy away from developing products, so venture groups are often not the fastest way to develop new products.

The original Skunk Works, established by Kelly Johnson at Lockheed, was a separate project, although it continues as an organization to this day. Skunk works have been tried by many others, with outcomes ranging from very good to very bad, and this has led to a variety of opinions on skunk works. The quality of its leader, the way in which senior management interacts with the team, and the team's ability to operate effectively without alienating itself from the rest of the organization are all factors in the differing assessments of skunk works. Too often, a skunk works is set up because all other approaches have already failed and the only way to complete the project is to go outside the regular system. This approach might get one product to market quickly, but it avoids the fundamental issue of creating a fast-cycle capability that will add to a company's competitive strength. It can be a useful short-term tactic but rarely has a permanent impact.

Yet there are cases where skunk works have been used to initiate broader organizational change. These cases are carefully designed to pilot new concepts, and the problem of reintegration is meticulously managed. For example, Chrysler used a skunk works, called the Viper Pit, to design its first Viper—and at the same time used it as a pilot for shifting to its successful platform teams.

The separate project should be considered an alternative development process, with its own appropriate control systems, that is established by management for use when circumstances suggest it. Just like the other forms, this one is not universally better, only better in certain cases. If executed properly, it will be too demanding of talent, resources, and management attention to be used on every project.

Although the separate project can get a new product to market quickly, its greatest value is often in providing an ongoing means of challenging and rethinking the less radical forms, to see if certain aspects of the separate project might be adapted to them. It is an experiment in rapid new product development with the ultimate power to revitalize the company, just as it did for Chrysler. Such experiments are covered in Chapter 15.

Picking the Best Form

Table 8-1 summarizes in a single view the pros and cons of the five forms discussed above. By the way, there is nothing special or all-inclusive about the five forms listed; they just provide five illustrative points along a useful continuum.

There is no clear "winner" in this table, so what do we do? We first look at the objectives—the drivers of success—for a particular project. We then choose the organizational form that best fits the primary objectives, adjusting it as necessary to these objectives. This chosen form will have some features that will most likely be undesirable, so we identify these weaknesses and put appropriate compensating mechanisms in place.

For example, Chrysler has found that a permanent separate project form, which it calls a platform team, is best for its strong emphasis on cycle time. Currently Chrysler has five such platform teams, one each for small cars, large cars, minivans, trucks, and Jeep®. However, lack of common standards and shared design experience across the teams is a weakness for this form, especially as Chrysler uses it on a permanent basis. Chrysler's means of compensating for this weakness is to form Tech Clubs in certain technical areas that span the teams. There are 10 Tech Clubs now in major areas, such as body engineering and thermal. Each has subgroups; for instance, the electrical and

TABLE 8-1

Strengths and Weaknesses of the Five Organizational Forms (The items shown here are general indications; ones more specific to the organization will be more useful in a given situation.)

	Functional	Lightweight	Balanced	Heavyweight	Separate Project
Strengths	Technical coherence	Identifies resource and schedule issues	Can allow strong functions with strong projects	Fosters task overlapping	Concentration on one project
	Consistency across projects	Functional management remains in control	Flexibility to move people and have dedication	Members grasp project drivers	Focus on the customer
	Individuals do what they know best	Each project has a focal person	Develops negotiation skills	Fits with dedicated staffing and co-location	Easy to co-locate
Weaknesses	Reinforces sequential development	"Team" lacks authority	Questions about "who is my boss"	Hard to find suitable leaders	Projects are linked weakly
	Weak grasp of project drivers	Illusion of greater strength than it has	Power struggles	Project can drift from other projects	Hard at end to reintegrate
	Weak commitment to project	Frustrating for the "leader"	Individuals don't get clear guidance	Flux when projects end	Little flexibility to move people

electronics group has a radio subgroup. These have evolved from a rather informal system a few years ago as Chrysler's platform team system has matured.

Notice that Chrysler violates our advice above that all projects should not be run as separate projects, due to the demands that such projects place on resources. This exception demonstrates that there is nothing inviolate about our principles. In some cases, running all projects as separate projects may be the best solution, but we have seen more companies stumble than succeed in attempting this.

If we take the approach of adapting the organizational form of each project to its specific needs, then we are going to have as many kinds of organization charts as we have kinds of projects. This was mentioned in Chapter 1 as part of the messiness that is a byproduct of going faster. There are various ways of dealing with this variability, especially in an ISO 9000 environment in which there is an expectation of an established organizational form and development process against which progress can be measured. One means, used by Chrysler and others, is to have an explicit step at the beginning of the project where the organizational form for that project is determined and documented. Another is to establish several predefined forms for different business circumstances, then assign each project to one of these predefined forms.

You may notice two trends in Table 8-1: as one moves from the functional form to the separate project, speed increases, but the potential for higher expenses also arises. To the extent that the forms on the right seem expensive, one must know the cost of delay, as discussed in Chapter 2; otherwise, the trade-offs will appear too expensive, and the slow, status quo system will prevail. Although there is the appearance of a trade-off here, the experience of many companies that have used the more "expensive" forms is that they actually find them cheaper once they are using them (see Figure 1-7, page 13, and its associated discussion).

DEVELOPMENT TEAM ISSUES

Teams Are Not Meetings

We mentioned earlier that *teams* is an overused term that has lost a clear meaning. Often we hear teams being equated with meetings, as in, "Susan's team is the one that meets on Friday mornings." Some teams form to make decisions or solve problems, and these teams may do most of their work in meetings. However, this connection is dangerous for development teams, which are instead teams that *do* things, such as designing parts, visiting customers, and testing prototypes. These tasks do not get done in meetings, and if the team equates membership with showing up at meetings, little will get done between meetings. Then progress will be slow, which is clearly disastrous for rapid development. Furthermore, the whole concept of letting a decision wait until the team next meets is incongruent with fast cycle time, which must be much more proactive in style.

Don't let anyone believe that they can be on the team simply by attending the meetings.

Team Size

Research done on teams suggests that a team of five to eight individuals works most effectively. Fewer than this and the group lacks the diversity of skills and viewpoints needed for effectiveness. With too many people, communication becomes complicated, geographic spread of the group starts to hurt, and consensus takes more time to achieve. This is wonderful news if your products just happen to be suited to development teams of five to eight people, but most products need either more or fewer than this. Let's consider both cases.

Just look around your office or home. The things you see—waste baskets, staplers, coffee pots—do not require great leaps of innovation or large teams of people to develop them. There are dozens of these mundane projects for each notebook computer project that gets written up in *BusinessWeek*. Yet a team of one or two individuals lacks a critical mass and tends to require an exceptionally broad set of skills from each member.

If you have small projects, some options are available. One is to move more toward multiskilled generalists. Although this does not increase team size, it does justify keeping the same people heavily involved in the project, rather than suffering hand-offs or more fragmented staffing. The next option is to only plan on using teams for your largest or most complex projects, where they will probably provide more value anyway. Lastly, consider lumping a few related products together under one project to reach the critical size. This has the advantage that, with some careful planning, the individual projects can be staggered, keeping the overall staffing by discipline fairly level. Also see Chapter 11, which suggests that management's bias is to understaff projects, because resources are always tight; thus, a small-team situation is an opportunity to add one more person to the team, which will simultaneously bolster the staffing level and get the team up closer to the ideal size, both factors to accelerate progress.

The more obvious problem is projects that are too large to be done by a small team. Chrysler prides itself on reducing its development teams to *only* about 700 engineers from ones that were almost twice this size a decade ago. Boeing used about 7,000 engineers to develop the 777. The challenge on such large teams is to achieve the entrepreneurial spirit that exists on much smaller teams.

Such large teams will often be hamstrung by communication difficulties if they are not properly organized. The basic architecture of the product provides an opportunity to organize the team for effective communication. When we use the concepts of product architecture to divide the project up into relatively independent modules, they can be developed by separate teams. Concentrating on designing clean interfaces, as described in Chapter 6, allows teams to proceed with less interteam communication. This is what Boeing did on its 777 project, using about 240 design-build teams, as they were called. For example, one team was responsible for the rudder of the aircraft, another for the passenger doors.

Can We Afford a Separate Team?

Management often is reluctant to set up a separate team or a heavyweight team. Such teams are not the automatic answer for every organization or every project, but they do have great power to bring new products to market faster. Because of reluctance to start using these forms, often they do not get applied in cases where they would really help the organization. So let's explore the resistance to making this change so that you can consider it more realistically.

Probably the most common concern is that the people needed for such a team simply have too many other responsibilities. Wonderful observation! If your prime new product developers are so overloaded and fragmented, then you have your problem right here. You might turn to Chapter 11 to explore it some more, but in essence, you will never be very fast to market until you can dedicate your principal human resources to what you say is important—rapid introduction of new products. In this case, using a dedicated team on one project on a trial basis, as explained in Chapter 15, is a good way to get started.

Related to this situation is one in which the key people or the leader needed for such a team just do not exist in the company. The company has encouraged individual contributors and a chimney-type organization to such an extent that it lacks people with the cross-functional skills needed to even start a team. As for the team members, this shortcoming will need to be addressed in your recruiting, training, and promotion policies, but usually most of a team can usually be patched together if the desire is there. For the team leader, we often find that management has not searched broadly enough. The leader of this team is a crucial role in the new form of your company, so it would be worth considering someone from your functional manger or executive ranks to fill it the first time. In the future, you will have to emphasize the development of team leaders if you wish to continue the practice.

An underlying concern often is that the people on the team will not be kept busy. On a well-functioning team with the proper training, we have never found this to be a problem. People start planning ahead to keep their, or their team mates', activities off of the critical path, which is the very essence of rapid development, as explained in Chapter 9. It may be uncomfortable to set up a dedicated team if you fear that people will not be kept busy. But you can swing the odds in your favor by training the team, using monitoring techniques such as management by walking around, and setting clear contractual objectives for the team (see Chapters 10 and 14).

The last possibility is that your products are minor enough that they cannot engage even a dedicated team of a few people. If this is a question, calculate the cost of delay, as explained in Chapter 2. This will enable you to decide whether dedicated teams are worth pursuing. If they are, refer to the material earlier in this chapter concerning small teams.

FITTING FAST DEVELOPMENT TEAMS INTO EXISTING ORGANIZATIONS

Teams and Support Functions

Teams, especially the more powerful forms of them, often find that they can move quickly but their project languishes in the test lab or the model shop. This can be solved on several levels. First, recognize that it goes right back to your project economics: do they drive you to keep support expenses to a minimum, assuring full queues everywhere, or do they suggest that time is more valuable? See our example of how Hewlett-Packard monitors its support queues (page 269).

Arrange for your teams to go outside for support services when this is faster. Standing agreements with machine shops, circuit board houses, and rapid prototyping services, for instance, will facilitate quick access. One company found that this external competition for the internal support services caused the internal shop to get faster, too!

Lastly, here is a secret trick, because it works best when your colleagues are not aware of it. On one consulting assignment we noticed that everybody was complaining about the long delays in the machine shop. Everybody except for one project manager. We asked her why it wasn't a problem for her. She explained, a bit flabbergasted, "I just go to the machine shop supervisor when I am planning the project and work out with him what I need and when I can deliver the drawings. He appreciates this, because nobody else lets him know their plans. Then I deliver the drawings as planned or make arrangements with him if plans change. He follows through with the parts responsively. That's all there is to it!"

New Roles for Functional Managers

If you have just an occasional dedicated team or two, they will not be too disruptive to the rest of the organization. But if much of your organization moves to these forms, many questions arise about the "residue" functions and functional managers. These issues must be dealt with explicitly, because if they are not, the organization will, over time, lose its functional strengths and the functional managers will wither.

If most of your product development work is being done with dedicated teams, the role of the functions must be redefined, especially for the technical functions supplying most of the people for the teams. Two such roles are critical to the ongoing vitality of the company. One is maintaining corporate competence in the function. Say in mechanical engineering, someone must continue to keep the computer-aided design (CAD) system up to date, assess new methods of replacing life testing with computer simulation, and evaluate new technologies for your products.

The other need is to keep the function's skills up-to-date, for those both on and off of teams. For example, the Manager of Software Engineering would oversee recruiting, training, and career growth for all of the software engineers in the company, making sure, among other things, that the software engineers keep up-to-date in new computer languages and structured programming methods. Some programmers may need to spend time back in the Software Department between team assignments learning new programming techniques.

Teams and the Parent Organization

Team members and leaders develop valuable cross-functional, time-to-market, and customer-awareness skills on teams, and when the project ends, these skills are too valuable to the organization for them to be left to chance, especially if the organization wants to move further toward heavyweight teams. Well before the project is over, planning of future assignments should start with each team member. Team members are naturally anxious about their place in the company when the project is over; they need something to look forward to. Some may move on to the next project; some may return to the home department to hone their skills or develop more advanced technology; and some may take on a challenging new assignment in another part of the company.

A certain healthy balance is needed between the teams and the functional departments. If the teams are treated as being special—which can easily happen—they can easily become resented by the rest of the organization. In fact, the team is not special, but it is playing by a different set of rules. Unfortunately, outsiders see the glamour of the team but do not see the sweat at three o'clock on Saturday morning when the prototype fails yet another test. Management and the team itself must modulate the amount of exposure the team gets to make it a desirable job for others to aspire to but not put the team on a pedestal, where others might try to undermine the team's work. Another balance is between the necessary technical interaction with others in the company versus the casual onlookers. A Black & Decker team handled this modulation quite effectively by posting a keep-out sign at the entrance to their area when they were forming and storming, needing their privacy. Then later, when they felt more comfortable and had a prototype to show off, they removed the sign and put down a welcome mat. You will have to decide, initially and continually, whether to build walls or tear them down; unfortunately, this dilemma is worst at the beginning of the project, when you have the least experience to deal with it.

Carrier Corporation's Team Conquest, which developed a new line of rooftop air conditioners for large retail stores and offices, managed its communication with the rest of the organization well by issuing a monthly one-page team newsletter. It had a standard format: project mission, update on project activities, future plans, and thanks to individuals who had helped the team. Team members took turns writing it, and it was both distributed and posted on bulletin boards.

To Whom Does the Team Report?

In Figures 8-3 through 8-6 we have shown the team reporting to the General Manager. These teams are intended to be cross-functional and are encouraged to take a broad business perspective. Reporting to the General Manager reinforces the team design objectives. Unfortunately, in many organizations one must go quite far up in the organization to find a General Manager. Often, it is impractical to have individual development teams reporting to such a high-level General Manager.

In this case, the normal alternative is to have the teams report to the Vice President of Engineering, since most of the team members probably come from Engineering anyway. This complicates the problem of creating a true cross-functional entity. The team can too easily become essentially an Engineering team and may have difficulty retaining its Marketing and Manufacturing members. Should the team report to another functional executive, the outcome is essentially similar. In theory, it is possible to find an executive from another function, such as finance or human resources, to shepherd the team, but in practice such people usually have little interest in or knowledge of new product development.

Finding viable alternatives takes some creativity. Many organizations today, including Black & Decker, are appointing Vice Presidents of Product Development, to whom development teams report. Others have teams assigned on a rotating basis to Vice Presidents of Engineering, Marketing, and Manufacturing, and they hold these executives responsible for providing general management leadership to the teams assigned to them.

CO-LOCATION

At the outset of this chapter, we stated that enhanced communication is what drives an effective organizational design for rapid product development. Perhaps the most potent tool for providing that communication is physically getting team members close together, what we call co-location. By close, we mean close enough that they can overhear each other's telephone conversations. The team members co-located include those from Marketing, Manufacturing, Engineering, and any others, such as Purchasing, who are heavily involved in team decisions.

Many companies claim that they are co-located, because they sense its power, but they haven't really made the change to the type of co-location described above. Often, members are in cubicles spread around on the same floor, but they are not within earshot of each other. Often, a critical member, usually marketing, does not sit with the team.

The classic data supporting this closeness comes from Professor Thomas Allen at MIT, who has quantified the effect of distance on technical communication. By measuring the frequency of communication of 512 individuals in seven organizations over six months, he developed an analytical relationship between the likelihood of technical communication and separation. That relationship is shown in Figure 8-7. The "knee" of the curve is at a surprisingly short distance

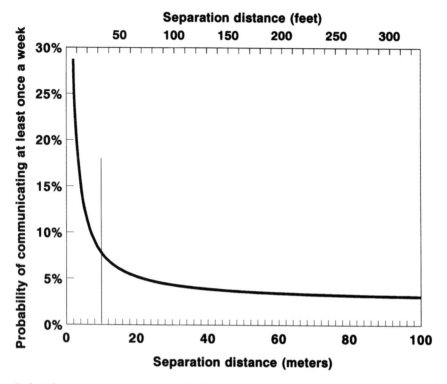

Technical communication is much more likely to occur between team members if they are located close together. *From Allen,* Managing the Flow of Technology, *Figure 8.3, p. 239, MIT Press, 1977.*

FIGURE 8-7

(about 30 feet, or 10 meters). Beyond about 100 feet (30 meters) the curve is so flat that further separation becomes immaterial. (See Virtual Co-Location on page 159 for an update of Allen's work.)

The Pros and Cons of Co-Location

In the seven years since the original edition of this book appeared, no subject in it has prompted more discussion than co-location. We have added to this discussion by asking many of our audiences who has actually participated in a co-located project. Then we ask these actual participants if they would do it again if time to market were crucial. The answer is always yes, from those who have experienced it.

However, those who have not tried co-location have many quite valid concerns:

- Lack of space.
- Concerns about distractions (especially from software engineers) or lack of privacy.
- Lack of a permanent office home or lack of status.
- Functional bosses worried about losing control of "their" people.

Co-location is a principal tool in shortening development cycles at many companies, such as Chrysler, Black & Decker, and Motorola. If you ask product development managers in these companies about how they now develop new products, one of the first things they are likely to mention is co-location. The implementation takes on its own character in each company. Black & Decker uses a team of about 10 people, and employs such "fusion cells" for all major projects. Chrysler has invested $1.1 billion in its state-of-the-art Technical Center, which houses all development activities, including test labs and model shops, under one roof. Each platform team, as Chrysler calls them, occupies one wing of one floor of the building, and Chrysler believes that this facility has given them a real advantage over their competitors, domestic and foreign, none of which has such consolidated facilities.

NACCO Materials Handling Group (makers of Hyster and Yale lift trucks) had no room for a co-located team, so it found unused land at its test center and leased a prefabricated building, which now houses a cross-functional team that includes members from the United States development center as well as from the target factories in Japan, the United Kingdom, and the United States.

We will provide just one sample of how NACCO accelerated problem solving with its co-located team. The team had just built the new truck's first frame, which was about to enter stress testing. The co-located manufacturing engineer happened to notice that pockets in the structure were too inaccessible to be cleaned and painted adequately, thus inviting rust later. Even NACCO's state-of-the-art CAD system would not have revealed this design mistake. It took "people around the metal," as they put it, and the manufacturing expert was right there, co-located. Then, because all of the skills needed were instantly available, the team decided on the design change needed and redesigned and rebuilt the frame, all within 48 hours. Without the co-located manufacturing engineer, probably no one would have even noticed the problem until the product got to the plant.

In order to foster co-location, many companies ensure that team artifacts, such as competitive products, broken test parts, supplier samples, the project schedule, large QFD charts (see Chapter 5), and design aids are in the team area. This draws team members, because it is where they must go to find the things necessary to do their work on the project. These "magnet" objects also help keep team members from drifting away from the team area later in the project, which can be a problem. Also consider providing conference room or quiet room space that can be reserved for activities that aren't effectively done in the co-located space, some portions of software development, for example.

Consider co-locating key supplier engineers too. Toyota achieves about seven times more face-to-face contact with supplier engineers than its North American rivals; the company credits this with advantages in both cycle time and product quality.

Dispersed Product Development Teams

Many product development teams are spread around the world or around the country. Management either believes that such spread is essential, or is not willing to pay the high price that Chrysler did to get its teams close together.

Sometimes, management just is not aware of how inefficient its dispersion makes its teams. Once we visited a client to gather information prior to teaching a time-to-market class. When we spoke with several executives of the company, they proudly told us how they had beat co-location by having three teams, one in San Francisco, one in London, and one in Tokyo. When the San Francisco team finishes its work for the day, it ships its work electronically to the Tokyo office, which then works on the design for a shift. Then the design moves on to London, so that they actually get three times as much effort per day as the design circles the globe. Electronic miracles! When we taught the class to the company's product developers, we related their bosses' story. The rank-and-file's view of the efficiency of this floating design was quite different, because they saw firsthand how designs tend to get redesigned each time a new designer takes over. What management thought was three times as much work was really three redesigns per day.

When they must spread out their teams, shrewd managers use as much co-location as they can. For example, a chemical company found that the chemists' daily work had to be done in vent hoods that could not be moved around the building; so they arranged a team desk area and had the team members sit together there for the first hour of each day while they did the day's paperwork.

Some companies discover that the team really must have two nuclei, so they form a strong co-located team at each nucleus and assure that the nuclei are well connected. Carrier's Team Conquest had a co-located team at the manufacturing plant, but also needed another team at headquarters, where they had some critical environmental test cells. Conquest's solution involved lots of travel in the beginning for training and team bonding. Then Conquest permanently booked video conferencing for eight hours a week. This setup included a video sketch pad, printing whiteboards, and faxes to pass graphics quickly.

Battelle helps manufacturers to develop their products, especially when the client manufacturer needs to get the new product to market quickly. Inevitably, in this contract development mode, part of the development has to be done at Battelle (in Ohio) and part at the client site, such as in the case of a sonic technology toothbrush project at Teledyne Water Pik (in Colorado). Battelle and Teledyne Water Pik planned in early team training and lots of initial travel to build trust and alignment on goals. Then they scheduled conference calls every Monday, Wednesday, and Friday, and these ran as long as necessary. At each nucleus the teams were co-located, where team members found that the ability to spontaneously collaborate and overhear telephone conversations helped everyone to anticipate issues faster and minimize redesign and formal meetings.

Virtual Co-Location

Allen's data (Figure 8-7) date to a period before there were communication tools such as voice mail, faxes, electronic mail, video conferencing, and the Internet. Some people, especially in high-tech industries, suggest that the need for physical co-location has been superseded by electronic media—what we might call virtual co-location.

We believe that the virtual co-location tools available today can supplement physical co-location but not supersede it. Everyone knows that phone tag and its e-mail equivalent are not fast ways to resolve issues. When we do not get the information we need to make a decision quickly enough by electronic means, we tend to make the decision without the missing information and move on. It is situations like these— where being able to overhear another team member's conversation or having them immediately available for a face-to-face conversation—that can keep a project moving ahead much faster and with fewer side trips.

NACCO Materials Handling Group clearly embraces physical co-location, but they also use their high-end CAD system to communicate with other marketing groups around the world. The group employs four remote workstations in different countries where marketing can watch solid models of the latest design and have them rotated, exploded, and recolored.

Each medium of communication has its advantages, and fast product developers recognize these and exploit them. Similarly, they understand where a particular medium should not be used. For example, e-mail is effective for non-urgent documentation (meeting minutes, parts lists, and memos), but it is poor for getting a rapid response or for interactive problem solving. The Internet may be the fastest means of passing a data file overseas, but it may be poor for explaining the nuances in using the preliminary data in that file.

Electronic (and face-to-face) media can be enhanced with techniques such as feedback, paraphrasing, and requesting verification. A useful exercise here is to listen in on air traffic control conversations (some airlines provide this on their audio channel, or you can purchase a receiver for this channel). Fast, clear communication is a life-or-death matter here. How do they make sure they are talking about the same thing—quickly?

Studies in human communication reveal that less than half of what is conveyed in a conversation comes from the words themselves; the majority of the message is communicated via intonation, body language, and timing. Electronic communication, depending on the medium involved, often fails to capture these other elements. The electrical engineering concept of bandwidth provides us with a helpful way of thinking about the range of available communication media. An e-mail message requires little bandwidth to transmit, but it cannot convey any intonation or timing information. Telephone messages need more bandwidth but convey more dimensions of the message. Video is another step up in both bandwidth requirement and communication richness. Finally, face-to-face communication would require a staggering amount of bandwidth but adds elements of body language that even the best of today's video cannot capture, as well as smell and touch.

As electronics provides new forms of virtual co-location, such as personal video, team communication will switch more to them. But these forms are unlikely to ever completely displace the full richness of real co-location. The astute product developer will recognize the pros and cons of each alternative to real co-location and in each case use a form that fits the need at hand.

TEAM TRAINING

Every rapid development team needs time together at the beginning of the project to concentrate, not on the project at hand, but on how team members will work together effectively. We used to think of this as a nice-to-have, as good insurance against the possibility of destructive friction within the team. But every team must understand how members will work together, what each person's roles and responsibilities will be, how they will operate proactively to keep work off of the critical path, and the types of methodologies they will use together. Every team eventually figures these things out, through what is often called the forming and storming stages, but to save the considerable time this adjustment can take, we find it much faster and surer to provide for it explicitly near the beginning of the project. The very beginning of the project is a bit too early, though, because a little initial turbulence can help team members to appreciate that there may better ways of working together and that they could use some help at it.

Normally, the best solution is a couple of days off-site for the whole team with a trainer. Many companies have professional trainers on staff for this kind of work, or you can find outside specialists who do it well. For your initial teams, you will also benefit from regular "booster shots" from the trainer as you advance from one stage of team effectiveness to the hurdles of the next stage. As the company becomes more experienced with teams, the need for these sessions will lessen. But the need will always be there, because each team will have to reassert its commitments and working style and make new covenants pertinent to the project at hand.

The heavyweight and separate project forms are quite demanding on team leaders, so training and developing these leaders is wise if you plan to use these forms. Like many other companies, DuPont has found that the skills needed to both lead a cross-functional team and manage a complex project were not abundant in its organization. So DuPont offers a three-day training class on project management and continues to facilitate and coach team leaders on styles of leadership. More broadly, DuPont strengthened the team leader position, making it a developmental position for future leadership in the organization.

The communication issues covered in this chapter take on vital importance as we move on to the next chapter to look for opportunities to execute activities in parallel, to save time. As we will see, having parallel or overlapping activities requires participants to work with bits of partial information, because the tasks from which they must draw their information will not be completed yet. This partial information is the seed of chaos unless high-quality communication linkages are in place. Consequently, communication issues receive a great deal of emphasis here, because in addition to their direct value, they are critical to the successful overlapping of activities.

SUGGESTED READING

Allen, Thomas J. 1977. *Managing the Flow of Technology.* Cambridge, Mass.: MIT Press. Interesting findings on the effects of communication and structure on R&D effectiveness. Chapter 8 in particular discusses the relationship between physical separation and the frequency of communication between technical workers.

Allen, Thomas J. 1986. Organizational structure, information technology and R&D productivity. *IEEE Transactions on Engineering Management* 33 (4): 212–17. Allen argues that the decision between using functional or project structures depends on how rapidly the company's technologies are changing. If they are evolving rapidly and the company's technologists are sequestered on a development project for too long, the company could lose its technical expertise.

Katzenbach, Jon R., and Douglas K. Smith. 1993. *The Wisdom of Teams.* New York: Harper Business. There are dozens of books on teams, but few of them pertain to the cross-functional project teams of professionals that characterize development teams. This book offers fresh insights by concentrating constantly on the connection between teams and performance.

Majchrzak, Ann, and Qianwei Wang. 1996. Breaking the functional mind-set in process organizations. *Harvard Business Review* 74 (5): 93–99. Although it covers a quite different activity (assembly of printed circuit boards) than product development, this study shows that just reorganizing into a cross-functional group has little effect on cycle times, but creating a collective, overlapping sense of responsibility can reduce cycle time dramatically.

C H A P T E R   9

Designing Fast Development Processes

Some managers focus solely on the process of product development, thinking that if they can just get it right, it will be the perfect recipe for their rapid development. Process is certainly an important element, but not the only one; furthermore, it connects strongly with many other topics in this book, such as the development teams just addressed.

The Importance of Process

Process has become a more important topic in recent years, as companies have delayered their organizations, thus de-emphasizing the role of organizational form and emphasizing process in its place. ISO 9000 has encouraged the shift to an established development process. Our emphasis here, as always, will be on the aspects of process that facilitate speed.

A development process is effective in a particular organization to the extent that it has been adapted to the specific needs and strengths of that organization. Borrowing someone else's process is not the way to fast development. The good news here is that once you have an effective process, it is a valuable corporate asset of limited value to your competitors. The bad news is that you will have to put effort into building your own process. However, the material in this chapter will focus your attention on the most fruitful areas for accelerating your process.

Another aspect of process is that the companies that are good at it continually work at it, modifying and honing their processes to suit ever-changing conditions. Chapter 15 describes how to institute this continuous improvement of your development process.

MOVING BEYOND THE "PHASES" MENTALITY

The product development process used in many North American and European companies was originally patterned after the phased project planning (PPP) process. In this process a project passes through checkpoints sequentially to ensure that all the items required by that checkpoint are in good order. Any problems are corrected and the project proceeds sequentially to the next checkpoint.

The PPP process is wonderful for catching items that have been forgotten and for assuring that company funds are not spent without justification. Unfortunately, we pay dearly in development time for this security. These processes are slow because of their sequential nature and because of the inevitable delays in review and approval that occur between phases.

PPP processes are difficult to move away from, because they fit our instincts as managers. We know it is important to catch problems early, and what better way to do this than to review work and approve it before moving on?

Tollgates and Stage Gates

A decade ago in the United States, a popular PPP process was the tollgate process, created by General Electric and adopted by other companies as they acquired GE managers or businesses. As anyone who has traveled on the Garden State Parkway or the autostrada knows, tollgates do not speed up travel. In fact, tollgates send an interesting message to developers that it is more important to stop traffic and collect the toll than it is to keep the flow moving. Black & Decker is an illuminating case in point. It inherited GE's tollgates when it acquired GE's small appliance business. Recently, however, B&D switched to a "milestone" system, because its new message is that the checkpoints are not to be stopped at but noted as the team passes them at cruising speed.

The terminology used does reveal management's intent. Nellcor Puritan Bennett (see page 171) uses the term *facets* for portions of its development process, because it wants to get away from any notion of the portions following each other sequentially.

In recent years the PPP process has evolved into the stage-gate process, popularized by Robert Cooper of McMaster University (see his book listed at the end of Chapter 3 and his paper at the end of this chapter). A typical stage-gate process has five stages, each preceded by a gate. Its improvements over a typical PPP process, as explained by Cooper, include:

- Each stage is staffed cross-functionally, not associated with a specific department as before (note that in this book we handle this crucial point in the teams chapters instead of tying it to the process).
- The process includes Marketing and Manufacturing as equal partners, rather than viewing product development as primarily Engineering.
- The process extends from the early planning activities through delivery to the customer, not just the engineering activities.

Users of stage-gate processes, and Cooper himself, are working to streamline the stage-gate process, but it remains primarily oriented toward control rather than speed. The economic analysis in Chapter 2 and an assessment of some of your recent projects will help you to determine how much emphasis to place on stages and gates as opposed to a more free-flowing process.

What Happens at the Gate?

Gates may seem essential to any development process, but Black & Decker (discussed above) has removed four of seven gates from its critical path, thus eliminating them as an impediment to speed. Some companies have no checkpoints. NACCO Materials Handling Group runs major development projects without any checkpoints, instead using a quarterly review system to monitor progress without delaying the project.

DuPont has adopted a rather formal checkpoint process with an effective twist. Upon analyzing its prior projects, managers saw that much time slipped away in reaching a decision at each checkpoint. So they have implemented a policy that a management decision will be made on the spot at each checkpoint review meeting. This may seem like a small change, but it is an effective one for them and a real cultural shift for an organization as established as DuPont.

The basic idea behind gates is that they give management an opportunity to kill a project or put it on hold at each checkpoint (note that management always has this prerogative, even without gates). This is the benefit, but there is also the cost of delay associated with each checkpoint. Thus, it is worth assessing the cost and benefit of each checkpoint. You may find, upon checking some completed projects, that certain checkpoints are rarely used to kill projects, but the cost of delay associated with them is substantial. Such checkpoints are then candidates for removal from your process.

At each checkpoint the effort required to pass it can either be provided mainly by the reviewers (normally management) or the reviewees (the developers). This assignment of reviewing burden should be a conscious decision in designing your development process, because if the reviewees assume the bulk of the burden, they will be diverted from doing productive development work, thus your process will become slower and more formal. If you do not address this balance explicitly, it is likely to shift toward formalism. For example, a formal process might have rehearsals of the review, whereas an informal one would let reviewers cope with some errors and inconsistencies in draft documentation.

Another useful question to ask is, "What is supposed to happen at a checkpoint?" Presumably, the checkpoint is there to keep the project from proceeding if it does not pass the checkpoint review. But do you really want work on the project to come to a standstill if it does not pass all of the checkpoint criteria? Will the people working on the project be reassigned or let go? Usually, this is not management's intention, and if not, then the documented process should be changed to reflect management's realistic intent. This alignment between management's intent and the official process is important because any discrepancies in the two put the project in limbo and thus slow it down. People are not going to work on the project with full energy if they are not sure that they should even be spending time on it.

The Critical Path Mindset

The concept of gates or checkpoints seems to be deeply etched into development managers' minds. However, among the managers we know who do well at accelerating projects, another concept is at least as dominant: the critical path. The importance of the critical path is not its ability to be calculated by project management software and portrayed on a schedule network. Instead, its real value stems directly from its definition: any activity on the critical path that slips by one day will directly cause the project end date to slip by one day.

Experts at rapid product development are constantly aware of which activities are on the critical path, and they actively work to remove activities from the critical path. The critical path is the hot seat; it is not a pleasant place to be. We can keep activities off of the critical path by assigning more resources to them, completing them before they get onto the critical path, removing or relaxing the requirement for them (making them not critical to project completion), or rearranging project activities to allow more time for them. Critical path management is a juggling act: when something is removed from the critical path, something else replaces it. Such is the life of a fast-track product developer.

Keeping activities off of the critical path and doing what they can to accelerate activities that are on the critical path are the responsibilities of members of a rapid development team, regardless of who is "responsible" for each task. This may seem obvious, but what often happens instead is that those whose activities are not on the critical path figure that they now have more time to polish "their" piece of the project. Then the extra resources to work the critical path tasks do not materialize, and worse, tasks that never should have been on the critical path get delayed or expanded until they are on it.

We find a critical path mentality to be an extraordinarily valuable one for anyone who is connected with an accelerated development project. To use it effectively we must know the cost of delay, covered in Chapter 2, because decisions to shorten the critical path require economic trade-offs. Only tasks that are on the critical path are worth the cost of delay.

THE KEY ROLE OF PARTIAL INFORMATION

Overlapping and Partial Information

Overlapping—working on multiple activities simultaneously—is a basic tool of rapid product development, and it will be a principal topic in this chapter on designing development processes. Product development is a process of gradually building up a body of information until it eventually provides a complete formula for manufacturing a new product. Overlapping influences the pattern of accumulating this information. In the traditional, more comfortable approach, information about a topic builds up until it is virtually complete, then is transferred to the next activity, where it is used to build the body of information needed for that task. Figure 9-1A illustrates this gradual accumulation and lump transfer of information. Notice that since the modus operandi is to provide complete information, the second activity cannot start until the first one is complete.

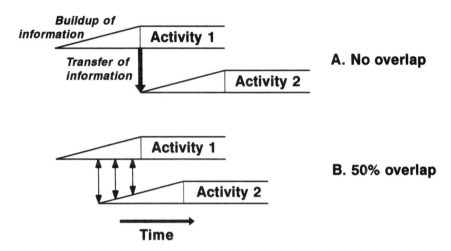

Overlapped and non-overlapped activities, showing essential differences in their information transfer processes.

FIGURE 9-1

In Figure 9-1B the two activities overlap. Because the first activity is still incomplete when the second one starts, the information available to it is by necessity incomplete. Working with this partial information requires a completely different style, as indicated by the difference in the arrows in Figures 9-1A and 9-1B. In the former case the information transfers in a single large piece, in just one direction. In contrast, in the overlapped case the information is transferred in small batches as it evolves. Because the information is incomplete, communication must go both ways as recipients ask questions about the data to find out what it means and provide feedback as to how well it meets their current needs.

Using partial information has its price, because we occasionally make incorrect assumptions when applying it and then some work has to be redone. The more traditional and safe approach is not to use any questionable partial information, but then we also forego the benefits of overlapping. Consequently, such situations should not be avoided but instead viewed as opportunities to trade time for money by assessing the cost of delay, as discussed in Chapter 2. Moving ahead without having all of the answers is a calculated risk, but we know how to do the calculations.

The Link Between Teams and Overlapping

Although overlapping is clearly a major opportunity to shorten overall cycle time, it places a burden on the developers. The partial information that is inherent in overlapping is fragile, and the only way to use it safely is to have a strong communication infrastructure among the developers that can assume the increased communication burden that partial information imposes. Without the strong team characteristics discussed in Chapters 7 and 8, attempting to overlap activities will create chaos.

A somewhat different way of looking at this situation is that additional skills are needed to handle partial information effectively. These include the communication skills emphasized in the last chapter. They also involve understanding the potential weaknesses in the technologies and market research methods being used. More specifically, partial information recipients must learn to probe information they are receiving sagaciously, and partial information providers must learn to be forthright about the possible pitfalls in what they are offering. In general, the new skills involve increased awareness of the implications of one's work on others and vice versa. A strong sense of team interdependence helps here, but specific skills are also needed relative to the content of the partial information.

Overlapping Examples

Often we think of overlapping in a rather formal way that appears in the written development process. But the more powerful types of overlapping are often more subtle and company specific. This is why you always have to be scouting for them. We provide two examples from clients, both involving machined castings.

In the first example, the casting was the machine base, a large, complex part with a long lead time that therefore established the project's critical path. The machine base is the last part the designer wants to release, however, because it is the part to which everything else attaches and is thus the most susceptible to change. This firm's solution was to design the raw casting by providing surplus material in the attachment areas. The casting drawings were sent off to the foundry to have initial castings poured while the designer refined the fit of the mating parts and completed the details of machining the casting. In essence, these cast parts were being designed even as they were being poured. (After the product was in production, its drawings and pattern could be modified if necessary to minimize the machining of surplus material.) In this case, the partial information surrounded the exact geometry of the attachment pads.

Another example is provided by Neles-Jamesbury, which manufactures quarter-turn valves used in chemical plants, pulp mills, oil refineries, and similar demanding applications. Neles-Jamesbury requires high-quality castings, and often the first batch or two to come from the foundry for a new design have dimensional or porosity defects. Normal practice was to return these defective parts and wait for the foundry to send acceptable ones. This company found, however, that once it started machining the castings it then faced another round of learning in debugging the machining process. So it now accepts and pays for the initial defective castings and uses them to debug machining operations. Thus, by machining bad castings and scrapping them, Neles-Jamesbury is able to overlap two learning processes. Here the partial information involves the nature of the flaws and their influence on the machining processes.

OVERLAPPING HARDWARE AND SOFTWARE DEVELOPMENT

Many products that were once entirely electromechanical—telephones, photocopiers, automotive ignition, and fuel systems—now incorporate microprocessors and depend on software for much of their functionality. Consequently, software development is a required new ingredient in many companies' development processes. It is a major ingredient, as evidenced by the fact that two-thirds of Hewlett-Packard's technical staff are now software engineers. Because it is a new phenomenon, many "hardware" companies are now struggling with software development issues.

One major opportunity and challenge is to overlap hardware and software development and testing. Such overlapping is not natural and will not occur without some specific attention to it. In some companies software engineers are often a scarce, rather exotic, expensive resource, so they are typically kept in a specialized department where they can focus narrowly on their task. As we discussed in Chapter 7, such specialization often leads to delays.

The opportunities to overlap hardware and software activities often relate to testing, where complex scheduling linkages often exist. The software people need hardware to test their code, and the hardware people need some software to even make their hardware work. Potential solutions include:

- Using modern requirements-driven software development methods, which defer the need for a testbed for the software and reduce tail-end debugging effort when the testbed is available.
- Planning the hardware and software testing early, so that scheduling challenges can be identified while there is flexibility left to resolve them.

- Recognizing that interactions between software and hardware will complicate the testing, and using the techniques of incremental innovation, architecture, and risk management (Chapters 4, 6, and 12, respectively) to overcome them.
- Employing a simulator, based on the target microprocessor, as a software testbed; this allows some early software testing and later provides a tool to isolate hardware–software interaction problems in the real hardware.

(A Suggested Reading at the end of this chapter pursues such topics further.)

CREATING OPPORTUNITIES FOR OVERLAPPING

Fortunately, there are many ways of discovering opportunities for overlapping. First, recognize that using dedicated project team members, as discussed in the last two chapters, encourages overlapping. Think about how a project is usually staffed. In its early phases Marketing may provide most of the effort, then Engineering gets heavily involved, and finally Manufacturing becomes the dominant player, as illustrated in Figure 9-2.

Now consider a team staffed from Day One with full-time members from various functions, and compare Figure 9-3 with Figure 9-2. The part-time, phase-in, phase-out type of staffing in Figure 9-2 condones a sequential approach, but in Figure 9-3 the different functions are *forced* to act in parallel; for example, Manufacturing is forced to be involved from the beginning. If the Manufacturing people join the team full-time from the beginning they will either have to work on engineering or marketing tasks or identify opportunities for overlap so they can begin work on manufacturing tasks, even if this must be done with only partial information.

Encourage Overlapping

Everywhere developers turn, they are subtly reminded to do things sequentially. We portray development as sequential stages and gates, we require deliverables to get approval to qualify for the next funding, and we publish a uniform development process that all teams must use. To avoid the delay inherent in a standard, sequential process, Nellcor Puritan Bennett quite explicitly tells its developers to do otherwise. This company is a global provider of monitoring and treatment prod-

**Staffing
level**

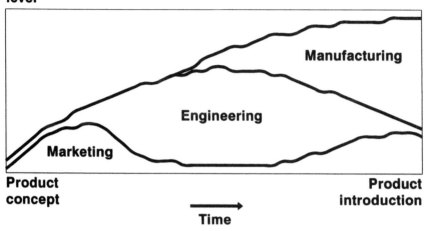

**Product
concept**   **Product
introduction**

Time

Conventional staffing practices force development efforts into phases
that become dominated by specific functions.

FIGURE   9-2

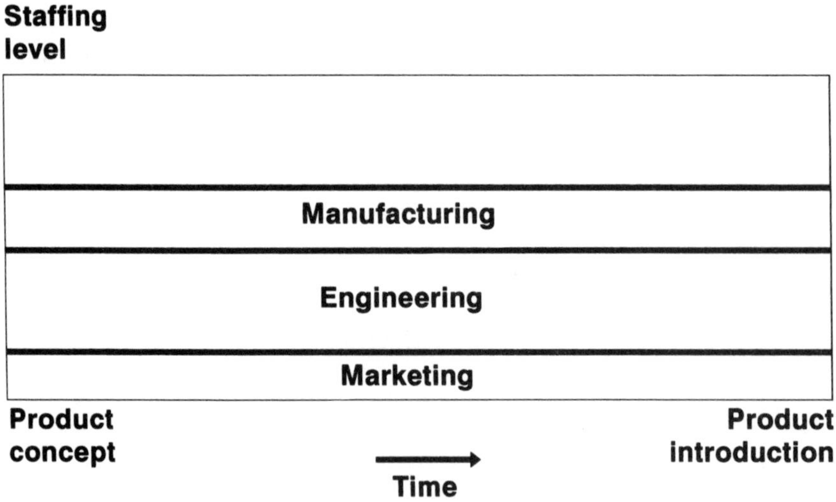

**Staffing
level**

Manufacturing

Engineering

Marketing

**Product
concept**   **Product
introduction**

Time

Dedicated staffing forces overlapping and cross-functional interaction.

FIGURE   9-3

ucts, such as pulse oximeters and ventilators, for respiratory-impaired patients. Because it serves the global medical-device market, NPB operates under ISO 9000 and must abide by the good manufacturing practices regulations enforced by the United States Food and Drug Administration and similar regulatory standards abroad. Nevertheless, it specifically encourages developers to work concurrently and adapt the process to fit the project. Consider these statements from Nellcor's *Product Development Process II:*

- "Concurrence is the philosophy of doing something as early as possible and not waiting to finish one task before beginning another.
- "PDP II is . . . an iterative task structure within facets that encourages concurrency and closely models the way rapid development work is actually performed.
- "No project is expected to incorporate every task contained in the PDP II. If a development project were a game of Scrabble®, then PDP II would be the unabridged dictionary used as a reference during the game. It contains every possible word you might use during the game, but for any one game, you'll use only the handful of words that fit the problem at hand.
- "No project is expected to order tasks exactly in the temporal order shown in the PDP II task diagrams. In fact, some iteration and concurrency is expected and encouraged within facets and clusters.
- "The project planner has wide latitude to vary the time-order of the tasks within a facet. The order in which tasks are executed within a facet should fit the project at hand. It is not rigidly fixed by the PDP II process maps."

Watch for the Triggers

If we look at a Gantt chart, as in Figure 9-4 (Before) it may appear that activities cannot be overlapped: we must build the prototype before we can test it; a part must be designed before it can be built. But if we dissect these activities, by looking inside them on the Gantt chart, we usually find that part of the succeeding activity can be started before its predecessor is complete.

The concept of triggers is helpful here, as illustrated in Figure 9-4, which illustrates the design and building of tooling. The trigger for starting the tool-building activity is buying the piece of tooling steel. This trigger occurs not when the tool's design is complete, but much earlier when the overall dimensions of the tool are available. Once we recognize that the tool-building trigger occurs relatively early, we can overlap many of the design and building activities. And once we find an early

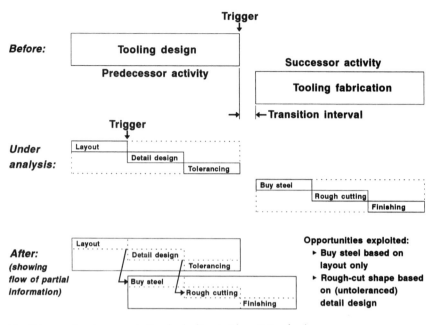

Identifying overlapping opportunities by looking inside activities for the earliest trigger for the successor activity (illustrated here for the design and fabrication activities of a piece of tooling).

FIGURE 9-4

trigger for the successor activity, we can reassess both activities to optimize the flow of their subactivities so that they can be run simultaneously. Discovering an early trigger thus becomes the starting point for designing overlapped activities. The key to finding such triggers is to probe into the internal structure of larger activities like tooling design and tooling fabrication. As long as we see them as one big activity we will never find the opportunities for overlap.

Clearly, partial information plays importantly here. If the length of the tool increases after we have bought the steel, we have a problem. However, if we are not completely sure about the length of the tool, we might want to pay more for the longest piece of tool steel we might need, because the time value of having the steel early might outweigh the extra cost of buying a bigger piece.

How Fast Could It Be Done?

In Chapter 1 we explored publishing a newspaper relative to publishing a book to discover the potential for improving time to market in book publishing. Such an unconstrained approach can expose large opportunities for overlapping. For the moment, do not let money, people, or other resources stand in the way. Try to find a similar situation that was done much more quickly. If you let yourself go here, your speedy alternative is likely to be rather outlandish. But now you have something against which you can start comparing real-world solutions. For example, if a newspaper composes half of an edition before the news comes in, why can't we buy half of our parts before we have a design? Maybe we should be relying more on standard parts.

Alternatively, look for examples where something got done exceptionally fast, even if it was only once, in your own company. On one consulting assignment we were assisting a task force trying to pare part of the organization's development process down from 13 months to three. The task seemed hopeless to these old-timers, and we weren't making much progress. Then a respected member of the group noticed that, once before, they had done the job in only four months. By studying this example they soon had a plan for routinely doing the job in four months. Mathematicians often do their work by starting with an "existence proof," first demonstrating that there is in fact a solution without worrying yet about its nature. Sometimes some of the rest of us need an existence proof to spur us into finding a solution.

Use Prototyping to Set the Pace

The timing of many development programs, for example, those for automobiles or semiconductor manufacturing equipment, often revolve around prototypes. Successively more refined prototypes assure that higher levels of fidelity, product performance, or yield are being attained.

In such cases, prototype generations can be effective ways of setting project milestones. For instance, Stage One is complete when a prototype demonstrates technical feasibility, Stage Two when a prototype achieves the basic performance objectives, and Stage Three does it with tooled parts. Such milestones are cross-functional; they are performance based and measurable; and they encourage overlapping.

Perhaps even better for pushing the schedule along aggressively is to use periodic prototyping. Here we decree that a new prototype will be built at certain pre-established intervals. Any new designs or parts that are available by a given prototype's deadline go on that prototype; if they miss the deadline, they go on the next one instead. The prototype gets better and better almost continuously, and we can adjust as we go to reach the level of maturity needed to ship the product. Periodic prototypes fit best when the product is not too expensive (keeping prototyping expenses within reason) and when system integration issues are paramount.

Microsoft develops software by using daily to weekly "build" cycles for operating system and application products, and any features developed and initially tested go into the next build. The builds are tested routinely by Microsoft employees as they use the prototype in their daily work. When a product acquires enough features and is stable enough, Microsoft decides to ship it. This approach has several time-to-market advantages. First, it is the ultimate in incremental innovation, because the product improves on almost a daily basis until it is good enough for a next version. It avoids most of the huge difficulty in software products of having a long, unpredictable debugging cycle at the tail-end of the schedule. Finally, it encourages programmer accountability for code quality, because if a bug in a programmer's submission "breaks" the build, this programmer's flaw is apparent to many people quickly.

Generational prototypes, and especially periodic prototypes, are effective for accelerating schedules, because they keep constant attention on the schedule. In effect, they allow us to control product, and thus project, performance against time.

Either generational or periodic prototyping can accelerate the pace, but they are also likely to raise development expense, simply because prototypes cost money and we are building more than are necessary to just develop the product. This is a clear example of building a tall junk pile, trading off the expense of "excess" prototypes against the schedule acceleration they bring us.

Overlapping Requires a Cultural Change

The extra money that overlapping might cost is the easy part; the harder part is that to really gain the benefits of radical overlapping, we must change the way we think. In essence, it requires an ability to move ahead proactively with much less information than we would like, constantly assessing whether the muck ahead is firm enough to support a few more steps.

The overlapping mindset is reflected in the types of questions we ask when seeking overlapping opportunities:

- What is the bare minimum of information I need to get the next step started?
- When is the earliest I can produce this information in the preceding step?
- Is there anything I can do to make the requirement for having this information unnecessary?

- Are there assumptions I can make about this information that will provide a high likelihood of its being accurate enough to begin work?
- How great are the consequences of being wrong, and how long will it take me to get back to where I am now if I am wrong?
- Can I save enough time by starting early to allow for making a mistake and still finish early?
- What information would allow me to take another step?
- Who could use the information I have to enable them to take another step?

In general, team members should be the ones creating the overlapping. This process requires a keen sense of the data that must be transmitted from one activity to another to support the actual sequence of decisions that must be made in successor activities. Since the exact sequence of development decisions is a notoriously foggy path, it is usually best identified by those who will have to do the work. They have the greatest understanding of the issues involved and ultimately will have to own the solution.

Like many of the other cultural transitions suggested in this book, you can do some overlapping on a pilot basis without having the whole organization on board. However, if you want to make it standard practice, the corporate values, reward systems, etc., will also have to be adjusted to be in alignment with the new behaviors you desire in your developers. Otherwise, people will gradually revert to what the system encourages them to do.

THE ROLE OF TECHNOLOGY TOOLS

For the most part, this book covers what we call management tools for accelerating product development, but technology tools are also available. These include computer-aided design (CAD—both mechanical and electrical), computer-aided analysis (for example, finite-element stress analysis), computer simulation (such as is used for circuits simulation), rapid prototyping (for instance, stereolithography), and product data management (PDM) software.

Although both the management tools and the technology tools are valuable for cutting time to market, we place emphasis on the management tools first, for two reasons. First, we believe that the management tools have broader potential to shorten all portions of the development cycle, from product need to first shipment. Second, overemphasis on the technology tools can result in automating—thus further entrenching—poor management practices.

That said, the technology tools do have great power to accelerate certain portions of the development cycle, and any company that is truly interested in rapid product development uses both technology and management tools. These excellent companies do not just buy some software and workstations and install them. Instead, they procure technology solutions to meet certain identified needs, train their people well in the use of the technology, and ensure that the technology is well integrated with their management processes.

To illustrate where the technology tools fit and how they can help, we provide three case studies. They were chosen to illustrate how several of the technology tools can work together and be integrated with the management tools—the kind of solution that provides the greatest competitive advantage.

Case Study: Senco Products

Senco Products, Inc., is a global manufacturer and marketer of powered nailers and staplers, and the fasteners they drive. Their SNS45 project aimed to bolster Senco's leadership position in heavy-duty pneumatic construction staplers. This project applied recent technological advances in CAD, QFD, finite-element analysis (FEA), and rapid prototyping. The project team comprised a Project Engineer, a second engineer, two designers, a Manufacturing Engineer, a member from tool and die, a buyer, a marketing member, and the team leader, all but two of which were dedicated full-time. Most were co-located in a 10 meter by 10 meter (30 foot by 30 foot) area. This heavyweight team followed much of the guidance in Chapters 7 and 8. They also employed the financial analysis suggested in Chapter 2 and kept their trade-off rules in mind by printing them on a laminated wallet card that each team member carried.

The team collectively used simplified QFD (see Chapter 5) to translate and prioritize the customers' requirements into a form better suited for engineering and manufacturing decisions. They accelerated this analysis by using commercial software that managed the voluminous data associated with QFD and allowed them to analyze several alternative formulations quickly. Beyond the anticipated advantages of their QFD analysis, the QFD data paid off later when a Senior Sales Manager forcefully protested the team's design approach for loading fasteners. The Manager of Product Development and Team Leader, Scott Allspaw, and the Project Engineer, Jack Schloemer, worked to prevent the issue from derailing the team by using the QFD and market research analyses to solidly support their design approach. The QFD analysis software supported them well here, because they were able to recast the results quickly to shed light on the fastener loading issue.

Project Engineer Schloemer faced a tough decision regarding the CAD system. After the project began, an upgrade package became available that would provide more capability, but would require training for the designers. He pondered, "Should we spend time (and money) to be more effective later?" He concluded and convinced the team that the CAD upgrade would not only bring benefits to this team, but position the company better for future projects. Note that usually it is better not to change the CAD system after the project has begun, to avoid unnecessary disruptive change during a project. In this case, however, the new CAD package was available early enough to make such a change feasible. Team Leader Allspaw was skeptical initially, seeing a clear parallel between CAD upgrades and the disastrous creeping elegance phenomenon that afflicts product features. However, Schloemer did not let the upgrade affect the schedule; as Allspaw puts it, "He had the designers on the airplane headed for training before the final signature was on the upgrade approval."

The Project Engineer's wisdom also paid off on one part that presented subjective ergonomics and feel issues that affected the product's differentiation in the marketplace. He helped the team to retain focus and reach closure on the design so the tooling could be finalized. To do this, he worked with the designers in helping them leverage the CAD system, without becoming enamored with the CAD's ability to "optimize" the design. Schloemer assessed the amount of time this part should receive compared with the balance of tasks required to complete the entire design. With the flexibility of the new CAD system and the creativity of an outside industrial designer, the possibilities were endless. The team simplified the part, made some decisions on aesthetics, and moved on.

Another part was to be investment cast. Previously, such prototypes for functional confirmation were machined from solid stock. As this was clearly time inefficient, the team turned to stereolithography (a rapid prototyping technique). In addition to the primary advantages offered by rapid prototyping of having a part that could be touched and felt, the SNS45 project took the technology further. The team shared the rapid prototype part with the foundry, which was able to give instantaneous feedback on manufacturability improvements. Then the rapid prototype was used as a pattern for functional prototype parts.

The Buyer, Tom Kent, and Manufacturing Engineer, Dan Reed, uncovered an opportunity to fundamentally change the way the company acquired prototype aluminum castings. Reed explains, "We modemed the CAD file (without tolerance details) to a stereolithography service bureau, who in turn supplied a prototype core and shell to the pattern maker. The pattern maker then constructed a mold for the foundry, which poured functional aluminum parts. The team used these parts to build staplers for initial testing. This accelerated means of making parts shaved 10 to 14 weeks off of Senco's normal approach. And nobody even asked for a toleranced print!" Allspaw observes that this opportunity to consider making parts differently emerged from the proximity and dedication of the Buyer, the Manufacturing Engineer, and the Designer. Furthermore, because the team wasn't required to seek management approval before proceeding, the decision to pursue this new method took place in a team meeting lasting less than an hour.

The SNS45 team decided to use FEA as an engineering tool to locate high-stress areas in one of the most critical parts on this new tool. This part had to be strong enough to withstand abuse and contain air pressure. The team saw FEA as a way to get this information quickly and hopefully shorten testing time for this component. Senco was in the process of training an employee in FEA analysis, so team members decided to use this part as a training exercise that would also give them the stress information they needed. But the FEA model of the component turned out to be more complex than anticipated. As a result of this complexity, it took almost three weeks to complete the analysis. They did get a robust design right the first time, but the time savings was not as great as it might have been had the team given the job to an expert in this field. Senco learned that the decision to use FEA requires careful consideration and that an experienced analyst is needed to gain the most benefit from FEA.

As the SNS45 team integrated many of these technology tools, they sent CAD files to several suppliers to obtain parts for testing and prototype tool builds. Often, these files first had to be translated to another format (e.g., DXF, IGES) and then sent to the supplier via modem. Sometimes suppliers have trouble using such files and must make certain corrections before they can begin making parts or tooling. Senco has learned that these problems can be minimized by early involvement of their CAD Administrator with the suppliers. They identify differences in their systems and file format requirements far in advance. Then they send sample files back and forth for evaluation and to work out the bugs, off of the critical path. This approach helps ensure that the time saved by these new tools is not offset by delays encountered in file transfer and translation.

This case study reveals a strong inclination toward learning from past projects at Senco. The company applies the continuous process improvement tools described in Chapter 15. Consequently, cycle-time continually decreases, as illustrated in Figure 1-3 (page 5).

Case Study: Lathrop Engineering

Lathrop Engineering specializes in the rapid development of new products for client companies. A major pacemaker manufacturer approached them to develop an instrument used to set up the pacemaker and adjust it after it has been implanted in a patient. The client urgently needed a next-generation instrument to preserve its core market for the pacemakers themselves.

To start design, the team had to understand how users interact with the instrument and how frequently they use various interfaces, such as the touch screen, modem connections, and built-in printer. The team generated some preliminary solid models of the system configurations under consideration. Then the multi-disciplinary team discussed and refined positions of the user interfaces and internal components. This was important because team members needed to minimize the instrument's height without compromising the vital, sensitive communication link between the instrument and the implanted pacemaker. Concurrently, Rick Emerson, the Industrial Designer on the project, developed hand sketches and foam-core models of the concepts. The team then converged on the form and look of the instrument. In a little over a month this cross-functional team synthesized an overall shape, a user interface configuration, and a layout of the key internal components, setting a strong basis for the detailed design work in the next phase. Notice how they mixed their high-tech solid modeler and low-tech sketch pad to exploit the power of each medium to reach certain decisions quickly.

During the detailed-design phase the team reviewed progress on its CAD model every week. This weekly review allowed them to make design corrections before designers wasted time going down unfruitful avenues. For example, they recalled that the instrument's carrying handle had been a problem in previous models. So they ran a finite element analysis, which took just a few days, to assure that the handle design would not fail. This saved weeks of prototyping and testing time. The analysis allowed them to identify areas of high stress and even to eliminate some material in low-stress areas.

Thermal performance of the system was critical, due to the thermal printer, which generated heat, being packed closely with the hard disk, which would not work reliably at high temperatures. They started with classical thermal analysis, to get an understanding of the important thermal parameters. The tool of choice here was Mathcad, a relatively simple software package that let the engineer set up the natural convection and fan-forced airflow calculations and adjust them easily as the configuration changed. This level of analysis showed that using even a small fan gave reasonable safety margins, but the system would not have met specifications without a fan. This relatively simple but flexible technique eliminated the need for time-consuming and complex FEA analysis and thermal testing–redesign iterations.

The solid modeling capabilities of the CAD system proved to be a time-saver for Steve Wilson, one of the engineers on the project. He could easily monitor the design's mass properties and check for interferences as the design team worked to stuff all of the required electronics into the small interior space. These interference checks before parts were made saved several weeks of modifications later when the initial prototypes were built.

Several technology tools helped Lathrop integrate suppliers into the project. Early in the design phase the team contacted about 20 molders as potential suppliers of the plastic parts. Molders were given files of the plastic parts to create preliminary budgets for tooling. The suppliers were able to bring the files up on their CAD systems, which accelerated and improved the quality of their tooling quotations. Before the design was 80 percent complete Lathrop selected the final molder, and this molder's involvement during the design phase cut weeks off the development cycle.

When the CAD model was complete, final CAD files were sent to the molder and suppliers of the non-plastic parts to start the prototype procurement process. First, the rapid prototyping house used the CAD files to create a stereolithography model of the instrument, which took only a week. This model was used to verify that all of the components fit and to give the electronics subteam a platform to start system integration.

In the past it would have been risky to go straight to production tooling on a project of this complexity, but due to the solid model's database and the stereolithography prototype the team decided to commit to production tooling in the prototype phase. This decision saved the additional time needed to create both prototype and production tooling, and also enabled early pre-validation testing. To fill the gap from the one-off stereolithography prototype to the production injection molds, 15 urethane cast prototypes were fabricated in about two weeks. Marketing used some of these units for user feedback, Manufacturing started planning the manufacturing process with them, and Engineering built functional units to use for software development.

After prototype testing some changes had to be made to the design. These changes resulted from EMI (electromagnetic interference) testing and from focus group feedback. Most of the changes were minimal and none of the plastic injection molds had to be scrapped. This project was completed in just five months, from the start of the initial concept to availability of pre-production models (these models are used for clinical trials and other regulatory and safety approvals that can take up to a year for devices of this type).

Case Study: BroadBand Technologies

BroadBand Technologies, Inc., provides equipment to advance telephone network technology by adding broadband digital services to residential dialtone lines. Our last case study ended with some EMI issues, but the magnitude of the electronics and the frequencies involved in BroadBand's products makes EMI a major concern. Let's see how the company kept EMI problems off of its critical path by integrating technology tools into the development process.

Early in a high-speed multiplexer project the team had a mechanical design concept, but wanted to do early verification testing to ensure the approach would work. The concept included a rack-mountable sheet-metal card cage and 30 circuit cards plugging into a backplane. Four multiplexers would be stacked in a seven-foot equipment rack with a fan to force cooling vertically. The need for cooling created a conflict with the need to control EMI. The top and bottom panels of the card cage had perforations that were large enough to allow cooling but small enough to minimize EMI. The front of the card cage presented even more challenges due to penetrating fiber cables connecting to the cards and alarm indicators that had to be visible. These requirements led to individual, electrically conductive faceplates on each circuit card. In order to minimize cost, the faceplates were injection-molded parts with electroless copper/nickel plating. Due to the importance of the program and the expense of the faceplate mold, BroadBand needed to verify early that its design would provide adequate EMI shielding.

The developers sent CAD files of the faceplates to a supplier that produced a master part using stereolithography. From this, they made a rubber mold, then they cast urethane faceplates. These were painted with copper paint to simulate electroless nickel/copper plating. Simultaneously, they sent CAD files for the card-cage parts to a sheet-metal supplier. Notice that all of this was done directly from the solid model without any drawings or tolerancing. Elimination of the detailed drawings reduced time to prototypes by a month.

EMI test lab results indicated that the design would provide adequate shielding with only minor design changes. These early test results increased confidence in the design approach, so BroadBand committed to faceplate hard tooling. BroadBand continued to leverage use of the faceplate CAD files by selecting a tooling supplier that could build the injection molds from the CAD database without drawings. This allowed the tool-building process to start three to four weeks earlier than if detailed drawings had been required. Detailed drawings were eventually created, but they were done off the critical path. BroadBand conducted a final EMI test with hard-tooled parts, and the design passed without further modification.

SUGGESTED READING

Clark, Kim B., and Takahiro Fujimoto. 1991. *Product Development Performance.* Boston, Mass.: Harvard Business School Press. Chapter 8 provides great detail on overlapping of activities and the use of partial information in automobile development.

Cooper, Robert G. 1994. Perspective: third-generation new product processes. *Journal of Product Innovation Management* 11 (1): 3–14. Cooper predicts the evolution of stage gates to processes with "fuzzy gates" and more fluidity and flexibility.

Rauscher, Tomlinson G., and Preston G. Smith. 1995. From Experience: Time-driven development of software in manufactured goods. *Journal of Product Innovation Management* 12 (3): 186–199. Describes several techniques, including overlapping, for accelerating the development of embedded software.

Takeuchi, Hirotaka, and Ikujiro Nonaka. 1986. The new new product development game. *Harvard Business Review* 64 (1): 137–46. A classic on accelerated product development. Includes a good section on overlapping that draws on examples from Honda, Canon, and Fuji-Xerox.

Wheelwright, Steven C., and Kim B. Clark. 1992. *Revolutionizing Product Development.* New York: The Free Press. Chapter 10 covers prototyping, including periodic prototyping, in detail.

CHAPTER 10

Controlling the Process

Controlling the progress of activities has always been identified as one of management's basic roles, and almost no business activity screams out that it needs control louder than product development. As a result there is a perennial quest to bring control to this activity. But the challenge is tremendous, due to the inherently unpredictable nature of the problem-solving process. It simply is difficult to predict the amount of time needed to solve an unknown problem and how adequate the solution will be when it is identified.

This difficulty exists for any development project and will be even greater for an accelerated project. The overlap of rapid development projects makes such projects inherently less predictable than the same projects done as groups of sequential activities. To see this imagine three activities. If these three activities are being done in parallel, all three must be completed on time to meet the schedule. In contrast, a more generous sequential schedule for the same three activities might permit one of these activities to be taken off the critical path, thereby reducing uncertainty in its completion date. This higher unpredictability of overlapping schedules is often troubling to developers and managers, because they have learned by painful experience that their superiors and shareholders are not pleased with surprises. This drives them to seek tools to reduce this unpredictability.

The traditional tools that we use for increasing predictability are often counterproductive on a rapid development project. They often consume our scarcest resource, time on the critical path, in return for modest improvements in predictability. They too often lead to slow decision making and time consumed on administrative activities that do not move the project forward.

In this chapter we will propose another way of controlling projects. It involves shifting the locus of control down to lower levels in the organization. This approach demands a fundamental shift in management attitude away from controlling and toward empowering and enabling the success of the team. Only by using team members to control their own progress can a truly rapid process be created. These empowered teams are replacing the "robot" teams of the past, which relied on the superior wisdom of management to make or approve decisions. Instead, we are recognizing that an imperfect decision made quickly may be more valuable than a perfect decision made slowly. Moreover, we frequently find that decision quality and decision speed are not conflicting objectives. When we push decision making down to the team level, decisions can be both quicker and better. Often the team is closer to the underlying market and technical data needed to make good decisions. This is particularly true when we are dealing with rapidly moving markets and rapidly changing technologies. The manager trained 20 years ago may not be the best decision maker on a technology that is less than five years old.

In Chapters 7 and 8 we focused on creating a team with the competence and motivation to control itself. In this chapter we will discuss the implications of these choices for project control. We will begin by exploring our underlying business motive for process control. Then we will establish an overall strategy for achieving this. Finally we will discuss specific control tools.

THE LOGIC OF PROCESS CONTROL

To understand the underlying logic of controlling a development process we need to understand what is really going on in a development process and be clear about our true objective in controlling it.

Engineering Is Inherently Unpredictable

Managers who have little experience with engineering often have a distorted view of what engineers really do. They observe the precise calculations done by engineers and assume that all of engineering is a precise science. In reality, the precise techniques that comprise the bulk of an engineer's academic training are ultimately of only limited use in actual design problems. When established techniques fail to apply, the process quickly becomes more empirical than analytical.

Engineering professor Billy Vaughn Koen, of the University of Texas, is noted for his research on the theory of engineering design. In a monograph, *Definition of the Engineering Method* (American Society for Engineering Education, 1985), he provided his definition of the engineering method:

> The engineering method [is defined] as the use of engineering heuristics to cause the best change in a poorly understood situation within the available resources. This definition is not meant to imply that the engineer just uses heuristics from time to time to aid his work, as might be said of the mathematician. Instead my thesis is that the *engineering strategy for causing desirable change in an unknown situation within the available resources* and the *use of heuristics* [Koen's emphases] is an absolute identity. In other words, everything the engineer does in his role as engineer is under the control of a heuristic. Engineering has no hint of the absolute, the deterministic, the guaranteed, the true. Instead it fairly reeks of the uncertain, the provisional and the doubtful. The engineer instinctively recognizes this and calls his ad hoc method "doing the best you can with what you've got," "finding a seat-of-the-pants solution," or just "muddling through."

If "muddling through" is an apt characterization, this has consequences for controlling progress. One is that it is both difficult and impractical to control progress at the microscopic level, where a design's progress looks pretty chaotic. Here it is two steps forward, one back, another sideways, and finally a hop to avoid an obstacle. Trying to use elaborate, highly quantitative control methods on process that is this variable is wasteful and likely to be frustrating. We will have to develop an alternative to this sort of microscopic control.

Why We Control Product Development

If we know that the engineering process is inherently uncertain, this will allow us to choose appropriate tools to control it. But before we explain *how to control the process,* we must be clear on *why we are trying to control it.* There is only one reason to control a development process, which is to influence its economic performance. The financial analysis that we discussed in Chapter 2 will allow us to determine whether a schedule delay will have a major impact on profitability. In situations where it does we should concentrate our control efforts on ensuring schedule objectives are met.

As obvious as this point seems, we frequently find companies concentrating on control of project expenses and spending rates. Several years ago a Vice President of Engineering at one company cynically pointed out to us that he would lose his job if he overspent his budget, but if he missed his schedule it would be considered an unfortunate but tolerable accident. Times are changing, and Vice Presidents now lose their jobs for missing schedules, but the vast majority of companies still incorrectly concentrate their control efforts on development budgets instead of schedule.

Effective control of time relies on two principles in Chapter 2: time has quantifiable economic value and decisions affecting it should be assessed by comparing their cost against their benefit. Schedule impact must be factored into both the costs and benefits of applying any control system. By this standard, many of today's tools fall short of our needs. For example, a project manager at a medium-sized electronic company recalled the moment he learned to put his company's project management software in perspective. He had just spent a week inputting a detailed schedule for his project, faithfully following the rules of the project management course he had just attended. A day after he finished entering the information the detailed schedule became obsolete. He then faced a choice of repeating the exercise or taking a different approach. He decided that there were more useful things for him to do in managing the project than spending all of his time in caring for and feeding a scheduling system. Instead, he simplified the plan to critical milestones and spent his time removing the obstacles threatening the team's progress.

This contains a valuable lesson for managing rapid product development. In many cases it is more effective to react to some aspects of the future when they arrive than it is to predict them. For example, it is useful to forecast a year in advance that April is usually a month with a lot of rain. However, it is not useful to try to predict a year in advance whether it will rain on April 5. In fact, the cost of an accurate forecast, if one were possible, would exceed the cost of an umbrella.

In a similar manner, on many rapid development projects we do not achieve our control by becoming better at anticipating all possible changes. We will forecast as much as we can usefully forecast, but we will respect the fact that there will always remain a large component of uncertainty. Instead of trying to make all this uncertainty go away, we will deal with it by using different tools. We can either attempt to reduce the magnitude of the change or we can make our project less vulnerable to this change. For example, in Chapter 4 we discussed the technique of incremental innovation. One of the key benefits of this technique is that it permits us to shorten our planning horizon and therefore reduces the likelihood of changes. In Chapter 6 we discussed the use of modular architectures and the importance of architectural flexibility. Such approaches make the project more tolerant of change. As we mentioned, the original IBM Personal Computer was designed with both a cassette port and floppy disk capability. When it became clear that nobody used the cassette port, it was eliminated from the next product. In this case, it was unlikely that any amount of money spent on market research would have accurately determined in advance which choice would be preferred. When reacting is less expensive than forecasting, it makes business sense to react.

If our control system will rely on our ability to react quickly to change, we must be very sure that we design our development process to make this possible.

DECENTRALIZING PROJECT CONTROL

The capability to react quickly to changes on the project requires decentralizing control down to the team level. This goes beyond simply shifting control to a lower level of the organization by empowering the team to make decisions. In our experience such empowerment will not be successful without taking careful measures to ensure that these empowered teams are adequately prepared to handle this new authority. It is only when the team has both the authority and the capability to make project decisions that it can react quickly and surefootedly to the constantly changing terrain of the rapid development project.

Let us examine the logic for decentralization of decisions and the associated need for highly capable teams.

Fast Decisions Require Decentralization

Rapid development projects must make many decisions in a compressed time period. Such decisions can only be made quickly when we locate them at a level in the organization that has sufficient bandwidth or capacity to process them quickly. Invariably this means that we cannot leave them with high-level managers, because such managers have too many other things competing for their attention.

Unfortunately, high-level managers frequently delude themselves as to how quickly they make decisions. They conclude that they create little decision-making delay because they observe their own decisive behavior as they quickly glance at a set of facts and resolutely choose a course of action. Since this happens in a matter of minutes, it surely cannot add much delay to a project.

The reality of high-level decision making is quite a different matter. There are hidden delays that make the manager's five-minute decision cost the project several days of critical path time. Whenever a management decision is going to be made, somebody has to prepare the data for the manager to review. The team has to wait for the manager to have time in his or her schedule to make the decision. They have to generate new data when the manager is unhappy with the data he or she receives to justify the decision. It is these hidden delays that make high-level decision making a huge source of delay for most development projects.

But, you say, "Our system isn't so bureaucratic as this. I can just phone the General Manager and get a decision instantly without all this paperwork." Well, what are the odds of catching the General Manager live on your first phone call? What happens if the General Manager is visiting customers or traveling? Invariably, the average delays in reaching the decision maker are longer than the time it takes to make the decision.

When we consider the number of decisions that must be made on a typical project the burden of high-level decision making becomes intolerable. When a thousand decisions are each delayed by a day, we have a thousand days—three years—of decision-making delay! It is crucial that we push these decisions down to lower levels to ensure we do not incur these delays.

Decentralization Requires More Talent in the Trenches

However, there is much more to decentralized decision making than simply delegating the decisions. We must ensure that the level of the organization that acquires this new decision-making authority truly has the capability to make good decisions. This turns out to be a major stumbling block for many organizations. For example, one company de-cided to create cross-functional teams. It had a very small marketing organization, so when it assigned the marketing representatives to the teams, the only person who could be spared was an inexperienced new employee. Because the marketing representative lacked experience he was reluctant to exercise his decision-making authority. Instead, he would delay making the decisions until he could talk to his boss. The net effect of this behavior was to frustrate other team members and achieve no improvement in decision-making speed. Instead, the company became disillusioned about the benefits of cross-functional teams.

It is critical to deploy the talent of the organization down in the trenches where we intend the decisions to take place. If the functions retain their most talented people for functional activities and release the least talented ones to serve on the teams, then we will never achieve the benefits of cross-functional teams. We will either get bad decisions made by people who are underqualified, or we will fail to improve decision-making speed because the teams are reluctant to take the risks of deciding without the prior approval of the powerful functional staffs.

Often this deployment of talent to the team level will require heavier staffing in some functions that have traditionally operated with very lean staffs. For example, groups like Marketing and Manufacturing Engineering may simply lack the resources to adequately support cross-functional teams well. In such cases, we encounter the classic conflict between our drive to utilize these resources efficiently in a centralized structure and our desire to accelerate decisions by decentralizing these resources to the team. Such conflicts should be resolved by taking a careful look at the economics of the project. As we explained in Chapter 7, the true cost of experts may be the delay that they add to the project, not the expense of the task they perform.

Providing staffing in these departments adequate to run several cross-functional teams is a daunting task. We will describe a pilot project approach for getting started on this in Chapter 15. Once we demonstrate the effectiveness of adequate staffing on a single project, it is easier to sell it on others.

KEY CONTROL TOOLS

Let us now consider some important tools for controlling the development process on rapid development projects.

Let Schedule Be the Primary Goal

As mentioned earlier, meeting the schedule of the project becomes the primary objective of a rapid development project, because a schedule delay will do more economic damage than variation in another project goal. The entire organization must understand this and manage activities accordingly. One simple way to do this is to have the team complete the financial analysis described in Chapter 2, and present it to the functional managers. This will ensure that the entire organization is thinking about the economics of delay in the same way.

When we achieve this common understanding, many of the traditional expense-oriented controls driven by the accountants begin to look unproductive for rapid development projects. Such controls need not be totally discarded. Instead, they should be tailored to meet the needs of the rapid development project. For example, an engineering manager at one company explained that he would approve travel, even on chartered aircraft, for any number of his people without justification if they wanted to travel to another company facility. His company has several facilities, and he knows that separation hampers communication, which in turn slows progress. Besides, the plants are in locations where it is not likely that the travel privilege will be abused. For other destinations the normal travel-justification procedures apply. Another company simply establishes a generous travel budget for the team. This enables them to make quick decisions regarding travel without being encumbered by lengthy approval processes, while still setting an overall cap on travel.

Another common source of delay is corporate capital-authorization processes. One firm took an average of nine months to obtain approval to order tooling. Too often such capital approval takes place on the critical path of projects and cannot be initiated until all details of the investment are resolved. On a rapid development project it makes sense to modify such procedures. The goal should be to keep capital authorization off the critical path. In some cases this can be done by authorizing the project capital in increments. Tooling suppliers can take weeks off the critical path of projects by procuring material early. In other cases we can carefully integrate the capital-authorization process so that capital is preapproved subject to certain conditions; once these conditions are met the approval is automatic rather than requiring another trip through the authorization process.

For instance, at one client firm Finance used to be heavily involved in approving projects, emphasizing return on investment rather than strategic fit or project objectives. It would take months for approval. In addition, funding was controlled at significant phases of the development process, and the annual budgeting process further impeded progress on projects. Finally, when the team ordered specific tooling for a project, more management signatures were needed. Today, however, Finance plays a more supporting role. This company still allocates funding at milestone reviews, but it has streamlined the approval process. And the biggest difference is that team leaders are authorized now to approve any purchase already in the project plan.

Misplaced control on small-ticket items is just as destructive. Many companies place excessive controls on the use of petty cash to support project objectives. For example, how liberal is company policy about dispensing petty cash to an engineer who is working on a

Sunday and has to buy some parts at a hardware store? The company's exposure here is minimal, and the effect on the schedule may look small. Sometimes, however, just one day can make the difference between getting a CAD file to a supplier on Friday, in time to get it into the weekend work schedule, or having the supplier start work sometime the next week. Furthermore, the true damage of some of these apparently inconsequential control systems lies in the underlying message they convey about corporate values. If an engineer's reimbursement is challenged, that is a powerful message from the system about the relative importance of following the accounting rules as against exercising initiative and trying to design the product quickly. Chapter 14 covers this subject in greater depth.

Let the Team Build the Detailed Schedule

Give the team responsibility for creating the detailed schedule. People frequently get tripped up in doing this by falling into a obvious trap. They tell the team to prepare a bottom-up schedule. This bottom-up schedule is too slow for management's needs. Then, management cuts the allowed time in half by mandating a top-down schedule to the team. As a result this top-down schedule is viewed with cynicism and not owned by the team.

The defect here is in the process of scheduling. The target introduction date should be given to the project team as the *primary constraint on the project.* The team should be explicitly told to propose whatever modifications in project scope and resourcing that might be necessary to meet this date. Then the team can build a detailed schedule to meet the mandated introduction date. There is always a certain scope of work that can be fit into any allowed amount of time. If we are willing to be flexible on scope and resources we can get any schedule we need. If we attempt to tightly constrain schedule, scope, and resources simultaneously we will create insoluble problems for development teams who will respond by refusing to buy-in to these objectives.

Prepare Detailed Project Plans

Many managers misunderstand the role of detailed planning for rapid development projects. They assume that the purpose of a detailed plan is the same as it would be for a repetitive activity like manufacturing. In repetitive activities we establish detailed targets and measure variances against these targets. This permits us to constantly reduce the variances, making our activities more and more predictable. This is not, however, the purpose of detailed planning in product development. In product development we prepare plans for some things that we have never done before. The purpose of these plan is not to reduce variances, but rather to coordinate these uncertain activities. By preparing a plan we establish a common baseline from which to coordinate the project. When we have to deviate from this baseline, as we inevitably will, everybody on the project is using the same reference point.

Detailed planning is essential for rapid development projects. We cannot reasonably estimate resource requirements without such detailed planning, nor can we identify task dependencies. The detailed plan fills an indispensable role for coordinating the activities of people inside the team and outside the team. For example, in one project a special carton with its graphics, drop testing, and related tasks added an unexpected four months to the project's schedule when the organization thought the project was complete. Detailing planning would have avoided this surprise. In another case the team almost failed to allow time for the creation of an assembly procedure because they thought the design was complete when the parts reached the factory floor.

Although such planning is valuable, we always must remember that the plan is likely to change frequently throughout the project. This change is both necessary and healthy because new information is constantly emerging during the development project. Most experienced project managers do not respond to this change by repeating the detailed planning activity in response to every change. Instead, they manage the project off a subset of higher level milestones. This allows them to exploit the advantages of detailed planning without experiencing the disadvantages of trying to micro-control the project.

Create a Product Development Procedure

As much as some engineers resist the idea of having a procedure for something that is inherently non-repetitive we always encourage our clients to develop such procedures. The point is not that everything is predictable, but that if we make some of it predictable we can concentrate our creativity on the part that is not.

We discussed the design of the product development process in the last chapter. We normally find that the larger the scope of the project and the size of the team, the more we can gain from having some defined procedures for doing development. Communication just becomes too difficult on a large effort if we have no agreement on vocabulary or method.

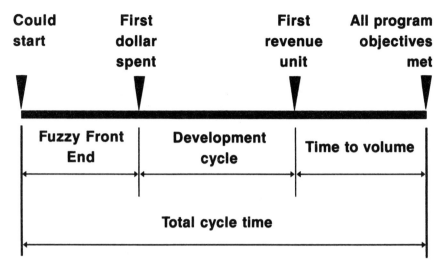

Cycle time metrics for the development process.

FIGURE   10-1

You should note that the amount of control needed depends on the project's size, not the company's size. Too often we see small companies that believe they can do business with no procedures and large companies that develop a "one size fits all" development process that overburdens small projects with bureaucracy. It is the size of the project, not of the company, that determines the degree of project control required.

Establish Overall Process Metrics

Once they have a process most companies find it very useful to establish overall metrics for their development projects. Metrics focused on speed should give quick indications of the health of the development process. The most common metric for the development process is development cycle time. Usually this should be measured as the time from when people start developing the product until when they ship the first revenue producing unit. This metric is shown in Figure 10-1.

As companies get more sophisticated they realize that they should also measure the adjacent processes. To do this they begin to measure the Fuzzy Front End as we explained in Chapter 3, and the back end of the development process, which we call "time to volume." Time to volume is the time from when the first revenue unit is shipped until when all project objectives are met. These objectives include things like reaching the target manufactured cost, reaching target production yields in the factory, and reaching certain availability levels of the product.

It is important to separately measure these adjacent intervals because they represent significant opportunities to improve profitability. The Fuzzy Front End is the bargain basement of cycle-time reduction opportunities, as we explained in Chapter 3. Time to volume is important because it is very expensive to be manufacturing a product that has not yet met its project objectives. Yield and cost problems on the factory floor can be expensive.

A hybrid measure introduced by Hewlett-Packard is the break-even time of the product. It focuses on the point at which a product's early earnings just offset the cost of developing it. This end point captures not only the development time but also provides a measure of how well the product is satisfying marketplace needs. This comprehensive measure is ideally suited to the purposes of business planning because it emphasizes both profitability and timing. However, it is weak for controlling the progress of a development project, because its end point is far in the future, is not tangible, and is not entirely under the control of the team. In general we need metrics that produce information quickly while the team that must act on them is still in existence. A metric that gives you a score months after the team has disbanded is less useful than one that gives results while the team can still do something to change things.

Although development cycle time is valuable for seeing long-term improvements in cycle time over several projects, this measure comes too late in an individual project to be helpful in making changes in that project. As a result many companies measure the cycle times of specific project activities that represent hot spots on the project. Examples of activity cycle times are:

- time to reach full project staffing;
- time to process an engineering change;
- time to create a CAD drawing;
- time to process a purchase order;
- time to make a prototype part;
- time to assemble a prototype;
- time to test a prototype;
- delay time associated with a phase review.

The value of such activity metrics is that they allow you to take action during a project while you can still influence its success.

Define Milestones and the Critical Path

Once we have some overall metrics for the development project we need intermediate milestones for tracking events. As we have mentioned earlier in this book it is only time on the critical path of a project that is worth the cost of delay. The implication of this statement is that we must know where the critical path of the project lies.

The technique of identifying the critical path of a project is covered in all project management books. The most common technique is to use a type of precedence diagram called a PERT (Program Review Evaluation Technique) chart. This is a very useful way to identify critical path activities, which are those whose slippage can delay the project. Only critical path activities are worth the cost of delay.

Once the critical path has been defined by using a PERT chart we generally find it is more useful to manage high-overlap projects with a Gantt chart. The problem with PERT techniques is that they treat project activities as if they are either 0 percent or 100 percent complete. Real tasks are often partially complete. When we treat them as binary events, as a PERT chart does, it causes people to delay beginning the next task until the precursor activities are complete.

In contrast, a Gantt chart can easily depict activities in parallel at a slight offset from other activities, as shown in Figure 10-2. This allows us to communicate to project team members that the upstream activity will have produced enough useful information to permit the downstream activity to commence even though it has not produced enough information to allow the completion of the downstream activity. A further advantage of the Gantt chart is that it can be drawn to depict task dependencies, which is sometimes claimed to be a unique benefit of the PERT chart.

With the critical path defined we can establish frequent, meaningful, measurable milestones along the way. These should be fairly frequent, because the near-term goal always seems more concrete and instills more urgency than the remote one. In a fast development project there is less time for corrections, so it is more important to have frequent goals to catch problems before they can have serious impact on the schedule. The next criterion, meaningfulness, is important because only if a goal is clearly related to an essential activity in the project will it be taken seriously.

Measurability is perhaps the most difficult feature to provide in a goal for a development project. Because innovation is a journey into the unknown, it is often difficult to know how much work lies ahead or how far one has proceeded toward the destination. The process of prototype debugging provides a good example of how difficult it can be to measure

PERT Chart

1. Prepare part drawing, stage 1
2. Prepare part drawing, stage 2
3. Prepare part drawing, stage 3
4. Prepare part drawing, stage 4
5. Prepare part drawing, stage 5
6. Procure material, stage 1
7. Procure material, stage 2
8. Design tool, stage 1
9. Design tool, stage 2
10. Design tool, stage 3
11. Machine tool, stage 1
12. Machine tool, stage 2
13. Machine tool, stage 3
14. Machine tool, stage 4

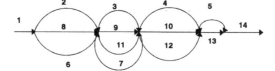

Gantt Chart

1. **Prepare part drawing**

2. **Procure material**

3. **Design tool**

4. **Machine tool**

Gantt chart and the more complex PERT chart depicting identical overlapped activities.

FIGURE   10-2

progress. When an engineer is working on a bug in a prototype it is often impossible to know whether it will be fixed in 10 minutes or 10 days. Then, when it is fixed it may uncover a new layer of bugs, or the fix may introduce problems of its own. It is usually impossible to know whether one has found and corrected all the bugs. *The Soul of a New Machine* (see Chapter 7's Suggested Reading) provides a vivid description of the frustrations of debugging, the immense effort that can go into this activity, and the uncertainty of not knowing when it will terminate.

The project's intermediate goals must also be individuals' goals. The team leader should develop goals jointly with individuals to ensure that they are realistic and establish ownership. This can be a difficult step requiring a considerable amount of negotiation to arrive at an acceptable solution. It is nevertheless an essential step in an accelerated project, because until individuals sign up for the plan there is no real plan. We have seen many plans drawn up by Marketing to satisfy sales deadlines, but because others did not help create the plan and thus buy-in to it, the desired schedule was never maintained.

Make Schedules Visible

Once the schedule has been created it must go into active use by the team. The easiest way to do this is to produce a giant project schedule chart and post it on the wall of the team area for all to see. (A CAD system is sometimes better than project management software for making these giant charts.) If the schedule is important, it deserves to be displayed prominently to demonstrate its significance. This schedule will also be handy for the team to use in discussing progress and pitfalls, and it will be an aid when management visits to see how things are going.

Once the schedule goes up on the wall, it should stay there. On effective teams it is heavily annotated and covered with sticky notes. This is a healthy sign that it is in active use. Too often when the schedule resides in some computer file it is hidden from the team's view and can begin to slowly diverge from reality. We have yet to see project management software that can be annotated as easily as a large chart pinned to the wall of a team room. We strongly believe that project managers are most useful when in face-to-face contact with team members solving problems, not when they are at the computer terminal updating schedules or creating schedule reports. Their job is not to record the unfortunate accidents that occur on the project but to spot them quickly and engineer a way around them. This is best done with direct contact with the team members.

Leave Excess Capacity

In the next chapter we will cover the crucial issue of capacity management. However, we cannot discuss the issue of process control without touching on this issue. As we mentioned earlier, we need to structure projects so they will not unravel when obstacles arise. The most crucial element of this is to leave enough capacity to deal with the inherent uncertainty of the rapid development project. This is perhaps the hardest concept to get across to managers who have been indoctrinated through years of experience to believe that the elimination of waste is the holy grail of management. In fact, excess capacity is critical to making a development process work. *If you fail to have excess capacity you will pay the price in cycle time.* Excess capacity in development only looks like waste to the manager who does not understand what really happens in product development. Those who do understand recognize that it is a key tool for controlling the performance of the process. Without it the smallest obstacle could unravel an entire project. By doing post-project reviews of many projects (see Chapter 15) Microsoft has learned that, even with totally honest planning, applications projects take 20 to 30 percent more effort than anticipated, and systems projects take 50 percent more. So Microsoft plans this in as "buffer time" and is careful not to spend it on predictable items such as feature enhancements. This is their way of dealing with the uncertainty of innovation.

Formal Project Reviews

Formal reviews are a traditional means of monitoring progress on development projects. There are two basic types of reviews. A review of technical design decisions is called a design review, whereas a review of project status by management is a management review. Many com-panies choose to combine both reviews into a single meeting, but this is generally a bad idea.

Design reviews should be focused on the past, reviewing technical decisions that have been made since the last review. The people doing this review are generally technical, and the purpose is to ensure that the best technical choices have been made. The design review ensures that the product will function as intended and that its manufacturing cost is acceptable. It is important to use outsiders to the team who do not have a stake in the project, because such a stake renders reviewers less objective. These outsiders must be prepared before the review, since a superficial understanding of the design will reduce the quality of the review. Such reviews are normally done infrequently on a project.

In contrast a management review is usually the precursor of a financial commitment. The organization is trying to assess whether there have been any changes in the basic nature of the project that render it unwise to commit further funding to it. Such reviews need to assess both technical developments and changes in the marketplace. As a result they include a group of managers familiar with all aspects of the business.

Unlike a design review which focuses on the past, a good management review should focus on the future, since this is the portion of the project that can still be influenced. In this sense the term "review" is an unfortunate one, because it automatically creates the wrong focus. We would prefer to call it a planning session and use it to look ahead 60 to 90 days and determine the roadblocks that are beginning to emerge for the project.

Interestingly, in most organizations the flow of information in both of these reviews is two-way. During design reviews key technologists from outside the team learn of technical solutions that may be relevant for other products. During management reviews functional department heads become familiar with the current status of projects and often get a chance to contribute to their success. This results in a greater familiarity and comfort with the projects when they finally near completion. The implication of this is that we must choose reviewers by two criteria. First, we must look for those reviewers who can contribute immediately to current project success, for example, by clearing roadblocks. Second, we must look for reviewers who will be in important positions to influence success in the future and get them involved early. For example, key members of the selling organization may participate in a management review more for the latter reason than the former.

Informal Project Reviews

Complementing our system of formal reviews we want a healthy system of frequent, informal project reviews. This is fundamental to catching problems while they are small and influencing them while they are still easy to influence.

Such informal reviews can be used for both design reviews and management reviews. In design reviews, informality reduces the time needed for the review and creates an atmosphere of trust in which the reviewer is more likely to make realistic suggestions. The reviewee will also normally be less defensive to outside ideas. When such reviews are frequent they catch design problems before they can solidify and require extensive rework. Furthermore, when such reviews are frequent the reviewer is less likely to be overloaded by the magnitude of the review.

As with design reviews, many management reviews can be informal. For example, the team leader can meet weekly with a key executive sponsor to discuss project progress and management issues. We recommend holding such a meeting in the team room where we have posted the project schedule.

To emphasize speed the reviews should be frequent because things can get out of hand quickly on an accelerated project. So if you normally have monthly reviews, consider weekly ones, and if they are weekly, consider daily ones. A Black & Decker team held daily team review meetings. Each meeting lasted 15 minutes, and each of the 10 members got time to describe what had happened in the last 24 hours and what they planned to do in the next 24 hours. Cleverly, they used a printing whiteboard and created a reporting template on it with automotive pinstriping tape. A scribe took notes on the board during the meeting, and at the end they printed and punched their meeting report, placing it in a three-ring binder as the permanent record of their progress. Top functional management reviewed all the teams' progress monthly and looked for ways to remove roadblocks.

Frequent, Open Communications

Frequent, open communications are the lifeblood of the rapid development team. When information flows rapidly and without distortion, problems can be identified early and fixed before they do much damage.

Communications on rapid development teams is such an important issue that most teams will use all the communications tools that they can lay their hands on. We knew one team that installed its own bootleg local area network, even though members were all located within 50 feet of one another. When asked why they violated the corporate MIS procedure, team members replied that it would have taken too long for the MIS department to install the network and that the local area network was the best way to exchange certain types of information.

In general we find that rapid development teams favor face-to-face, real-time communication. As we discussed in Chapter 8, such communication is dramatically enhanced by co-location. Written documents can be slow because they take more time to prepare and distribute. Furthermore, there is no guarantee that a memo will be read or responded to.

Electronic mail speeds up some parts of the process, but it still does not get around the three fundamental flaws of written communication. One flaw is that the very act of composing a written message can unwittingly draw a person into solidifying a position, advocating a particular sequence of events that will involve others, and making assumptions about how a reader of it will respond. None of this helps to keep communication open. In contrast, in verbal communication a position is taken progressively as a conversation is shaped by the reactions of the person with whom one is conversing. Second, written communication can easily go into inappropriate detail or neglect important information, because it lacks the feedback of an audience saying, "I know that" or "I don't understand." Written communication invariably provides both too much and too little information for its audience. Finally, the timing of a response to written communication is unpredictable. The recipient may call immediately and share just what he or she thinks of the memo, but if there is no response, what can you assume? Had you delivered the message in person and the recipient stormed out of the room without saying a word, there would at least be some information about the reception the message got.

Frequent, regular meetings are often the heart of the project's communications systems. Most commonly they occur weekly, but at certain times some teams will raise the frequency to twice a week, or even every day. These meetings focus on the project's status and share new information that may affect the project. The meetings are used for problem identification—most problem solving should be done in smaller groups outside of the meeting.

The tone of these meetings is important if we wish to create open communications. The team leader plays a key role in getting the meeting to focus on issues rather than people and on solving problems rather than fixing the blame for them. The tone for these meetings is typically set early in the life of the project and is hard to reverse later on.

Let us illustrate the use of meetings with the example of a 100-person company in the Boston area that manufactures computer equipment. Every day at the 10 o'clock coffee break (which encouraged informality and tied the meeting to something pleasant and regular), the team met to discuss the progress made in the past 24 hours and set goals for the next day. The group included Quality Control, Manufacturing, Purchasing, Field Service, and often Marketing. The meetings were sponsored by a Vice President, who attended them whenever he could. This attendance enabled management to keep in touch with the project and signaled the importance of the project.

The daily meeting concept just described is not limited to small companies. For instance, consider a large computer company with different requirements that handled its meetings differently, but still held them daily. Engineering and Manufacturing were interdependent in this company, but were located 50 miles apart. Their solution was to "meet" on a conference phone call every day at four o'clock. The parties on the two ends of the conversation would vary some from day to day, and sometimes they might not have much to report, but the call would always be made. Because phone calls have their useful limits, there was also a regular weekly team meeting, always held at a fixed time but alternating in location between the lab and the plant.

The discipline of holding these daily meetings forces people into thinking about making daily progress. In a fast project every day counts and no one can afford to lose a day, either because nothing got done or because the wrong thing was done because of poor communication. Monthly or quarterly reviews simply do not do the job in rapid product development.

Earlier in this chapter we pointed out that excess capacity was a critical tool to permit projects to deal with uncertainty. In the next chapter we will explore the issue of capacity management in more detail.

SUGGESTED READING

Hronec, Steven M. 1993. *Vital Signs: Using Quality, Time, and Cost Performance Measurements to Chart Your Company's Future.* New York: American Management Association. This book by a consultant from Arthur Anderson & Co. provides a good philosophical view of metrics, with many general management metrics. However, its breadth makes it a weak source of metrics for rapid development.

Kotter, John P. 1990. What leaders really do. *Harvard Business Review* 68 (3): 103–11. Conventional product development processes emphasize management systems to monitor and control progress through plans, reports, and reviews. Our alternative emphasizes providing the team with a vision and empowering and motivating the team to execute the vision. Kotter explains this subtle but crucial difference.

Randolph, W. Alan, and Barry Z. Posner. 1988. *Effective Project Planning and Management: Getting the Job Done.* Englewood Cliffs, N.J.: Prentice-Hall.

————. 1988. What every manager needs to know about project management. *Sloan Management Review* 29 (4): 69–73. Both of these pieces get right to the heart of managing projects for results with a message that directly reinforces the material in this chapter. The article nicely condenses the book above, which is just 163 pages itself.

CHAPTER 11

Preventing Overloads

Up to this point we have suggested many time-to-market opportunities: dedicating people full-time to a project, co-location, doing the project economic analysis, and many others. Each of these will reduce cycle time, and most of them will also reduce the amount of effort put into each project, which will eventually allow you to do more project work with the same resources. Yet many companies never can get started putting these tools into use, because all of them take some extra effort to learn, plan for, or set up. Many managers and developers are stretched so thinly just trying to finish what they have already been assigned that any improvements must wait until "tomorrow." Thus, the subject of dealing with project overloads is critical to not only executing projects quickly but also to even getting started in using these tools.

This chapter addresses the subject of resources head on. Clearly, we cannot create resources for you, but we can explain what you are going to have to do to get the resources needed to apply any of the other tools in this book. We will also show you how overloading resources directly dilutes effort and creates queues, which stretches cycle time accordingly.

The resource issue has gotten worse in the past few years, in the face of corporate downsizing, restructuring, and management fluidity. Companies that were doing well at accelerating their product development a few years ago have been set back today. A 1993 study by Kuczmarski & Associates found that the number one impediment (74 percent agreeing) to product development speed was lack of people resources.

We can think of this subject as resource shortages or as project overload. We don't have enough people to staff the projects we have to do. Or, we have too many projects for the people available. These are two sides of the same coin, and the common issue is an imbalance between the people available and the projects that "must" get done.

For convenience of presentation in this chapter, we equate workload with the number of projects here, but another powerful means of attacking overloads is by reducing the effort involved within a project. For example, the techniques of incremental innovation in Chapter 4 can cut the amount of work needed to get a product out the door dramatically. In addition, Chapter 6 discusses module reuse; for instance, if 80 percent of the modules in a product are reused, design effort for the project goes down by 80 percent, which means that capacity to turn out projects has increased by 400 percent. Please refer to the product-related chapters (Chapters 4-6) for techniques focusing at the project level. This chapter concentrates just on the number of projects, not their size.

PROJECT DILUTION

When individuals work on more projects than they can handle, cycle time suffers directly. Say, for example, that you give someone two tasks to do, and they could effectively work full-time on either of them. Then, each task is going to take twice as long to complete. When your worker is splitting his or her time between two projects, on average each project is getting half of his or her time, and each will sit waiting half the time. In this case cycle time doubles, just due to the dilution effect, not even counting any losses in efficiency that may stem from having to juggle tasks.

This is one major reason why project overload is so catastrophic to cycle time. It dilutes effort and stretches cycle time proportionately.

Splitting People Between Projects

Figure 11-1A suggests that each engineer should be working on two projects, if one considers only project expenses and ignores time to market. This chart is the result of a study conducted at a major R&D facility in the United States. It shows how value-added time changes, depending on how many projects engineers were working on at once. It rises in going from one to two projects per person, but it drops off after that. These results stand to reason: if a person works on just one

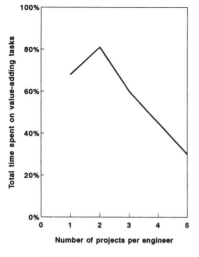
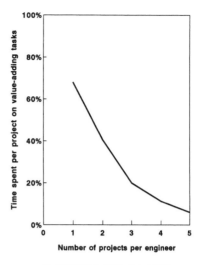

A. Engineer's value-adding time   B. Engineer's time per project

Value-added time considerations suggest that two simultaneous projects per engineer is the best solution, but the answer comes out differently if we wish to concentrate effort on a project to complete it quickly. *Adapted from Wheelwright and Clark,* Revolutionizing Product Development: Quantum Leaps in Speed, Efficiency, and Quality, *The Free Press, 1992. Figure 4-2, p. 91.*

FIGURE 11-1

project, there will probably be times when he or she has to wait on something related to the project, and this time is wasted. With two projects, the second one can fill any waiting gaps in the first one, so this makes more complete use of an individual's time. But with three or more, the overhead and switching cost of working on all of them cuts increasingly into the person's value-adding time.

However, if speed is the objective, then two projects per person is not the best solution; one project per person is. Figure 11-1B replots the data in the first chart using cycle time as the objective. Any time we assign more than one project to a person, we pay a large speed penalty, because the time they can devote to each project gets diluted.

The one-person-per-project loss indicated in Figure 11-1A may in fact not have to be a loss if the team is properly trained and motivated, because then there is little reason for idleness. If team members develop generalist skills, as suggested in Chapter 7, then every member can usually find a value-adding task to do even when their primary skill is not needed. In addition, the concept of critical path, discussed in Chapter 9, also contributes here, because with a critical path mentality throughout the development team, everyone will constantly be looking for activities they can either get off of the critical path or keep from getting onto it. This has the effect of making people more proactive and increases scheduling flexibility. Consequently, the apparent loss that one suffers with dedicated staffing seems to be something that we can avoid with good preparation. This is probably why some of the companies mentioned in Chapter 1 have been able to gain substantial cycle time and productivity improvements simultaneously.

The critical path mindset plays in another way here, too. People stretched among several projects are normally so busy just trying to keep all of their masters happy that they have little time to think about the critical path and keeping tasks off of the critical path proactively. Consequently, activities get onto the critical path that do not have to be there, and the project slows down. Giving people some time to look ahead, with proper training and motivation, clears the debris off of the critical path.

This point is so important that we will summarize. The normal situation, backed up by the data collected from a real company in Figure 11-1A, is that you may pay a slight efficiency penalty to dedicate a person to a project. In return for this slight penalty, you get a large savings in cycle time, which is usually worth more money. Moreover, if you apply the methods in this book, the efficiency penalty is likely to become so small as to be insignificant. Nevertheless, many managers do not take advantage of this opportunity, for two reasons. One is that going to dedicated staffing is an act of faith; one has to trust that the benefit will materialize. The other is that the manager just does not seem to have the resources for this "luxury." This is what we cover in the remainder of this chapter.

BECOMING SENSITIVE TO OVERLOAD

The medicine for overcoming overload is generic, thus quite cost-effective, but it is bitter. Therefore, before discussing the medicine, we will provide some indicators and an understanding of the disease so that you can determine whether you have a chronic case and need to take the medicine.

Some Barometers

 Four indicators will help you to measure project overload. The first is to look at individuals' workloads. Are they trying to work simultane-

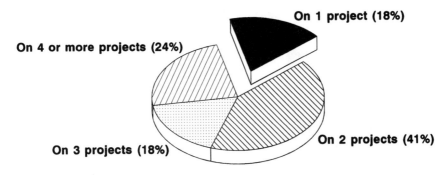

Projects assigned per engineer for one client's senior development
engineers, the client's most valuable development resource.

FIGURE   11-2

ously on many different tasks, to keep many masters happy? How long
does it take someone to start a given piece of work? Is the common response "I can't get to it for a few days, because I have thus-and-so to
do"? If those few days are on the critical path of a development project, this response has just delayed the product introduction date by
that interval. If this happens one hundred times in the course of a project, a delay of a few hundred days has crept in.

Figure 11-2 shows how you can measure this dilution of effort. It
illustrates how the senior development engineers in a client company
were splitting their time. Keep in mind that these individuals are the crucial resource, the engineers just below the manager ranks, those that would
be most valuable to have assigned full-time to one project. They were in
fact so talented and valuable that they were being pulled in many different directions. Although these senior engineers are a key resource,
sometimes the bottleneck lies elsewhere, and this is what should be measured. For example, if you have delays due to a bottleneck in the analytical lab, then chart the time split for your analytical lab technicians.

A related indicator is to watch how people are applying their time
to a project. Figure 11-3 comes from another client company that keeps
particularly good time-card data for its engineers. This is a chart for a
small project, showing how management had planned to staff a critical
mechanical engineering position on the project relative to how the staffing
actually worked out. The labor shortfall, apparent in the vertical dimen-
sion, is because this individual was also working on another project, in
contradiction to the plan. The stretch-out in the horizontal direction illustrates how this staffing dilution directly lengthens time to market.

The third indicator of overload is to look at the project list over
time. At what rate are projects being added to it, and at what rate are
they leaving the list? Is the list growing, or stable? Are there more dor-

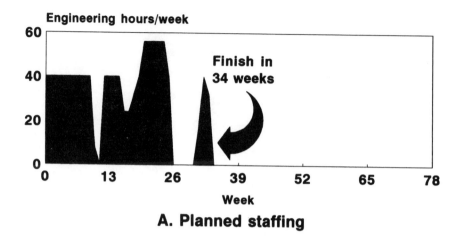

A. Planned staffing

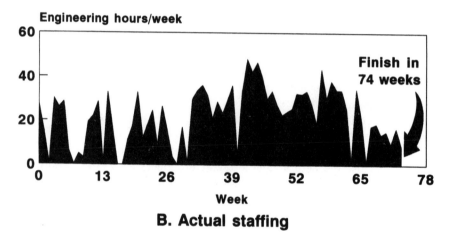

B. Actual staffing

Staffing levels and cycle time relative to the project plan for a client project.

FIGURE 11-3

mant projects than active ones? Figure 11-4 illustrates some of these issues. The top curve in the diagram represents cumulatively all the projects given approval to start, with the space under this line accounting for the outcome of each project. Some have been officially aborted, some completed (resulting in new products), some are still active, and some have become dormant (with, for example, no effort having been expended on them for at least three months). This diagram is fairly typical. Few projects are actually being aborted, the completion list is growing steadily as projects routinely complete, and the active list is fairly constant because it depends on the organization's product de-

Development projects

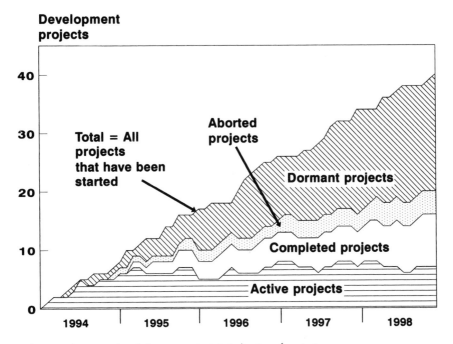

A large and growing list of dormant projects is indicative of project overload.

FIGURE 11-4

velopment capacity. However, the dormant list is growing steadily because projects are being added faster than they can be completed.

The projects on this dormant list have consumed effort that could have been put to work on active projects, so the dormant list is counterproductive. In addition, the dormant projects often are not so dormant. Managers put effort into managing and explaining the dormant list. Some of the dormant projects are likely to be the pet projects of certain developers, so they receive hidden attention, thus siphoning effort from the active list.

The fourth earmark of project overload is delay in starting new projects. How long does it take, once a project is approved, for management to marshal the resources to put a full development team to work on it (a couple of people just piddling with it does not count)? In most companies people are so heavily committed that it takes months to get up to full team strength on a new project, months that add directly to the length of the development cycle. This is why we strongly advise in Chapter 3 that you measure the end of the Fuzzy Front End as the moment when you have full staffing, not just ap-

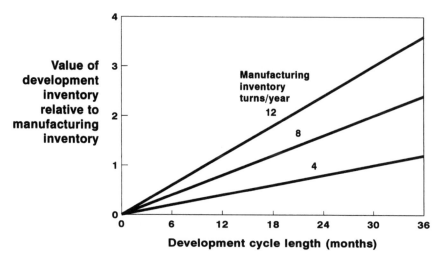

If the ratio on this chart comes out above one, your development WIP is more valuable than your manufacturing WIP, which you are probably managing quite carefully. Assumes a 50 percent gross margin and that R&D expenses are 5 percent of sales (results are in proportion to this R&D expense percentage).

FIGURE   11-5

proval. It may be more difficult to measure the full-staffing moment than the date of an approval signature, but using the later date makes the reality of staffing delay—and overload—more apparent.

Development Work-in-Process Inventory

The dormant projects in Figure 11-4 can be put in perspective by considering them as inventory. In the factory we have what is called work-in-process (WIP) inventory, all of the parts apparent in the factory that have not yet been assembled into a shippable product. Because WIP is a significant factory cost, factory managers are well trained to manage this inventory. They do it by increasing the number of times it "turns" per year.

Product development has the same WIP problem, but it is both a bigger and a less apparent issue than in the factory. Product development WIP is the result of the company's investment in its active and dormant projects, but since much of this investment goes toward ideas and documentation, it is less tangible than the hardware artifacts representing the factory WIP. Figure 11-5 allows you to estimate the value of your product development WIP relative to your factory WIP; it is not uncommon for this ratio to exceed unity. In addition, product development WIP is usually more perishable than factory WIP, that is, if it is not used quickly, it tends to lose much of its value.

THE BASIC RULES

The basic means of avoiding overload is to start fewer projects but get them done, then start a few more. Here is a simple, idealized model. Suppose that a company has a fixed amount of development resources, which we will take to be the R&D head count, as represented on the vertical axis in Figure 11-6. There are two projects on this project list, with time portrayed on the horizontal axis. There are two options, as illustrated. The more commonly chosen one is to divide the resources in half and work on both projects simultaneously. The other option is to put all the resources into one project, get it done, then put all the resources into the other project.

Option 1

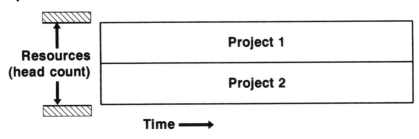

Option 2

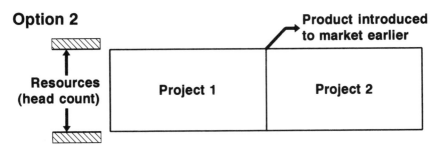

Simplified model contrasting simultaneous versus sequential effort on two projects.

FIGURE 11-6

The illustration shows the second option ending at the same time as the first one. In reality, the second option may take longer, which may occur if there are fixed time constraints, such as tooling lead times, driving the development cycle. If the limiting constraint is the amount of effort (labor hours) that can be put into the project, the second option will end at the same time as the first because the labor hours (the areas within the rectangles) are exactly the same in the two options. Notice that when working in an overload mode, the constraint that governs cycle time is labor hours, and the situation illustrated, with both options ending at the same time, is accurate.

Operating according to Option 2 offers several advantages. One is that the first product gets to market in half the time, as indicated, with no cycle-time penalty for Project 2 compared with Project 2's cycle time in Option 1. Another advantage is that Option 2 provides more flexibility because no commitments need be made to Project 2 until Project 1 is finished. At this point it might seem best instead to do Project 3, or do Project 2 in another way. A third advantage is that if you do decide to do Project 2, you will be doing it with more current market and technical data than in Option 1. The final advantage is that of cycling people through projects faster so that they learn more and keep their skills sharpened.

In advocating Option 2 we may seem to be contradicting the advice in Chapter 8 to keep the development team small, to facilitate communication. Certainly, carrying this concept to extremes and putting all the staff on one mammoth project would be inefficient. What tends to be the case in industry, however, is that even individuals and small groups tend to operate according to Option 1 rather than 2. These people are fragmented, splitting their time, and when they are working on two tasks simultaneously it will take them roughly twice as long to complete their tasks as if they had worked on them exclusively.

The observant reader may notice another apparent contradiction: we advocated a short front end in Chapter 3, but by delaying project starts until substantial staff is available, we are in fact lengthening it. In this case, however, the lengthening is balanced by a shortening of the development cycle. We incur no cost of delay because the project gets done at the same time as it would have starting earlier with lighter staffing. We could actually have a shorter project and a shorter Fuzzy Front End if another, more timely project became available to start before the end of Project 1. Such a project might be superior to investing in the less timely Project 2.

Even though Option 2 seems advantageous, it is not popular. Option 2 requires a great deal of management discipline to not start a project until adequate staffing is available for it. It is easier to tell the boss or the customer that you are working on their project than to explain that you will not start a project until you can staff it adequately.

Control the Project List Religiously

The solution to the project overload problem is very careful control over the project list, specifically over the start-up of new projects. This strict control over project starts is usually the responsibility of upper management or product managers. Ironically, product managers are usually rewarded in proportion to the number of development projects they initiate, the opposite of the restraint we are suggesting.

Most companies are working on far more projects than they can staff fully. This means that if they wish to get into the mode of staffing projects fully, they will have to make some tough choices in radically pruning their project lists, as Dade MicroScan, Inc., did. MicroScan makes hospital laboratory instruments, and the company suspected that it was working on more projects than it could support adequately. So we analyzed the project load, using project staffing diagrams such as the one shown in Figure 11-7. MicroScan found that, on average, the company could develop its products twice as rapidly with the same total resources by working on fewer projects at once but staffing them more intensively. So the MicroScan management team took action: they trimmed project starts for the next year from 41 (which was about normal) to 21.

Such reductions are not unusual for managers who are serious about staffing projects adequately. For example, in a division of a major chemical company, top management trimmed the project list from 47 to six projects. Interestingly, they haven't missed the 41 projects killed because new, better opportunities have arisen since, and they were in position to exploit them. Among the 41 aborted projects, they lost one customer (knowingly), but they have since regained that customer.

Another client example comes from a leading electrical machinery manufacturer that slashed its active projects list from 114 to 17. Always running to keep up before, now it finds that it can make commitments and keep them. Furthermore, controlling the project flow has enabled it to reengineer its product development process, thus leveraging its competitive advantage. When this company completed some projects from its shortened list, it soon had an opportunity to choose a new project to start. Surprisingly, it found that the top project on the waiting list (old number 18) no longer made sense, due to technology changes. Instead, the company chose a new idea that wasn't even on the waiting list.

In Australia, Initiating Explosives Systems, makers of blast initiation systems, killed 21 projects so that it could fully staff one. That project was completed in nine months, compared with 24 months that it would have taken, and IES has not missed the killed projects.

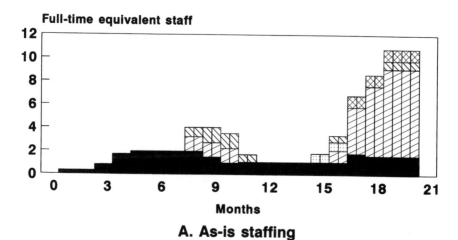

A. As-is staffing

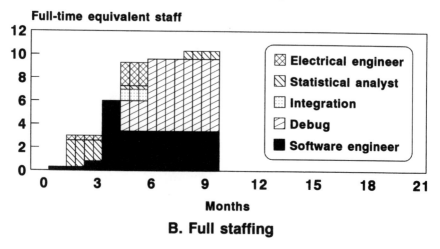

B. Full staffing

Typical staffing diagram from Dade MicroScan, Inc., shows how a
software upgrade project could be accelerated by staffing it fully.

FIGURE   11-7

Post the Project List

Shifts in development priorities are indicative of project overload. Priorities among development projects are often unstated, uncommuni-
cated, or constantly churning. What happens when management does
not send clear, steady signals about its priorities is that individuals
then establish their own, based on various individual objectives.

Once you have pruned the project list, the next step is to post it for all to see. This leaves less latitude for someone working on a pet project. A project is either being given full, official attention or it isn't being worked on. Clearly, there are some proprietary information issues in posting lists of product development projects, but these usually amount to smoke screens for not committing to project selection decisions. Projects can be given code names if necessary.

Create External Capacity

There will be times when you have bottlenecks in certain areas, so why not plan in advance for them? Develop a network of suppliers that can fill gaps in drafting, testing, assembling, or analyzing. Prequalify them and give them some work from time to time just to keep them interested in your business. Because scheduling is an imperfect art, especially when innovation is involved, these suppliers can be invaluable in giving you a larger, more flexible capacity.

This is a perfect example of trading time for money. Teams that have done their economic analyses (see Chapter 2) and posted the cost of delay on the wall of the team area know just when it is time to go shopping, and if they have prequalified their suppliers, they know just where to go shopping. To take quick advantage of this capacity, some kind of funding mechanism is needed, too. You might have a team budget for such services, or you might have key service suppliers on standing accounts. The key is to be able to engage them quickly.

Similar advantages accrue from using temporary employees. They can provide a means of quickly expanding staff to cope with temporary opportunities. As with suppliers, arrangements (recruiting, contractual arrangements, funding channels, etc.) should be made before the need arises. Another advantage of temporary employees is that they can be used as a buffer to protect the permanent work force from the demoralization that stems from cutting staff.

However, our clients have observed the downside of using temporary employees. Such employees usually are not motivated to the level of a permanent employee, especially when used in high-performance co-located, cross-functional teams. Another problem in a high-performance team situation is that such team members are getting training, just in participating on the team, that is valuable to the company. You cannot afford to lose much of this training, especially if it might go to your competitor. The solution is to monitor the temporary employee levels; if it turns out that you really have a permanent need for certain temps, they should be brought into employment.

TRAPS TO AVOID

Because it is so easy to take on more projects than the organization can handle quickly, there are many ways to go astray in adequately staffing projects. Here we look at some of these.

The Risk of Diversification

Project portfolios sometimes get compared with investment portfolios, which can be dangerous. Diversification, which works so well for investment portfolios, leads to dilution of effort in project portfolios. It is quite natural to minimize risk by taking on some "extra" projects, because with many different projects underway, uncertainties are diminished and some projects are certain to be successful. Unfortunately, when we are working on more projects than we can staff fully, we are incurring project delay due to dilution of effort, and this delay carries with it other types of risks, such as missing a market window or misforecasting a market that is excessively far in the future. There are also risks associated with the loss of flexibility one suffers when all resources are tied up in lightly staffed projects that will not complete for a long time. Diversification, if it gets to the point of diluting effort, actually adds risk.

Unanticipated Projects

Another reason for starting fewer projects is that it is counterproductive to run a product development operation at 100 percent of its capacity with known projects. Some slack must be provided for handling unanticipated projects. Such projects are not unwanted distractions or signs of an undisciplined organization, but rather an indication that the firm is responsive to market demands. Chapter 3 discussed the type of annual planning cycle that completely fills the product development pipeline for years in advance, thus virtually assuring that every project will start serious development long after its market need is identified.

Manufacturing planners do not plan plant capacity to run at 100 percent of current demand because they know that there is enough variability in demand and capacity to prevent a fully loaded plant from shipping on time. When it comes to product development, however, the same executives who allow for a margin on manufacturing capacity seem to be fearful of having engineering resources sit idle. They neglect to factor in the cost of delaying the market introduction of new products, but they are careful to provide enough capacity so that production orders do not slip.

Operating at full capacity on planned development projects causes another type of dysfunctional operation. Unanticipated projects will always come along and demand an immediate response, and current projects will sometimes require more effort than planned. Then the organization will have to shift people and priorities, which destroys productivity and commitment. Although a certain amount of shifting is inevitable, by not allowing some slack, development efforts will be in constant flux.

The Project Loading Rule

The standard way of assigning staffing to projects is to simply take the projects that "must" be done and divide the available people into them. Instead, we suggest that you rank order your projects. Then take your most important project and assign as many people to it as it can effectively engage. Next, go to the second project and do the same with it, using any people left after excluding the ones assigned to the first project. Continue until the people are all assigned. Any remaining projects—even "must do" ones—do not get started until a project completes, freeing some resources.

How do you know how many people to assign to a project? Ask yourself, "If I assign one more person to this project, can that person make a net contribution to the project's profitability?" Specifically, will that individual's added expense be exceeded by the cycle-time savings provided? If the answer is yes, assign them, then ask the question again. When you get to the point that one more person will not add to a project's profitability, it is fully loaded. (The tools of Chapter 2 will help you calculate a person's profitability contribution.)

When doing this, assume that the person you add will have a mix of skills to fit the project well, not that he or she is a specialist who would only be narrowly useful to the project (see Chapter 7 for guidance on using generalists rather than specialists). For the moment, don't let reality get in the way, telling you that you do not have people with the right skill mix. Once you have loaded the project with these hypothetical people, go back and note the shortfalls in skills. This is where you should be thinking about improving your people's skills, through recruiting, training, development, or other means. When you have completed this staffing exercise, you will have two useful pieces of information: (1) How many people you could put on a project to really move it along, and (2) Skills weaknesses that should be addressed.

The Fallacy of Adding Resources

Project overload can be expressed as either too many projects or too few resources. We have been concentrating on reducing the number of projects, but what about solving the problem in the more pleasant way, by just adding resources?

 Let's be as generous as we can for the moment, assuming that more resources are available, that they are instantly trained to our way of doing business, and that we could expand our infrastructure simultaneously to accommodate the extra resources. Even in this envious situation, adding resources is not the long-term solution. If we add more resources, sooner or later we will be back in the same situation with more projects than we have the resources to handle, and we will be diluting our effort and delaying projects again.

The permanent solution to the overload problem must be in the discipline to not start more projects than current resources can execute quickly. Adding resources without developing the skill and discipline to control demand will ultimately result in the same overloads we had before we added them.

This chapter is fairly far back in the book, but this does not mean that one can wait until late in the project to think about project loading. Indeed, the greatest flexibility to solve the problem is before the project starts, although managing overload is an ongoing issue that continues throughout the project. Risk management, in the next chapter, poses similar issues: there are powerful opportunities to anticipate risks before the project starts, but risk management requires ongoing attention every day of the project.

SUGGESTED READING

McConnell, Steve. 1996. *Rapid Development: Taming Wild Software Schedules.* Redmond, Wash.: Microsoft Press. One of the difficulties of managing capacity is estimating the effort required for a new project, an especially difficult task for software development. Chapter 8 of this book provides an overview of available methods, such as Boehm's COCOMO model.

Reinertsen, Donald. 1991. Managing the design factory. *Electronic Design* 39 (18): 65–72. Compares the "design factory" with the manufacturing factory, transferring some lessons on capacity management from the latter to the former.

Smith, Preston G. 1994. Saying "No" to customers. *Across the Board* 31 (3): 56–57. Ultimately, controlling capacity comes down to occasionally saying "no" to internal and external customers. This short piece emphasizes the discipline required.

C H A P T E R   12

Managing Risk Proactively

As we accelerate a development project, we often assume additional risks by overlapping activities and using partial information. There is less time to react to risky items that turn out badly. Correcting something that does not work out as expected takes time, and in an accelerated project time is of the essence. Consequently, the management of risk is an important part of rapid product development.

The key to managing risk is to deal with it before the problems occur—that is, manage it proactively. Otherwise, risk provides a constant excuse for project slippage. An important byproduct of effective risk management is that the developers start to assume the responsibility for risks; things going wrong no longer become surprises that call for slipping the schedule.

In this chapter we will take risk management out of its mysterious realm and subject it to the same kind of business-based logic that has been the theme of previous chapters. Consider what Peter Drucker has to say about risk:

> A year or two ago I attended a university symposium on entrepreneurship at which a number of psychologists spoke. Although their papers disagreed on everything else, they all talked of an "entrepreneurial personality," which was characterized by a "propensity for risk-taking."
>
> A well-known and successful innovator and entrepreneur who had built a process-based innovation into a substantial

worldwide business in the space of twenty-five years was then asked to comment. He said: "I find myself baffled by your papers. I think I know as many successful innovators and entrepreneurs as anyone, beginning with myself. I have never come across an 'entrepreneurial personality.' The successful ones I know all have, however, one thing—and only one thing—in common: they are not 'risk-takers.' They try to define the risks they have to take and minimize them as much as possible. Otherwise none of us could have succeeded. As for myself, if I had wanted to be a risk-taker, I would have gone into real estate or commodity trading, or I would have become the professional painter my mother wanted me to be."

This jibes with my own experience. We too know a good many successful innovators and entrepreneurs, not one of whom has a "propensity for risk-taking." ... The innovators we know are successful to the extent to which they define risks and confine them. (Peter F. Drucker, *Innovation and Entrepreneurship*, Harper & Row, Publishers, Inc., 1985, p. 139)

The Mathematics of Risk

As we attempt to quantify risk, we find that the overall degree of risk has two components: The amount at risk, and the probability of occurrence. It is useful to divide risk into these two components, portrayed in Figure 12-1, because one of them is more under our control than the other. The amount at risk is the first graph, which is the same in parts A and B of the figure. This amount usually depends on what we have invested to get to this point—in labor or money—and there is little we can do about this investment. If we attempt to reduce our investment, we are deferring progress, which is not the route to accelerated product development. So the risks will come, and in rapid development we actually attempt to make them occur faster.

The key to managing risk is usually to control the probability of occurrence, constantly driving it down as we progress. The risk is still there, but we manage the chance that it will hurt us or slow us down. This is the difference in Figures 12-1A and 12-1B.

Figure 12-1A suggests another link between risk management and time to market. The right graph in this figure portrays an increasingly unacceptable situation in which the level of risk is getting out of hand. What typically happens in such situations is that senior management finally becomes uncomfortable enough with the project that they intervene. Such changes in management direction usually have a negative impact on the schedule, and they are not pleasant for the developers,

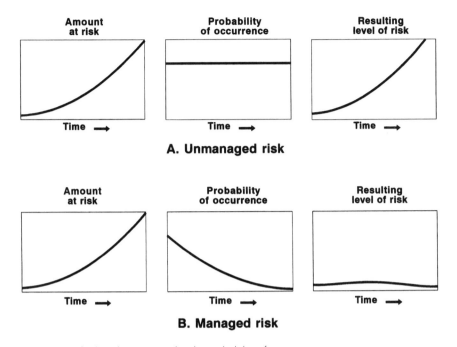

A. Unmanaged risk

B. Managed risk

The portion of risk under our control is the probability of occurrence,
portrayed in the center of each trio.

FIGURE 12-1

who lose control of their project and have to start conducting the project as management says.

The remainder of this chapter will concentrate primarily on techniques for reducing the probability that risk will delay our project. Clearly, this requires early identification of the risks and explicit, ongoing efforts to drive down their probability of impact on the project.

KINDS OF RISK

There is another useful distinction, one between technical risk and market risk. The dividing line between these is the product specification. Technical risk is the probability of failing to achieve the performance, cost, or schedule targets of the specification. It is the risk of poor technical execution, of missing the target. Market risk is the probability of not meeting the needs of the market, assuming that the specification has been satisfied. It is the risk of selecting the wrong target.

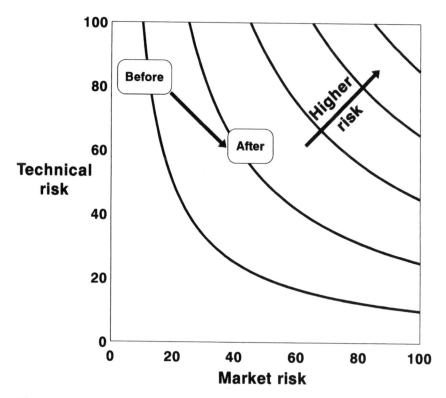

A focus on only technical risk can drive up market risk and thus total risk.

FIGURE 12-2

This distinction is useful because it focuses equal, simultaneous attention on technical and marketing issues. Studies of new-product failures find that about three-fourths of these failures relate to a misjudged market, and only a fourth have to do with poor technical execution. An underemphasis on market risk can affect projects in two ways.

Sometimes we become overly concerned with technical risk, say, overmanaging it with excessive reviews. These delay the project and force Marketing to look further into the future to predict sales. This increases market risk, as shown in Figure 12-2. Thus, overmanagement of technical risk actually increases the total risk level.

The second effect of an underemphasis on market risk is that this is a common cause of project redirection. Late in the project Marketing or Sales discovers that the product, as it currently stands, will not meet customer needs well, so it has to be redesigned. This is clearly bad news for the schedule.

Technical Risk

Organizations usually place more emphasis on technical risk than market risk, largely because technical risk is more apparent and is easier to manage. Technical risk can arise from the technology failing to perform as expected, from its cost being higher than projected, or from unanticipated side effects that arise from a particular technical approach. Companies are more accustomed to dealing with technical than market risk. For instance, they often monitor product and development costs, build checklists of technical problems experienced previously as a check on a current project, or create backups for a questionable technology. The outcome of having to resolve technical problems is usually schedule delay.

Companies can err by either overcontrolling technical risk or by undercontrolling it. Some companies focus heavily on the performance and cost dimensions of technical risk, which can indeed catch these problems and minimize surprises, but this burden of management overhead delays the project. At the other extreme, they can just react to design problems that could have been anticipated, consuming unnecessary time in making corrections. The effect of these two approaches on the length of the development cycle is different, however. In the lightly managed case the basic cycle can be short, but it will be extended an unpredictable amount by the unanticipated problems. Figure 12-3 shows this effect. In a heavily managed situation the cycle bears the extra management overhead, but the variation at the end of the cycle is smaller because the management attention improves predictability.

The amount of management attention to use depends on the timing demands of the business. In some markets the objective is just to get the product to market as quickly as possible. This emphasis is typical of technology-driven markets, such as computers. Other markets present specific market windows, such as snow throwers available by late fall. In this case, minimum cycle length is not crucial, but variations in cycle length will be costly, especially when advance commitments have been made with distributors, dealers, and advertisers. In selecting ways of managing development risk, keep your goal in mind. In some cases it may be advantageous to add a few extra checks to the process, to minimize tail-end variations.

Sequent Computer Systems, Inc. explicitly considers its risk management level by preparing three schedules, a risk schedule (designed for 90 percent confidence), a baseline schedule (50 percent confidence), and an opportunity schedule (10 percent confidence). Sequent uses three sets of assumptions to build these schedules. For example, for a hardware design task, the company might assume three, two, and one debug cycles, respectively. For the time needed to build a prototype,

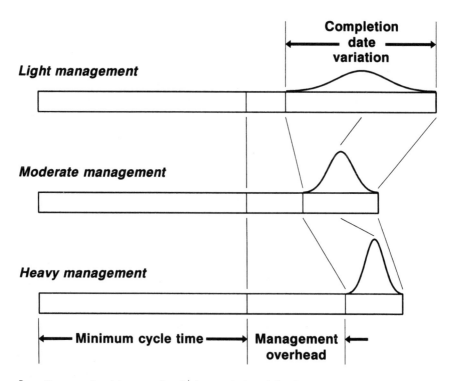

Light management

Moderate management

Heavy management

Completion
date
variation

◄── Minimum cycle time ──► Management ◄──
overhead

By putting more time into managing risk in a project, variation in
completion dates shrinks, but this management overhead can extend
the cycle's length.

FIGURE   12-3

the assumptions could be seven days, five days, and three days (with
a 50 percent pay premium), respectively.

Market Risk

Market risk can result from having done inadequate market research,
from not keeping in touch with customers as development proceeds,
or from following a weak specification due to unclear customer desires, changes in customer requirements, or the introduction of competing products.

Compared with how they handle technical risk, most companies
do a poor job of managing market risk. In part, this occurs because market risk is less objective and quantifiable than technical risk. The technical people who often lead product development may not know how
to deal with market risk, so they forget about it. In addition, compa-

nies resolve technical problems—or agree to ignore them—before a product is introduced. In contrast, market problems usually show up only after a product has been shipped.

Consider how your own company deals with market risk relative to technical risk. How vigorously, and when, does it react to a new product whose high unit manufacturing cost causes a million-dollar loss in profit compared with one whose weak sales are responsible for the same loss of profit?

Black & Decker provides an example of effectively managing market risk. After developing many cordless drills the company decided to add a cordless screwdriver to its line. So in June 1985 it introduced a cordless screwdriver with a comfortable pistol grip, a powerful unit that could be used for light drilling as well as for driving screws. The only problem was that it failed to meet sales expectations. Black & Decker later found out that customers did not consider it a screwdriver simply because it did not look like one. A competitor's product, shaped like a conventional screwdriver, was taking the sales. Consequently, B&D initiated a crash project to provide a new cordless screwdriver for Christmas 1987.

Engineering went to work on the functional issues. But Marketing could not decide on the handle shape, which was on the critical path because of mold-fabrication time. After conducting focus groups on handle size and shape, knowing this to be a critical issue, they were still unable to decide between two options: a slim one, holding two cells, and a somewhat fatter handle holding three cells for greater power. Unsure about handle size, Black & Decker decided to design both sets of handle tooling while doing more market research. The product design was purposely kept modular, with common interface dimensions (see Chapter 6 on product architecture) so that either handle could be used. Similarly, the handle molds were designed so that molds for either handle could be used in a common mold frame. The product went into production at full rate in August, assuming the larger handle, to build a supply for Christmas. But when the final market research showed a preference for the smaller handle, production switched over to it in October.

Without careful planning and a sound understanding of the critical parameters of a product, the outcome can be much less favorable. For instance, one company that builds electronic assembly equipment got itself into a trap with product flexibility problems. It was developing a machine to place a new generation of surface-mount components, for which there was yet no industry standard on component configuration or size. The engineers had found a clever way to transport these components quickly and cheaply. Their solution carried high market risk, though, because the transport scheme was sensitive to variations in component size and shape, precisely the issues that remained unresolved in the marketplace. Consequently, they were unable to move until the market stabilized because they had not maintained flexibility where it was needed.

The most obvious way of resolving market risk is to increase involvement with the customer, either through formal means like market research or more direct means, such as establishing routine designer contact with customers or actually having a leading-edge customer on the development team. Although additional market research may often be needed, we emphasize the direct approaches because they provide a quick means for the design engineer to remain surefooted as the terrain shifts in the marketplace. Market research seldom provides specific answers fast enough, particularly in the midst of the development process, when the inevitable design trade-off decisions arise.

Consider how Carrier's Team Conquest kept close to its customers by partnering with individuals from six of its major distributors from around the country. These six "distributor partners" began by helping prepare questions for a survey. They then provided access to their customers to administer the survey.

However, this was far from the end of their involvement. The six were flown in at Carrier's expense to review the specification, which was written around the survey results. Each of them, paired with one of their key building contractors or engineers, was again flown in for a review of the first prototype product. Using their input the design was modified, and a revised product sample was prepared for their review before production began.

By keeping these distributors and their customers involved throughout the program, Team Conquest assured that Carrier was keeping up with market shifts, the design was what the customer wanted, and the customers knew what they were getting before the pre-sale literature went out.

PROACTIVE RISK MANAGEMENT

Although keeping in touch with customers throughout the development cycle is clearly an important part of managing risk, it is just as important to constantly know what to be worrying about, both with customers and internally. We do this with a risk management plan. Unlike some planning, in which the major value is in the discovery while building the plan, or conversely, in executing any reasonable plan, risk management requires both. It is vital that important risks be uncovered and effective plans laid for them at project initiation, but in order to drive down the probability of occurrence, as shown in Figure 12-1B, the plan must be executed, too. Below we describe both of these activities, building the plan and executing it.

Building a Risk Management Plan

Risks are identified initially through some form of brainstorming, using its normal rules: quantity initially, not quality; write it down just as expressed; no judging; and building on others' threads. Cross-functional participation is essential here, and risks should be sought beyond the normal technical ones. Market risks are especially likely to cripple a project. Risks can occur in unsettled product requirements; the competitive arena; supplier relations (for example, bankruptcy); product literature, packaging, training, distribution, or installation; the beta testing program; budgets or funding; management changes; crises elsewhere in the company; weather; or illness or accident. Think about what has delayed recent projects. If product cost or performance is critical, consider the risks that might affect these parameters, because if they are critical, any shortfall is likely to affect the schedule.

Beyond the benefits that a diverse group brings to brainstorming, participation by the whole team gets them involved in being responsible for proactive risk management. Although all risks will never be identified and there will always be some surprises, our intent is have the team assume responsibility for what can go wrong.

Once you have your raw list of potential risks, clean it up by combining similar ideas, rewording them until everyone understands them, and so forth. Then assign each a number or letter-number pair. Using a chart like the one in Figure 12-4, map each risk on the chart. The horizontal axis of this chart is straightforward and normally runs from zero to 100 percent probability; if all of your risks are in a small part of this range, for example zero to 10 percent, just use the subrange. The vertical axis, the amount at risk, should be measured in profit dollars. Your discussions are likely to describe the amount at risk in terms of project expenditures, product cost, product performance, or schedule slippage, but these can be converted easily to profit numbers using the trade-off rules from Chapter 2.

This is all related to the mathematics of risk discussed early in this chapter. The level of each risk on the risk map is the product of its value on the horizontal axis and its value on the vertical axis, so lines of equal risk level are inverse curves ($y = C/x$, where C is a constant that makes the line come out where we want it). We draw one of these lines, as shown, to establish a risk management threshold at a level that we can manage. The risks above and to the right of this line

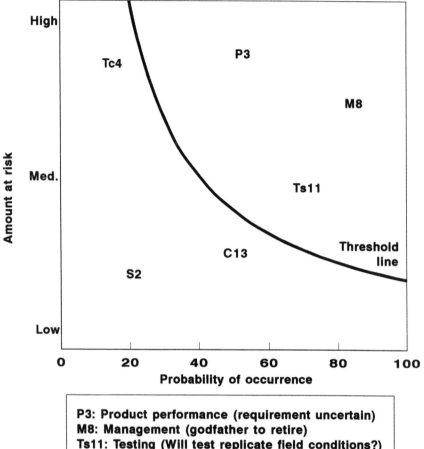

A risk map portrays all known risks for a project to facilitate risk
management; those above the line are managed actively.

FIGURE   12-4

get managed, and those below or to the left of it don't (until sometime
later should they rise above the line). It is important to set the risk
management threshold realistically. Each risk that gets managed will
take effort, so we cannot afford too many of them.

At this point a sanity check is in order. Are there risks above the
line that do not appear to be that important? More importantly, are

there sleepers below the line? Adjust as necessary, and reconsider where you have drawn the threshold.

The next step is to develop a risk management plan for each risk above our threshold. Each plan describes its risk and lays out what will be done to reduce its probability of affecting the project or its impact if it does. The detail plans will vary widely. Some may involve technology backups, some may call for market research plans to narrow uncertainty in what the customer needs, some may require frequent monitoring of a critical but erratic supplier, and some may involve cross-training to alleviate the impact of a strike. The section, "Other Risk Control Techniques" (see the next page), provides some tools for managing individual risks. As with all action plans, each should have an assigned responsible individual, a due date, and adequate resources to execute it. At this point it will become apparent if you have drawn your threshold line too low.

This risk management planning should be done at the planning stage of the project, along with the budgeting, scheduling, and product specification writing. The risk profile and what will have to be done to keep total risk under control is something you will want to know about before you get deeply committed to the project, just as you will want to assure that the schedule, budget, and product specifications are achievable.

The placement of each risk on Figure 12-4 is not highly precise and cannot be, because the underlying numbers are in many cases guesses. Thus, the same guidance given in Chapter 2 for the financial analysis is in order here. This risk management analysis helps us to make far better judgments than no analysis, but it should not be relied on to be exactly correct. Consider the extenuating circumstances, as necessary, and make adjustments if needed. Also, as is the case for the financial analysis, a major value of the risk management planning is that it gets all disciplines on the team thinking about, discussing, and attempting to quantify risk items jointly as they get into the project. However, do not let the plan lapse after the planning stage, because it also has great value during execution of the project, as discussed next.

Managing to the Plan

The risk management plan is an effective way to manage an accelerated development project. In the process of managing risk, the developers shift from a mindset in which risk happens to them to one in which they work toward a risk target, just like a cost, product performance, or manufacturing yield target. Most risk items no longer become an excuse to slip the schedule. In addition, schedules are likely to be shorter, because risky items are being taken off of the critical path methodically.

Managing to the plan amounts to regularly reviewing both the risk map (Figure 12-4) and plans for the individual risks being managed. The management interval could be once a week or once a month. We advise against tying it to phase reviews, because keeping track of a fast-changing risk situation is more akin to a frequent progress report than a deliverable at the end of a phase. At each review, the risk map is checked to see if there is any reason why the risks shown on it may have shifted on the map. If a certain risk(s) has moved above the threshold line, it needs to be put under active management, and if it has slipped below the line, its active management can be terminated. Also, it is important to look for any new risks that have appeared and should be placed on the map.

Once the risk map has been brought up to date, plans for the individual risks above the line should be reviewed. Is the plan still accurate or does it need updating? Is progress on track? Is the plan getting the resources and commitment called for? Has the risk been driven below the threshold line on the risk map, so that its active management can be terminated and its resources shifted to something more productive? Most importantly, is the overall risk picture improving so as to avoid the trap of escalating project risk portrayed in Figure 12-1A?

When Teledyne Water Pik jointly developed a new electric toothbrush with Battelle, using one team at each of these two sites, they found the risk management plan to be a critical communication tool for their dispersed team. Their plan, affectionately referred to by the teams as the "Master List of Things to Worry About," had a resolve-or-bail-out deadline for each item, and the list was under revision control. Establishing these deadlines forced risk assessment and decision making, and it assured that both teams and management were all working toward the same goals.

OTHER RISK CONTROL TECHNIQUES

Many of the basic tools for controlling risk are covered elsewhere in this book, particularly in product-related Chapters 4–6. For example, Chapter 4 suggests means for minimizing risk, from the overall project level (avoiding the megaproject) to the individual part level (for instance, by emphasizing the use of standard components). Also, keep as much risk as possible outside the development process, with a strong program of ongoing, product-oriented technical and market research, covered in more detail in Chapter 3.

Start with the Tough Issues First

When faced with several things to do, the normal human tendency is to do the easiest one first. This "bootstrapping" technique actually is quite sound in many cases. If we can complete a simple task, it will give us the confidence to tackle something harder. And for the procrastinator, the harder one may never have to be faced.

This sequence is unwise for product development, especially for accelerated development. Because the tougher tasks usually fall on the critical path, they should be started first. For product development, the procrastinator's rule also works in reverse, because if we cannot do the tough tasks, the project will be canceled and we will never have to worry about the simple ones.

Because the natural tendency is the opposite, explicit attention will be needed to identify the tougher or higher risk items and start with them. This is a place where management and the team leader can coach the developers to help them overcome the bootstrapping tendency. More importantly, however, make sure that the underlying motivational systems are aligned with doing the tough things first. For example, sometimes developers are rewarded or praised for the number of things they accomplish in a period, which clearly encourages them to knock off the simple items. The showstoppers then hibernate until they can do the most damage to the schedule later.

Assume Risk Only Where It Will Provide an Advantage

We have encouraged the use of standard parts to minimize risk. This is part of a larger concept of connecting risk with competitive advantage. Standard parts usually have little impact on competitive advantage, so we cannot afford to have them contributing to project risk.

It pays to think deliberately about which parts of your product enhance competitive advantage. These are likely to be tied to your business's core competencies. Cummins Engine Company has divided its product, diesel engines, into a continuum of value-adding categories, starting with standard parts and ending with those few portions of the engine where the company's creativity and expertise truly make a better engine (see Table 12-1). Parts such as the head fall into this final creative category. Chapter 13 discusses opportunities to reduce risk on standard or existing parts. In between, however, are perhaps the most interesting possibilities, the flywheel in Cummins' engine, for instance. A flywheel, although complex, can be designed completely analytically by specifying a few dozen values that determine its design—no creativity required. Cummins has thus automated flywheel design by

TABLE 12-1

Innovative Content Levels for Engine Parts

Product Attribute	Standard Parts	Parametric Parts	Feature-Based Parts, Restrictive Location	Feature-Based Parts, Free Location	Creative Parts
Dimensions	X				
Feature interchangeability	X	X			
Feature location	X	X	X		
Feature types	X	X	X	X	
Design specification	X	X	X	X	X

Courtesy of Cummins Engine Company, Inc.

X = Attribute not allowed to vary

writing high-level software that drives its computer-aided design (CAD) system and stress analysis software, producing drawings and machining tapes from the input values. This frees the designers to concentrate on the parts on the creative end of the spectrum where the competitive advantage—and risk—reside.

Stay Flexible on Unresolved Issues

If market risk can be narrowed to a specific issue, you may be able to leave it open indefinitely. Earlier in this chapter (page 227) we discussed a Black & Decker screwdriver that ran with two handle options until late in the project to cope with a market risk regarding handle fatness, and we mentioned a nameless firm that did poorly at selecting the parameter to leave open in surface-mount electronic components. Chapter 6 describes the original IBM PC, which provided both a cassette tape port and a floppy disk for data storage because the market was uncertain on this issue at the time.

Consciously Trade Off Expense and Risk Control

Most risk management options cost something. Black & Decker paid for an extra handle mold (although they were fortunate enough to be able to use it later for a higher-power model). IBM paid something extra for each unit it shipped with the unused cassette tape port. Most of the risk management actions are not free.

Use your financial analysis (Chapter 2) to assess the costs and benefits of each of these means of reducing risk, even if you can quantify some only approximately. You will have a superstore full of tempting buying opportunities to reduce risk, and only by using your decision rules will you be able to find the bargains and stay within your budget.

Provide Focus to Management's Attention

Good risk-control systems minimize risk by keeping the high-risk areas highly visible. Such systems allow management to make major resource shifts in response to emerging problems. Because in an accelerated project there is less time available to react, and because the cost of fixing a problem is much lower if it is caught early on, having early warning systems in potential risk areas is crucial. This is where "management by walking around" (MBWA) pays off (see Chapter 14). Another tool for drawing management's attention to high-risk areas is the risk management map (Figure 12-4).

Freedom to fail is another factor in keeping an early warning system vital. Communication on potential problem areas must be kept open, both horizontally and vertically. After all, product development is no more than a sequence of problems that arise and have to be solved, and if people are discouraged from talking about problems, nothing much will happen. In particular, if the messenger is shot for bringing bad news, the early warning system will vaporize.

Work Concurrently on Technical and Market Risk

For speed, work on technical and market risk concurrently. The traditional development approach is to address them alternately. Companies frequently work on market risk first, through market studies. Then a specification is written and Marketing basically waits while the technical risk is reduced through product development. When there is a prototype to work with, Marketing goes out for market tests to resolve market risk. Finally the project lands in Manufacturing, where the manufacturing process is debugged technically.

Although the market and technical risks interact and should be worked concurrently, it is usually best to resolve them independently of each other, because this decreases complexity (see Chapter 4) and provides more options to overlap risk-resolution activities. For example, if risk is to be resolved through testing, it is usually easier and faster to conduct two separate tests, addressing market risks, such as size, shape, and feel issues, through a nonfunctional styling model and technical risks with a crude-looking functional model.

Maintain Backup Positions

Backup plans are a common means of managing risk. Black & Decker's second handle mold was a backup against a market risk. More often, backups are used to cope with technology risks. If there is concern that a new technology may not work as required, develop an alternative in parallel, always keeping it ready to substitute for the new technology. Often, especially in electronics, the backup is a variation of the old technology, which lacks the desired price–performance characteristics. If necessary, the product can be shipped initially with the old technology and updated later. Backups can also be used in other areas, such as covering for a high-risk supplier or providing a secondary manufacturing method.

Although backups are a popular means of dealing with risk, they also often tend to be relatively expensive, because they consume two sets of resources solving the same problem. Unless the backup is an existing approach that requires little additional effort, explore alternatives to the technology being backed up before committing to a backup. Perhaps the risky technology can be deferred until an upgrade or next model. Maybe another technological approach will provide most of the benefit with much lower risk.

Find Accelerated Testing Approaches

Life or endurance testing often requires long periods of time and thus is likely to be on the project's critical path. If a product is specified to last for one million cycles, it simply takes a long time to amass a million cycles to see if it will survive.

Consequently, there is a premium on discovering ways of getting life-test results—or even indications—early. Identify the life tests that extend your development schedules considerably and search for means of getting leading indicators of the test results. We provide two examples.

When Pratt & Whitney was developing the engines for the Boeing 777, it had to run an endurance test of the engine in a test stand, which is industry practice. However, the developers observed that wear and other problems were related to imbalance that develops slowly in the engine as it operates. So rather than start the test with a factory-fresh balanced engine, they purposely built the new engine with the imbalance that it would typically have well into its life. Now the problems would start to show up sooner.

Chrysler has cut a month out of its development cycle by accelerating a vehicle durability test from six weeks to less than two weeks. This is a brutal test over potholes, railroad crossings, and the like, accumulating 100,000 miles (160,000 kilometers) of wear in 2,500 miles (4,000 kilometers). But it takes its toll on drivers, too; they last only about four hours a day. So Chrysler built a robotic test track that keeps the cars under torture 24 hours a day in any kind of weather.

Ideally, you can determine the effect of your acceleration technique on the real test and adjust the test results accordingly to estimate the actual life. In cases where this predictive capability does not exist, the accelerated test can still yield considerable value: failure modes, comparative life, etc. Usually, the accelerated testing provides enough confidence that the main development can proceed, using a verification life test that can be taken off of the critical path.

In Weak Areas, Model and Test

Two philosophies would appear to compete for resolving risk. One says to design, analyze, and simulate in the computer or on paper, producing a physical artifact only when there is a high probability that it will be correct. The other says to build something close first, test it or otherwise check it out, then make corrections. The question here, as always: which is faster?

The answer is not simply one or the other. Rapid developers know how to mix analysis and design with model making to obtain the advantages of each, dodging each's limitations. In general, analysis and simulation are precise but can be based on incorrect basic assumptions. Physical representations are great for getting a subjective reaction, but can be weakly tied to basic principles, making it difficult to know how to change the design if the model proves inadequate.

In recent years both model making and analysis capabilities have grown greatly (see the case studies at the end of Chapter 9), which has added more possibilities to this discussion. There are several rapid prototyping technologies available in a variety of materials, prices, and fidelities. This capability has extended into rapid tooling, which allows making short production runs using the final materials. Alternatively, one can use solid modeling and an array of analysis and simulation software to "optimize" a design in many ways before anything is ever built.

In designing integrated circuits, design automation is firmly established, with the objective of getting the first silicon to be correct. This is essential because the millions of individual components on a chip require design error rates that are lower than what could be achieved with manual techniques. In part, this is driven by the highly analytical nature of the product; subjective factors such as form and feel are not issues. However, the cost of iterating using physical artifacts is usually too high in terms of both expenses and time.

In designing its rooftop air conditioner, Carrier was able to use the precision and interference checking capabilities of the CAD system to eliminate many common problems in assembling the first prototypes. Due to the interference checking, no parts occupied the same physical space, which often happens in the initial build of a complex three-dimensional design. Carrier's designer provided the usual slots for sheet-metal screws to allow for assembly variation, but these were unnecessary, as all of the screws fell right in the middle of their slots. When Boeing assembled its first 777 using comparable CAD technology, total alignment error in the 206-foot (63-meter) long craft with four million parts was 0.023 inch (0.6 millimeters); typically, this error had run about half an inch (10 millimeters).

These results are a testament to the power of the computer, but there is more to new products than computing. Physical models help people to make firm decisions about a product. We once sat through a review of an electronic product employing sophisticated digital signal processing and housed in a small plastic case. The go–no-go decision was basically up to the Director of Marketing, and she reached her decision based not on how well the device could detect signals but on how it looked and felt. That organization was wise to get a physical model into her hands as quickly as possible.

Physical models are also invaluable as a reality check on the validity of your technical approach. As one of our clients who formerly developed products for a chain-saw company put it, "At some point, you have to cut the wood." Tom Peters talks about getting the "chicken test" out of the way. He is referring to the industry-standard test for a jet engine design. Since such engines have to be able to ingest birds without failing, and because science has found no substitute for the bird, jet-engine makers, as early as possible, send a live chicken through an engine running at full power to see if they have a strong enough design.

Our bias lies on the side of physical models rather than analysis, for reasons of speed. Models tend to reveal the big mistakes sooner. However, this is also their weakness, as developers would rather not have their misconceptions or oversights exposed. Thus, they tend to hide behind the analytical tools and need some encouragement to expose their design to scrutiny early on. Engineers in particular are trained in college to optimize solutions, so continual honing of a concept is instinctive to them. Analysis and simulation, which are certainly needed at some point, are the tools of this refinement. Models help to assure that the refinement is applied to an acceptable basic concept.

To use models for resolving risk, first identify the risk, using the risk management plan covered earlier. Then build models or design experiments intended to resolve that risk as quickly as possible. Strive for the very simplest models or experiments that will answer the question. If there are two questions, build two different models, which will likely be less complex than a single model built to test two separate ideas. Finally, always try to test at the lowest possible level of components or subassemblies.

SUGGESTED READING

McConnell, Steve. 1996. *Rapid Development: Taming Wild Software Schedules*. Redmond, Wash.: Microsoft Press. McConnell's Chapter 5 parallels our risk-mapping technique, and although it is aimed at software, there is helpful information here on hardware risk management, too. Good references to further sources on risk management are at the end of the chapter.

Peters, Tom, and Nancy Austin. 1985. *A Passion for Excellence.* New York: Random House. "Part III: Innovation." We have offered several tools for dealing with risk on a methodical basis. In contrast, Peters and Austin emphasize that innovation is an irreducibly sloppy process, so the best, fastest way of dealing with it is through constant experimentation; small wins, they call it. Full details on the chicken test on page 130.

Bridging the R&D– Manufacturing Gap

In our consulting practices we often see development projects that speeded through the design process come to a screeching halt when they reach manufacturing. At the same time we often encounter Manufacturing people who complain that they can devote less and less attention to a development project. No matter what these companies tell us about their concurrent engineering accomplishments, these symptoms speak the truth clearly. They are clear evidence that their process is still a sequential one. An abrupt transition is a sign that manufacturing activities did not begin early enough in the design process. A compressed manufacturing activity is a sign that most of the work waited to begin until the design was complete. The sad truth is that all too many companies are struggling to achieve a smooth transition into manufacturing.

One measure of the magnitude of this problem is the engineering changes that occur after parts are released to Manufacturing. It is not unusual to see more than one engineering change per part number, which in a certain sense means that each part is being designed twice, once in Engineering and again on the factory floor. Such practices can be wasteful, because a change on the factory floor is expensive in terms of both time and money.

Some managers have concluded that *any* engineering changes after release to Manufacturing are too many, but such a conclusion depends on the financial analysis discussed in Chapter 2. We need to determine the relative economic significance of cycle time and development expense to make the trade-off between refining the design in the design phase and completing it on the factory floor. The trade-off is not a simple one. When the product first hits the factory floor, we learn a lot about its limitations very quickly. We identify defects quickly and fix them. It might take 10 times as much time to find the same defects in Engineering, even though this is a cheaper place to fix them. We can only determine if the increase in speed is worth the added expense if we have done our financial analysis. Some rework on a design is healthy because it is a sign that we are making these trade-offs astutely. A design that experiences no changes after manufacturing release is probably a design that sat too long in the sterile environment of the development lab.

There is ample existing literature on the simultaneous design of product and process. Different observers have coined different terms for this activity including concurrent engineering, simultaneous engineering, and integrated product and process design. The bulk of the existing literature fails to distinguish among the ways that concurrent engineering impacts economics, or focuses on it as a tool to increase product quality and to lower product costs. This is appropriate in cases where this is the primary benefit of concurrent engineering. However, in this chapter we will focus on a different benefit of concurrent engineering, which is its impact on cycle time. Our perspective will be to treat concurrent engineering as a trade-off rather than an absolute good.

WHY WE NEED CONCURRENT DEVELOPMENT

The overwhelming conclusion of everyone who has delved into concurrent engineering is that the bulk of the leverage occurs in the product's conceptual design stage. Here we make the basic design choices that will determine a product's possible manufacturing processes.

We can view our design choices as having to meet the needs of both Engineering and Manufacturing. When a design fails to meet the needs of either of these groups, rework is required. The key difference in rework that comes from manufacturing issues is that it is expensive and late in comparison to rework originating from engineering issues. We illustrate this in Figure 13-1. By increasing the number of design choices that meet the needs of Manufacturing in advance we reduce this rework. The problem with most design processes is that they first

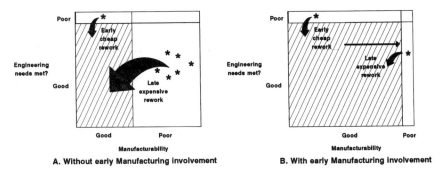

Using concurrent engineering to reduce rework.

FIGURE   13-1

design to meet the needs of Engineering and then assess manufactur-ability. This means that the needs of Manufacturing are poorly served until late in the design process. Instead, we do time-consuming rework of the design, frequently on the critical path where it can do the most damage to our cycle time. A better approach is to address the needs of Manufacturing and Engineering simultaneously. This reduces the num-ber of design decisions that fail to meet the needs of Manufacturing. As shown in Figure 13-1, this attacks a major source of rework.

The data generated in industry support this conclusion. Manu-facturing can not meet its objectives of attaining a low production cost without being able to influence early design decisions. For example, a McKinsey & Company study of an automobile body panel found that three-fourths of the manufacturing cost differential as compared to a competing panel was created by design choices. A British Aerospace study has reported that 85 percent of a product's manufacturing cost will depend on choices made in the early stages of its design. Rolls-Royce investigated 2,000 components and found that 80 percent of their production cost was attributable to design decisions. These find-ings are summarized in Figure 13-2, which is a composite of data from companies such as Ford, General Motors, and Westinghouse. As Fig-ure 13-2 indicates, 80 percent of a product's life-cycle cost has already been determined before the first design review.

Such data clearly show that we must get our experts on cost, the Manufacturing people and suppliers, involved before we can finalize the specification. Such early involvement provides two ways to shorten cycle time. First, it allows us to overlap product and process activi-ties. Second, it reduces the design rework arising from design choices that are unacceptable to Manufacturing.

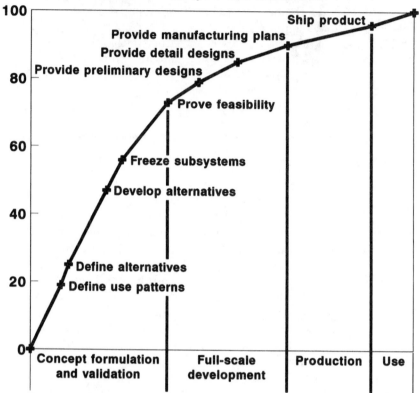

Product life-cycle costs are locked in at an early stage of development, when fundamental design choices are made. These choices, which include process issues, also influence a product's development time. *From Nevins et al.,* Concurrent Design of Products and Processes, *McGraw-Hill, Inc., 1989, with permission.*

FIGURE   13-2

STREAMLINING THE TRANSITION TO MANUFACTURING

It is the goal of every product to move from being a poorly defined concept in the minds of developers to become a well-characterized design that is built repeatedly, without defects, in a manufacturing process. In achieving this goal we can influence cycle time in three ways. First, we can keep manufacturing off the critical path. Any manufacturing activities that take place off the critical path do not consume cycle time. This applies to *all* manufacturing activities, not just those that involve the product design. For example, there is no reason that training of assembly workers should get on the critical path of product introduction. Second, we can reduce design rework. If our design engineers can meet the needs of the manufacturing process on the first try, they will not have to do additional design work. This reduces the total magnitude of rework and frees the designers to work on other issues. Third, we can force the inevitable rework to occur early in the process when it will do little damage to our schedule. It is much easier and faster to change the design while it is still a rough sketch than it is to modify the same drawing when it has accumulated a dozen approval signatures and has been put under configuration control within the documentation system.

Let us examine a number of the specific tools we can use to achieve these three objectives.

Put a Manufacturing Engineer on the Development Team

As we discussed earlier, most companies have too little feedback from Manufacturing early in the design process. The traditional model for getting this feedback is by inviting Manufacturing representatives to formal reviews of the design. Not only does this cause feedback to be too late to be useful, but it often results in less effective feedback because of the formal nature of the review. Too often we find busy Manufacturing representatives fail to adequately prepare for such formal reviews and miss even this limited opportunity to influence the design. Even if they do prepare, their ability to influence the design is far lower at this point, due to the design's built-up inertia in the formal documentation system and in the egos of the designers. Often it is easier and politically wiser to be a team player and overlook potential design problems as much as possible.

A far more effective approach is to maintain a continuous Manufacturing presence in the development lab. For example, one maker of restaurant equipment has a Manufacturing engineer permanently assigned at the company's design center. This engineer works directly with project managers to ensure that key engineering data is released early enough to support tooling lead times. The program has been so successful that a recent program was completed without tooling ever getting on the critical path. In contrast, previous programs would have tooling delays that added months to their development process.

Teledyne Water Pik routinely places manufacturing, tooling, or test engineers directly on development teams. One such team recently completed a new advanced performance water filtration product. Their challenge was to ensure that the influent (contaminated) water could not contact or mix with the effluent (filtered) water. In industry jargon, this means absolutely no bypass and absolutely no leaks. Senior Project Engineer Ed Giordano spent about an hour working on a design concept that, in order to meet the design requirements, was getting complicated. His concept involved many parts, including flexible seals, a rigid plastic closure with tight-tolerance-seal compression rings, and adhesive to hold it all together.

At that point Giordano knew he needed help, so he went to co-located Senior Plastics Engineer Len Haferman. They scrapped Giordano's initial concept and together started thinking about how they could achieve all of the requirements in one molded plastic part. They achieved this and also worked out the design concept for the associated multicavity mold. Although it was a rather complicated tool with several slide actions, the part it molds incorporates nine distinct design features that would have needed many parts otherwise. In addition, this design is much simpler to assemble and is far less likely to allow bypass. The time savings comes from the fact that designs of this part and its associated tooling design were the final ones released to production. Here Teledyne Water Pik achieved complete overlap between part design and tooling design.

Design Strictly to the Existing Process

One of the easiest ways to eliminate process design issues is to design strictly to the existing manufacturing process. When this is done well the product automatically fits the process. There are normally two steps to doing this. First, metrics must be identified that indicate when a design does not fit the manufacturing process. This gives Engineering accurate information regarding the limitations of the current manufacturing process and signals which product attributes are most critical to Manufacturing. Second, as the design takes shape it must be constantly tracked using these metrics and action must be taken when the design deviates from them.

For example, at one large electronics company all manufacturing processes have been characterized using a metric from quality engineering called a C_{pk} or process capability index. The designs are reviewed during development and compared to the capability of the process. Each design has a computed C_{pk}, which is tracked throughout the design process. This metric tells the development team if they have designed to fit the current manufacturing capability. At this company you cannot even release a design to Manufacturing unless you meet its C_{pk} target.

At another company, Manufacturing has identified the specific design choices that complicate the manufacturing process on its elec- tro-mechanical product. Each design is measured on the number of cables, fasteners, and springs included in the design. As a result the design teams try to eliminate these labor-intensive parts. On one design they were so successful at eliminating these parts that the company canceled plans to automate the assembly process and just assembled it manually. The product had such low labor content that the company could no longer justify automating its assembly.

We should caution you that strict design to the existing process works best when the manufacturing process is being proactively managed to achieve continuous improvement. If not, the existing process can become a millstone around your neck. If the existing process is less capable than that of competitors you will be permanently embedding cost disadvantages in the design. As we shall see later, sometimes we need to improve the process to meet the needs of the new design.

Design with Existing Components

There is an analog to this when we work with suppliers. Just as we can design to the existing process we can design strictly with existing components. This gives us proven, tested components from reliable sources. By increasing our volumes it will also usually give us purchasing scale economies. We can get reuse of components by providing Engineering with information as to which components are used in products that are currently being manufactured and encouraging Engineering to choose these components.

Unfortunately, most companies do a poor job of encouraging reuse of components. They provide cumbersome computer printouts of parts with cryptic descriptions. Does the description "Casting, aluminum" help an engineer decide whether it can be reused on the next design? We have found a simple test for the usefulness of information provided to design engineers. We compare the approved parts list to the information provided in a well-organized supplier's catalog. We find that if it is easier to select a new part from the catalog than it is to find an existing part in "Master Parts List," busy engineers will choose from the supplier's catalog. Our objective should be to make it very easy to identify key parts targeted for reuse. When we make reuse "the path of least resistance" we do not have to coerce engineers to reuse parts.

If we cannot make it easy to reuse parts, we must make it difficult to use a new one. An approach that is used by one manufacturer of test equipment is to penalize development teams for using new components. When the cost of the product is calculated for a part that is already in use, it is costed at 100 percent of its cost. In contrast, when a new part is added to the bill of materials, it is costed at 120 percent of its cost. This encourages the team to reuse parts. You need to be careful in using this sort of approach because it places a very small penalty on minor parts like fasteners, and a high penalty on high-value items. Furthermore, a standard part like a motor is treated the same way as a custom casting, even though it is much more valuable to get reuse on custom parts.

Get Product Engineers onto the Factory Floor

One of the tools that helps engineers understand the limitations of the manufacturing process is educating them on the manufacturing process. There appears to be no better way to do this than to get the engineers out onto the factory floor.

 In companies like Honda, engineers spend several months in manufacturing positions before they reach their final job as a Design Engineer on a product development program. This gives engineers direct experience with manufacturing. Furthermore, engineers who have been through such programs develop relationships with Manufacturing counterparts, and are likely to feel comfortable continuing to interact with Manufacturing. In contrast, an engineer who has never seen the manufacturing plant, who does not know how it is organized, and who doesn't know the name of anybody in it is unlikely to try to get a manufacturing perspective when facing a design choice.

When the factory is located at the same site as the design center, companies will insist on having design engineers spend time on the factory floor. At the Lockheed Skunk Works, which is famous for cutting-edge aircraft designs that push the limits of technology, engineers can spend 30 percent of their time on the factory floor working with the machinists who are building their designs. This is crucial for the success of their designs because they are frequently pushing the limits of the manufacturing process.

General Motors uses a powerful approach in its Flint Automotive Division. Its design engineers spend a full day each quarter assembling the part of the car that they normally design. They thus learn some valuable lessons that will eventually help streamline the assembly of new car models, lessons that cannot be learned from books. For example, when trying to push some parts like hoses onto a car as it is continuously rolling down an assembly line, it is much easier to push the part on from the side, because if you have to work from the rear, the target constantly recedes as you are trying to bring the two parts together. Designers also learn that threaded fasteners can be difficult to install quickly, particularly in tight places where it is impossible to get all of one's fingers on the nut to get it started. An engineer who had worked for GM told us that part of the benefit of working on the factory floor came from standing next to the hourly workers who had been doing the same job for months. These workers had many things they wanted to tell the Design Engineer.

We encountered another case where a design engineer visited the German plant that was assembling the product he designed. As he was being escorted down the line they encountered an assembly worker who made strong comments in German. He asked his guide what the worker had said. The guide translated: "If I ever meet the engineer that designed this I will wring his neck!" The engineer thought twice before identifying himself as the designer of the product.

Provide a Champion for the New Product in the Factory

It is not surprising that Manufacturing often sees new products as a problem rather than a benefit. After all, they get measured on the basis of monthly shipments and gross margins. New products do nothing immediate to help either of these objectives. Instead, they tie up valuable people and equipment which could be used to do profitable business. If Manufacturing is lucky, it will be reimbursed for the cost of its efforts, if not it will provide this support for free. There is simply very little short-term incentive for most Manufacturing organizations to support new products.

In the face of this lack of incentive, we have to find some way of getting adequate support for new product development. We need to get prototype parts made quickly, we need to get items from our suppliers through receiving inspections, and we need to get the Manufacturing workers to work on what are likely to be poorly documented and erratically performing designs. How do we do this?

There are three approaches. The first, a long-term solution, is to realign the incentives for Manufacturing so that they are motivated to support new product development. This may be done by simple approaches such as including support of new product development as a performance evaluation metric for the VP of Manufacturing and the plant manager. We have also seen companies develop more complex schemes such as giving revenue credit (which means that the plant earns gross margin) on work orders run to support new product development. Unfortunately, we find that most companies are slow to change their incentive systems, which means this first approach takes a bit of time to implement.

The second approach is normally faster to implement. It consists of creating a champion for the product on the factory floor. Such a champion will either come from Manufacturing or Engineering. We have seen both types of champions work, but usually find the manufacturing person has more credibility and influence within the factory. One very effective approach has been to assign somebody from the Manufacturing organization to report organizationally to the Engineering Department but be physically located in the Manufacturing organization.

Third, make sure someone from your development team spends real time on the factory floor, starting early in the project. This can be the team leader, the Manufacturing member, or a key design engineer. This individual who provides "factory presence" should start by getting production workers' opinions on design questions or alternatives as they come up for the team during conceptual and detailed design activities. This factory presence accomplishes three things at once. It gets valuable manufacturing experience into the design when it will do the most good; it gives the individual involved the factory experience we mentioned earlier; and it provides a point of contact on the team for manufacturing workers when they run into the inevitable snags in manufacturing the design. This link can be cemented with technology by having the liaison wear a pager for which everyone in the factory associated with the project has the number.

A simple test you can make to determine whether you have a clear champion is to ask one of the production workers who is in charge of the new product that they are working on. If the new product has become a stack of faceless drawings, they will have no clear idea who is driving the project. If there has been a visible presence on the factory floor by the project manager or his or her representative, the workers will quickly identify the person who is interested in moving the project forward. This is important because all projects compete with many other priorities on the factory floor. Without an advocate the rapid development project can easily slip into the background as work to be done when people get around to it.

This is a crucial point when it comes to cycle time. The typical factory has piles of work for everybody to do, and this work is well understood. Everyone gets measured on how much of this work they get done today. In this environment, if a new, poorly described, trouble-prone job comes along—our new product—it gets put aside in preference to the predictable one. When this happens it takes time, often on the critical path, to get the new product back on track.

Design New Processes Early

As mentioned earlier, in some cases the current manufacturing processes will not meet the needs of the new designs. To use the old process may be too expensive, due to low yields or high costs. Under these conditions we have to put in place new processes.

Obviously, there is increased risk when we change the product and the manufacturing process at the same time. One way to insulate ourselves from some of this risk is to develop the process before we need it for the new product. For example, new pieces of machinery can be brought in and used for old products. The looser tolerances on the old products will be more forgiving of processing problems. As soon as the new machinery is fully capable, Engineering can begin designing products to exploit the capability of this new machinery.

A variation of this approach is to use a low-volume existing product to test a new processing technology. If the new technology does not work we can always revert to the old processing technology. If the new technology works, we can begin to design new products that use it. For example, one company redesigned a low-volume product to take advantage of new surface-mounted electronic components. Once it was successful on this product, the company began to design other products using the same technology. A failure on this first attempt would have done no damage because boards made with the older technology were quickly available.

Consider how one company learned how to fabricate the high-precision parts associated with a new design, a task beyond the capabilities of its existing machinery. The conventional procedure would have been to design the product first, then select the high-precision machinery, order the machinery, wait for it to arrive, install and learn how to use it, and then—after the design had been sitting idle for months—refine the manufacturing process until it could make production parts.

However, this company took a different approach. It obtained the machinery before was required, and immediately started making parts of the best precision possible—more than needed for current products—putting them into the normal products. The company was in fact giving away precision because these parts cost more to make than those normally used, but its staff was learning, preparing for the new product's arrival. When the product design was finally ready to manufacture there was a stable, high-precision manufacturing process ready for it, with no start-up time needed for the new machinery and very few scrapped parts. Note that in order to use this approach, you must justify the acquisition of the new equipment before it is required by the new product—a substantial challenge at many companies.

Another example of this approach is seen frequently within the semiconductor industry. Companies use high-volume, low-complexity products like memory chips to perfect their production processes and bring them under control. These memory chips typically have less complex structures and fewer masking steps, each of which affects product yield. These simpler chips allow the manufacturing process to be well-characterized, providing the data that is needed to design the higher complexity chips where timing margins are more sensitive. Again, we see a case of developing process capability before it is used in the design instead of simultaneously.

Analyze Engineering Changes

We have found that there are few sources of data as useful as the engineering changes that occur on a product. These changes provide a detailed record of every design change that is made to the product. By focusing on the changes made after releasing parts to Manufacturing we will discover which groups were not given a chance to provide input to the design before it was released to Manufacturing.

This analysis requires a careful assessment of the root cause and purpose of each change. Make a careful distinction between changes that occurred because new information emerged, and those that occurred because available information was not used effectively. For example, if the market suddenly adds a new requirement to the product, an engineering change is simply being responsive to the market. On the other hand, if someone in Sales knew about this requirement, but failed to communicate it until late in the design process, this is a sign of a defect in the product specification and testing processes.

It is important to analyze each change back to its root cause because establishing causality is difficult. For example, consider the equipment manufacturer whose units began to fail in the field. The source of the failure was ultimately traced to the control electronics board, which would upon occasion self-destruct upon a power surge. Was this a defect of marketing, engineering or testing? Some engineers would argue that the need to tolerate power surges should have been identified in the specification. This sounds good in theory, but such a capability is unlikely to appear in the specification because it is not likely to be a key source of differentiation from competing products. Some Marketing people would argue that this was an engineering mistake. They should have understood the operating environment of the product. There is probably much truth to this view, but there is also a strong argument that an effective product verification process would have caught this defect. The true root cause of this problem is a two-point failure of engineering and testing. An effective stress testing or field testing program would have caught this defect before manufacturing release even if the engineers had overlooked it in their design.

Put Assemblers on the Development Team

An excellent method to ensure that the interests of assemblers are represented on development projects is to actually put them on the development teams.

Some companies use assemblers from the factory to build prototype units instead of the skilled engineering technicians that would normally be used. Although these assemblers must struggle with the sparse documentation typical of prototype designs, they offer important manufacturability comments for the designers. Furthermore, when they go back to the factory they become experts for other people in the factory. This not only helps Manufacturing to get up to speed on the new product faster, but it also helps Engineering to focus its effort on the parts of the assembly documentation that are the most valuable to Manufacturing. In addition, the mere fact that the assemblers went back to the lab to build a prototype is a sign that there is a new product that will soon arrive in the factory. This causes this product to get higher levels of attention from all areas of the factory, not just from the assemblers.

Enhance Data Handling and Control Systems

The "toss it over the wall to Manufacturing" system may be slow but it is elegantly simple. Manufacturing knows that if the drawings are on the Engineering side of the wall they are susceptible to change and therefore should be regarded with suspicion. Manufacturing is reluctant to spend time on the drawings or do anything important with them, such as designing associated fixtures or discussing them with suppliers. Once the drawings are tossed over the wall they belong to Manufacturing, and can be trusted. Any change in the drawings after this point must be approved by a change review board, so change is harder and therefore less likely.

As we move to concurrent engineering there is a compelling need for new tools. It is very difficult to achieve early Manufacturing involvement without changes in our management of design data. For example, in a sequential design process we could use a physical drawing because it was used by one department at a time. In a more concurrent process we must give many departments access to the drawing while Engineering is still working on it. Once we give simultaneous access, we need to distinguish between levels of access so that people are not trying to change the same drawing at the same time. This problem is a natural application for computerized data management tools, which is why we so commonly see these tools implemented when people shift to more concurrent processes.

We also observe significant changes in drawing control procedures when companies make their processes more concurrent. A traditional process has at best two release levels. The first might be a preliminary release for limited quantity purchases of the part, and the second would be a final release of the drawing. As people implement concurrent engineering they add other levels of release for different purposes. For example, a drawing can be released for purposes of material procurement, and then be released at a different level to start fixture design, and finally released at another level to finalize machining dimensions. For each release level different information will be frozen. For material procurement we need to know the type of material and the rough size of the part. For fixture design we need to know the dimensions at the points at which the fixture will come in contact with the part. Only in the final machining drawing do we need all dimensional information on the part. Such a system with multiple release levels is common in highly concurrent processes. For example, on the Boeing 777 the drawing release procedures often had six to eight distinct levels of drawing release depending on the type of part.

Get Suppliers Involved as True Partners

The traditional approach to product development requires a detailed design of a particular component to be as supplier-independent as possible. Once the design is completed Purchasing finds the supplier that provides the right combination of price, quality, and delivery. This means that the suppliers begin to look at our design very late in the development cycle. By then it is too late to influence any important design decisions.

Such an approach does not take advantage of the enormous benefits that can be achieved with early supplier involvement. Suppliers involved early in the design can help designers specify components that are easier to manufacture and ones that fully exploit the capability of the component.

For example, Nissan's British subsidiary worked in a true partnership with its suppliers on the 1989 launch of the Primera. When some suppliers were unable to deliver workable parts on time Nissan put teams of Nissan engineers inside each supplier to improve their key processes. By the time Nissan launched the Micra, two years later, these suppliers had become Nissan's best suppliers instead of their worst.

This willingness to invest in the long-term relationship with a supplier is crucial. Usually such investments do not make sense when the supplier base is too diverse. As a result it is common to see companies implementing concurrent engineering also reduce the size of their supplier base. For example, Chrysler's supplier base has been reduced from 2,500 suppliers to 1,120. Such a reduction dramatically increases the value of any time spent in helping a supplier improve its processes.

Take Long-Lead-Time Items Off the Critical Path

For most products certain components take longer to obtain than others. When cycle time is important it is natural to procure these long-lead-time items much earlier than other components. The logic of doing this is simple, but the implementation of this approach can be tricky. It requires that design processes be structured to identify these items, complete their design early, and test them well before other elements in the product structure. Unfortunately, this is incompatible with many phased development systems, which require that the entire product be designed before any of it is tested, and that the entire product be tested before any of it is procured.

For example, in the manufacture of high-speed hardened and ground gearing, one does not need to decide on the final geometry of the gear tooth to begin procuring steel for the shafts and gear blanks. Instead, the steel can be procured as soon as the rough diameters of these parts are known. Since large diameter pieces of 4340 steel are only made during certain mill runs, they can have a significant procurement lead time. This lead time can be taken off the critical path of the process if this material is procured before final gear dimensions are decided.

An analogous approach is used in the manufacture of certain integrated circuits (ICs). It is true that you may be unable to complete the manufacture of the IC until you know the final configuration of the circuit. However, you can design the circuit so that all of the variability is contained in the final layer of metallization. This means that you can complete all the processing steps prior to this metallization step before you know the final configuration. Such an approach takes most of the processing lead time off the critical path of development.

The key question to ask on long-lead-time components is, "When do we have *enough information* to *begin* the procurement process?" Usually this is well before we would normally procure the part. This approach stands in stark contrast to the traditional approach of asking,

"When do we have *all the information* that we need to *complete* the procurement process?" It requires a fundamental change in the way we do purchasing and requires us to assess the risk involved in procuring parts that may need to be modified or even discarded. The most effective tool we have found for balancing this risk is the decision rules that come out of the financial analysis that we discussed in Chapter 2. For example, if we had a tool costing $50,000 that could be speculatively started four weeks before a final drawing became available, we would need to assess the costs and benefits of doing this. Four weeks on the critical path might be worth $500,000. We might have a 25 percent chance of having to discard the tool. As Figure 13-3 illustrates, in the long run you would average a savings of $362,500 by procuring this tool early. In fact, even if you had an 11 percent chance of the tool being used, you make money by procuring it. The key point is that the decision to pull work off the critical path should be backed up by a sound understanding of project economics.

Use Prototype and Pilot Builds to Verify the Process

The initial prototype of the product will verify that the design works; however, because it is not built with the workers who will ultimately be building it, or using the tooling and methods that will ultimately be used, it cannot tell us that the design will work when we manufacture

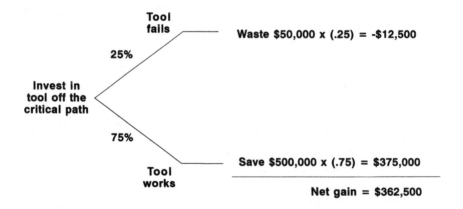

Note: Save 4 weeks on critical path = $500,000

The economics of buying tooling before the design is complete.

FIGURE   13-3

it. This is the purpose of pilot builds, which are the first controlled test of our production process. Pilot builds are used to find problems when they will be cheaper to correct than during full-scale manufacturing.

There is no need to do such builds unless we expect to learn something from them. In some industries, such as publishing, there is no need to do a pilot run. In other industries, such as the auto industry, there can be a need to do even more than one pilot. The important point is to plan prototype and pilot builds so that we obtain as much manufacturing process information as possible early, which will keep most initial production glitches off of the critical path. Fortunately, we have many approaches available to us here:

- Use assembly workers to assemble prototypes (mentioned before).
- Use production tooling or methods selectively to test high-risk areas early.
- Make early trial short-runs of critical assemblies through the regular assembly line.
- Make existing products using the new methods.

This is not a comprehensive list. For example, Carrier's Team Conquest used a seemingly simple tactic that had far-ranging power to keep pilot production problems off of the critical path. A Vice President simply stated that he expected the pilot production units to be "perfect," which to him meant that they would be as good as salable merchandise, not scrap as pilot units had traditionally been. This spurred a great deal more planning for the development team and the factory. They did more risk assessment up front than usual. In addition, the team arranged to have selected production associates and supervisors undertake both hands-on and classroom training on the new model prior to pilot production. This training even included two weeks of taking prototypes apart and putting them back together again. By the time the pilot run began, Team Conquest had a production crew that could assemble the new product with their eyes closed. This resulted in a faster, cleaner production start-up with fewer errors and much less confusion. This "perfect pilot" program was aided by work the team had done earlier to involve production associates in drawing corrections, assembly sequence development, service instruction development, and work station layout.

A BROADER CONTEXT

The ideas presented in this chapter can have a profound impact on time to market, because of their ability to remove surprises from the tail-end of the development process. Recovering from late surprises, when very little time is left, is particularly difficult and costly.

This book has focused on what we can do inside the four walls of our own company to improve cycle time. Yet we have suppliers and customers who also can affect our cycle time—and we can affect theirs. Every technique discussed in this book can be as applicable to our suppliers and customers as it is to us. Suppliers can learn to use more overlapped processes and to request critical information early. Customers can restructure their processes to exploit the early arrival of vital information and prototype products from our process. For example, we often see customers who want to work with prototype versions of products even before they have been fully tested by their suppliers. They acknowledge that it would be better to have fully characterized parts, but insist that this is not the issue. What is really important to them is that they can learn about the limitations of the new part off the critical path of their development program. If they wait until the supplier is fully prepared to release the part, then the learning curve associated with its use will lie on the critical path of their project.

Thus, our development process is really just a microcosm of a larger development system that includes the processes of our suppliers and customers. All of these processes can be changed to enhance development speed. Of course, the place to start making changes is the portion of the system which is in our most direct control, our own development process. When we make such changes we will need to get the support of management, which will be the topic of our next chapter.

SUGGESTED READING

Carter, Donald E., and Barbara S. Baker. 1992. *CE Concurrent Engineering: The Product Development Environment for the 1990s*. Reading, Mass.: Addison-Wesley Publishing Company, Inc. A thorough treatment of concurrent engineering by a recognized expert in design automation. Appendix B contains a useful 83-question assessment tool to determine your level at various concurrent engineering practices.

Dean, Jr., James W., and Gerald I. Susman. 1989. Organizing for manufacturable design. *Harvard Business Review* 67 (1): 28–36. Several thought-provoking options for ensuring manufacturable designs, but these ideas must be considered in view of their impact on development speed. For instance, one suggestion, giving Manufacturing a veto power, may eventually yield a producible design but may also waste design time.

Nevins, James L., and Daniel E. Whitney, eds., and Thomas L. De Fazio, et al. 1989. *Concurrent Design of Products and Processes*. New York: McGraw-Hill. A wealth of engineering information on product-process design, but weak on fabrication concerns relative to its stress on assembly issues.

Pisano, Gary. 1996. *The Development Factory.* Boston, Mass.: Harvard Business School Press. This book points out the importance of process design. The title is a bit misleading since the focus is on process design in the pharmaceutical industry.

The Role of Top Management

Top management's leadership and support are crucial to sustaining any significant improvement in development time. Unless top management is truly interested in faster product development—and shows it—little can be done by lower-level managers and workers that will have a sustained effect on time to market.

This chapter describes what top management must do in order to make time to market a company priority and discusses the ways it should, and should not, be involved in specific accelerated-development projects. The next chapter then explains in detail how the organization as a whole can make the transition to this faster mode of operation.

Who should read this chapter? Certainly senior management: those heading Engineering, Marketing, and Manufacturing; general managers; and on up to the CEO. However, many of the principles, for instance, coaching rather than directing subordinates, also apply right down to the first level of management. Also, all managers—and developers—will be interested in knowing why their bosses are trying to change their own styles.

New Product Development as a Core Activity

Chapter 1 mentions several companies—Black & Decker, Chrysler, Motorola, Senco, and others—that have made enviable improvements in development cycle time. Every one of these companies recognizes the value of new products to its business and has put real effort into improving its development process. This effort starts at the top of the organization, as top management sees a linkage between new products and business success. In particular, these managers do not regard new products as happening in some mysterious way in the Engineering Department. New products are just too important to be left to the engineers alone.

Once the organization is this serious about new products, we are ready to start speeding up the process.

TOP-MANAGEMENT LEADERSHIP

It has become a cliché that top management must lead in any program of corporate change, and the changes suggested here are clearly in the realm of significant organizational change. We know that senior management's time is scarce, so we will be specific as to what management should and should not do.

Clarifying Strategic Intent and Time-to-Market Goals

Developers, right down to the designer and technician level, *must* understand deeply how a particular development project is linked to the company's strategic thrust. This is crucial because these individuals will be making decisions daily that affect the direction of the project. Without a compass, the path is likely to look rather like that of an ant on the kitchen counter. It simply is not very fast for developers to have to guess at what is needed, have to go get management guidance, or have management constantly second-guessing developers' actions.

 This probably seems obvious, so let's consider what happened in a real company—one that has contributed examples of excellent practice to this book. Several years ago an executive, who now oversees company product development, joined this company. To get up to speed, he asked to see its strategic plan. He was told, "Well, I guess you are senior enough and have a need to know, but remember that this is a numbered, confidential document, and return it as soon as you have read it." If this executive had so much difficulty finding out where the company wanted to go, you can imagine how little a lowly team leader understood about the firm's strategic intent.

A company's strategic plan usually has two parts, language that describes missions, goals, growth areas, and competitive strengths, and numbers, which make the objectives hard and measurable. Fortunately, the portion that is less sensitive, the prose, is what could be most useful to developers. However, this portion also happens to be the one that is less well developed in most cases. All too often, goals and mission statements are too generalized, so they provide the developers with little power for making distinctions. Even if the text were released, it may not be sufficient to guide anyone in making daily decisions. To sharpen the competitive battle lines, an occasional "rap session" of developers and management can be valuable. Here, developers can ask the tough narrowing questions, such as, is it more important to be the industry technology leader or to serve our installed base well?

Senior management can be most helpful, then, in formulating a clear strategy regarding the role of new products in achieving the firm's objectives and communicating this strategy directly to all developers. The firm's time-to-market rationale, strategy, and objectives must be a part of this message, too.

When we start working with a company we typically ask several people at various levels and in different functions why they are interested in developing new products faster. In doing so we are simply trying to understand the agenda at the company so that we can address the proper issues. However, what we hear is often surprising. People are not sure why they should be racing new products to market, or they will have diverging explanations for it. Although the top individual in an organization usually has strong views on time to market, these views often do not permeate the organization, so each person operates from a different script. Until top management establishes—and communicates—the firm's rationale for rapid product innovation, results will remain sporadic and fragmented.

Unless there is a clear, consistent, compelling connection between time to market and business success, rapid development simply will not be taken very seriously. The program will be regarded as the latest management fad and dismissed accordingly. Worse, the program may be misinterpreted, either as a skip-steps-for-speed message or as a ploy to squeeze more work out of people.

Consequently, top management must establish the linkage between speed and profit. As discussed in Chapter 2, this linkage is usually more profound than just getting initial revenues sooner, but it may take some high-level, market-oriented thinking to build a solid explanation. The material in Chapter 2 will help you to strengthen this explanation, because the linkage is also needed to complete the economic analysis there.

Management Presence

Management communicates the importance of time to market through its actions. For example, if management continues to emphasize shipments of current products, to the detriment of a new product that needs some production line time for a pilot batch, the developers will remember the choice management made more than its rousing speech on time to market. This is why it is so important for top management to really know how development cycle time affects the business. Without this, management's actions will not match the words, and disbelief will grow like weeds in the garden.

Many of top management's opportunities to act in support of time to market have to do with its visibility to a specific development project. We illustrate some of these project-specific opportunities below. Then the following section covers other types of actions management should take to support a specific project.

Top management's presence in various parts of the organization sends amazingly strong signals to the troops about what is important. For instance, some senior executives spend their time with the accountants. Others show up frequently in the research labs or industrial-design studios. Even happenstance appearances can carry considerable weight. A team leader once said he knew that his project was important to the company because, as he put it, "I ran into the President in the rest room and he asked me how the project was going." This interested executive even monitored progress in the rest room, not by passively scanning progress reports in the office.

Senior management's time is precious, so it should be used to gain the greatest visibility. Short, unannounced, relatively frequent visits to the developers' workplaces provides strong messages about the importance to the company of new products and certain development projects. A five-minute swing through the lab each week is far more effective than a one-hour dog-and-pony show in a conference room every quarter.

This management by walking around (MBWA) benefits management too, because it provides managers with unfiltered, real-time information on the project's progress. In a fast-moving project, management simply cannot afford to wait for the next gate review to get scrubbed-down, secondhand information on the project's problems. Sampling

the pulse of the project directly and frequently gives management confidence that the project is indeed on track, and if it isn't, MBWA supplies them with the information they need to take whatever action may be indicated, such as asking about alternative approaches or offering to provide some type of needed support.

MBWA is a natural style for some managers, who need no encouragement. Some actually overdo it by interfering as they walk around, and they could benefit from paying more attention to their questioning style. Others feel uncomfortable in just walking around, either because they lack a naturally gregarious personality or because they feel uncomfortable in a high-tech setting that they do not understand. These managers can benefit from some coaching on the technique of walking around and encouragement to put such "random" visits right on their calendars, say five-minute visits twice a week.

Although MBWA basically involves asking questions of the developers, these questions must be asked quite perceptively. The biggest risk here is that, in the asking and answering of the question, authority for running the project will subtly shift from the developer to the manager, thus disempowering the developer. The judgment as to whether this has occurred, unfortunately, rests in the perception of the developer. In order for the manager to really sample the health of the project—clearly within the manager's need to know—pointed questions should be asked:

- What is on the critical path today?
- What is the next major difficulty you will face?
- Are you getting adequate support from _____ (a part of the organization that has been a bottleneck in the past)?
- What is getting in the way of success?
- What would help the next project to run more smoothly (or faster)?
- What good events have happened recently? (to tell others in the organization)

However, each of these questions must be phrased in a way that the authority for the next step remains with the developer. The critical distinction here is between coaching and directing.

In one consulting assignment, for example, we found that little MBWA was happening, so we went to some developers and asked a few questions about it, including what their fears might be if the boss were to visit their cubicle. Although they appreciated the idea of a visit, they were concerned that this executive would give them an assignment. So we suggested to the executive that he be careful to leave each visit without giving any assignments. Both parties benefited from the ensuing visits.

OTHER WAYS OF SUPPORTING AN ACCELERATED PROJECT

In addition to the presence that top management provides to signal the importance of rapid product development, there are concrete ways in which they must be involved in each particular rapid development project.

Initiating a Project

Because top management's leverage to influence a project is greatest at its beginning, concentrate management time put into a project at its beginning to get the team off to a good start. Senior management's leverage basically stems from the product design decisions that have not been made yet. Once these decisions are made, the team will have passed a fork in the road. After this point it will proceed to make an increasingly interwoven sequence of decisions, all dependent on the one made at that first fork. The farther the team proceeds from the fork, the more costly in both time and money will any changes become. If senior managers are going to influence the product—say, on its complexity, which determines its development time (see Chapter 4)—they should set the tone in these initial decisions.

Sadly, the typical pattern of top management involvement is just the opposite, as illustrated in Figure 14-1. There is normally a small flurry of management activity at the kickoff point, but then upper management often gets heavily involved only after the design is essentially complete and decisions are needed on large financial commitments. As the project moves into production it has a high profile, so upper managers are naturally drawn into any problems that arise at this stage. Except for the kickoff blip, management's typical involvement parallels the project's spending curve, which is basically the inverse of management's leverage curve.

Actually, the role needed early in the project is more that of a leader than a manager, showing the developers the vision of the journey ahead and preparing them for it, setting expectations for the project. Relatively few analytical management tools are available at this stage, but this does not reduce the potential to influence key decisions. Later, a flood of specific management decisions arrive and the management analytical tools to use on them are abundant.

Sometimes this detailed, reactive management is called fire fighting. Yet it is interesting to reflect on how professional firefighters operate. They actually spend most of their time in advance trying to prevent the fires, rather than racing around in noisy fire engines putting the fires out.

Just having top management involved in the front end will establish a sense of urgency regarding the project, especially as they communicate a message of concentrated effort during the project's start-up activities to overcome the Fuzzy Front End syndrome. This is also their

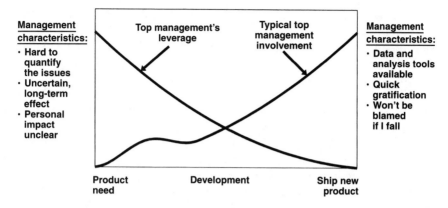

Management characteristics:
- Hard to quantify the issues
- Uncertain, long-term effect
- Personal impact unclear

Top management's leverage

Typical top management involvement

Management characteristics:
- Data and analysis tools available
- Quick gratification
- Won't be blamed if I fall

Product need   Development   Ship new product

Typically, top management's involvement in a project is just the opposite of its leverage to influence the project's outcome, and often the management characteristics required in the front end do not match the skills and motivations of operating managers.

FIGURE 14-1

opportunity to create clear scheduling urgency by identifying a fixed end point for the project.

Establishing an Effective Team Environment

Upper management must provide a team setting in which the team takes full responsibility for the project. There are two parts to this issue. One is to weaken the linkages between the team and the remainder of the organization so that the team can in fact move with some freedom. The other is to create a motivational structure where the team must indeed complete the project on schedule.

Luckily, these two parts work together, because the best way of helping the team take responsibility for the schedule is to place it in an environment where the external reasons for schedule slippage have been removed. By providing the required resources while establishing a separate identity for the team, upper management encourages it to apply its own resources rather than rely on others who do not have a clear stake in the project's outcome. This type of organizational and physical structure is not common in most companies, so management must have a strong voice in setting it up and maintaining it. The last section of this chapter suggests how to set up such agreements between management and the team.

Senior management must also make some changes in its own involvement in a rapid development project. The basic issue here is to stay off the critical path of the project. Management has set the team up so that it can make most of its own decisions—quickly. But a few decisions must be made by top management. Because of its limited availability, it is important that upper management's decision points be kept to a minimum and that the essential decision points be carefully planned into the development schedule so as not to cause delay. It would be ironic to have top management cited as an excuse for delay after it had worked so carefully to close all the schedule's loopholes. Nothing demoralizes a charged-up team faster than a hurry-up-and-wait response from management. Although there may be many other equally urgent demands on management's time, the development team cannot see these, and any management delay will be interpreted by the team as mere lack of interest.

Keeping the Team Focused on the Objective

Rapid product development comprises more than just rapid execution. As covered in detail in Chapters 4 through 6, it is also essential to frame the product concept so that it is capable of being developed rapidly. Upper management has several opportunities to influence the way in which the product concept is framed, both initially and as the project evolves.

Without vigilance, newly available technologies and market pressures will encourage the product team to enhance the product concept continually following the phenomenon called creeping elegance. Creeping elegance destroys development schedules, because the team now finds itself aiming at a moving target. This is an insidious phenomenon, as an expanding product concept stretches the schedule, opening the door for more changes to appear over the longer time horizon. As the schedule stretches, other developers believe they have an opportunity now to enhance their part of the design, placing it on the stretched critical path. Top management's role here is to hold the schedule inviolate and thus control creeping elegance.

Although top management's role is to control this phenomenon by forcing adherence to schedule or global constraints on product scope, there will be legitimate cases when it is recognized that the product concept is seriously off the mark and it will have to be changed. This should be recognized as being a major upset, not just a deviation, and upper management should then renegotiate the entire project plan with the team. By making the restart special, management will help to keep it rare.

In explicitly focusing the team on the task at hand, senior management takes on the obligation of watching for important events that are outside of the focus set for the team. Indeed, management essentially puts blinders on the team so that the team will concentrate straight ahead. For safety then, management must watch outside of the team's restricted field of vision for broader events that could upset the project.

Overseeing the Use of Resources

Even though our principle is to turn the vast majority of the decision making over to the development team and hold it accountable for its progress, top management still remains responsible for effectively employing the assets assigned to the team. Consequently, upper management must monitor the team's progress to ensure that the company's assets are being put to good use. Chapter 10 explained how this can be done without delaying development or infringing on the team's tactical decision-making process.

Occasionally, the project will need changes in human, facility, or financial resource levels—usually in the form of an increase. When an increase or adjustment in resources is needed, top management must be prepared to respond quickly. This is one situation in which upper management should be keeping itself off the project's critical path, as discussed above. Doing so means two things here, first that top management should be informally keeping apprised of the team's progress, by using MBWA, for instance, so that the request for resources does not come as a surprise. Second, it means that top management should be planning its resources so that they can be made available on short notice if need be (see Chapter 11).

Many products are late to market simply because of being starved for engineering resources, such as model-shop time. Once these bottlenecks have been discovered, it is up to top management to bolster these resources so that time-critical projects are not left sitting in an obscure in-basket in Engineering while the market clock continues to tick. Hewlett-Packard management, for example, monitors model shop queues on an ongoing basis using lead-time metrics. When lead times become unacceptable, management knows that the problem has gone beyond simple priority setting, and it takes steps to add capacity.

Overcommitting resources is an enticing trap that is destructive to development schedules. The conscientious manager wants to ensure that his or her resources are being engaged productively, and is tempted to keep some development work in reserve to cover potential slack periods (see Figure 11-1, page 207). Moreover, the ambitious leader normally expects a little more out of people than they can deliver. To cut development cycles, however, the challenge must be directed specifically at the schedule, not the workload. Ask to get a product in half the time rather than requesting twice as many products in hopes of forcing people to work faster.

On occasion a project will prove to be technically infeasible or not viable as a business proposition. It is top management's responsibility to detect and analyze these situations and pull the plug on a project if necessary. If it is properly motivated, the team is operating in a charged-up entrepreneurial mode and may be oblivious to the storm clouds overhead. Stopping such a motivated group is one of the more difficult and unpleasant tasks of management. Usually, the best approach to aborting a project is to separate the project from the individuals (in an ongoing project the objective is to connect the individuals to the fate of the project) and offer them encouragement as you help them redirect their efforts. Fortunately, if the project has been set up and run according to the principles suggested throughout this book, this option should not have to be exercised very often. Nevertheless, it is still an essential responsibility of management in its role of employing corporate assets constructively.

Encouraging Cycle-Time Improvement

If management desires improvements in cycle time, it must watch for and encourage changes in behavior toward this end. This may not be as easy for management as it might seem, though, as the following example shows. One client wanted to accelerate its development process, so it assigned a cross-functional team to a project and co-located them, as suggested in Chapter 8. Team members then took the initiative and decided that they first needed a product specification, so they wrote one, having all the engineering, marketing, manufacturing, and purchasing expertise they needed right there on the team. Again, this is very much in line with what we have suggested in Chapter 5. When the specification was complete, which did not take long, they were ready to dive right in to the design work. Thus, they issued the specification under a cover memo stating that they were starting to design to it immediately and would consider it final unless they received objections within a week.

At this point the new style met the old one head-on. This company had always regarded specifications as documents that evolved over months as they floated among departments and executives gathering refinements. In particular, the President, an engineer, and the General Manager, who had come from Marketing, were normally contributors to product specifications. The executives' first reaction to this quick specification was "Wait! You can't do this so fast. We have to think about it." Fortunately, they quickly reversed this position as they realized that they were getting precisely what they wanted: vast reductions in cycle time. Consequently, the executives called a meeting within the week to address the specification, which was then approved with only minor changes. It perhaps lacked some of the nuances that would have resulted from a longer process, but it was good enough. More importantly, the team had already signed up to execute it.

These managers were wise to learn from and support the team in this situation. By nurturing such changes that are headed in the proper direction, even if they are not complete successes, management encourages the team to initiate further change. The team and those who interact with them will thus be learning by trying new approaches, which will sometimes result in mistakes. Although managers would rather not have the mistakes, they cannot afford to squelch the learning that occurs during this critical period of transition. Furthermore, the way in which management responds to such changes will send significant messages to the organization regarding the sincerity of its time-to-market emphasis.

SOLIDIFYING AGREEMENTS

Fast, effective product development depends on having clear agreement between managers, who want the new product, and the developers, who will provide it. Throughout this book we have emphasized the importance to rapid development of

- an accountable, committed team;
- a team with sufficient authority and resources to get the job done;
- clear, stable project direction.

Any differences in opinion between management and the team on these issues are likely to lead to project schedule problems later. Most projects start with a tacit agreement at best on these items. Even though gaining such agreement will take some effort, it will be well repaid later. This section will show you how to make such agreement a part of starting each project.

Motorola and Origin Medsystems, Inc., a subsidiary of the Guidant Corporation and a producer of medical devices primarily for the surgical market, formalize these agreements into contract books. Whether they are called contracts or agreements, these pacts signify a meeting of the minds between the two groups involved. Qualities such as commitment and "stable project direction" are soft enough that they cannot be enforced in a strict sense, so the real enforcement is in crafting a win–win situation that both parties see as workable and in their interest. Origin's contract books are also the project business plan, so agreement between management and the developers on the project contract and business plan yields buy-in by all principal project participants that this project is something the company really wants to do, a marvelous way to kick off a project.

What Agreement Covers

The first and most important part of an agreement is the product strategy. What is the raison d'être for this product? What gap does it fill in our product line or in the marketplace? What prime benefits does it offer? What will drive its success? Such information is guidance from management that will help the developers to fill in all of the gaps in the detailed specifications, and it assures that everyone has the same big picture in mind.

The scope of the product is next. This includes product specifications, at least on critical attributes. Over several years of using contract books, Motorola has learned how to focus better in defining the product attributes that count, leaving implementation details to the developers.

Agreements should also identify any easily forgotten parts of the project beyond the product itself. Depending on the nature of your products, these might include packaging; sales, user, or service literature; training; or spare parts. In addition, agreements should define exactly what constitutes project completion: passing some drawings to Manufacturing, shipping the first unit, or achieving break-even in cashflow, for example.

Agreements also specify the project schedule (especially any critical time-to-market goals), project budget, and cost targets for the product and often also quality of reliability targets. These are all areas on which management and the developers are likely to have different opinions, which is precisely why they must be hammered out. Otherwise, there is no real agreement on key project factors, and the project is likely to unravel later. The budget is an opportunity for the developers to propose items they believe would facilitate or accelerate the project, such as customer visits, additional workstations, or a kitty for rapid prototyping.

Finally, an agreement specifies the human resources allocated to the project. Inadequate human resources is perhaps the most prevalent reason for slow development, so this issue cannot be ignored. Failure to provide the promised resources is also a great demoralizer for the team, so resources is the most important item management commits in a project agreement.

A standard template is helpful for the written agreement. This assures that the critical topics are addressed, it helps to keep the agreement short and to the point, and it saves reading time by providing a format familiar to the reader.

Making Agreements Work

Agreement does not come easily or automatically, so the process surrounding the document must be built in a way that gains real agreement, given the culture of your organization. For example, Origin has found that the important element is not the written contract book but the meeting in which the decision is made on the contract. Moreover, in Origin's culture it is essential for senior executives and the developers to be at this meeting, even when it is very difficult to schedule such a meeting. Seasoned project leaders have learned that without certain individuals at the meeting, they do not have a deal, and the project is more likely to falter later. This is Origin's key to success, but you will have to have to discover the key for your organization, knowing how it reaches solid group agreement.

Keep the written agreement short. Origin's, including the business plan elements, is about 25 pages. They are thinking of putting their supporting financial analyses in a supplementary document to get the contract book itself down to under 10 pages.

Don't let the negotiation grow into a major event. Keeping the document short helps, but there is more to it. Whenever two parties decide to make their agreement more formal, they automatically start to be more careful about what they agree to, because they may actually be held to it. Consequently, strike a balance to achieve an agreement that will be taken seriously while avoiding one where the parties believe their future hangs on each word. Motorola deals with this phenomenon by specifying, at the outset, how long the contracting will take, depending on the complexity of the project.

Have a means for changing the agreement and an understanding about the degree of project change that requires a change in the agreement. If the product specifications, the project scope, or the financial or human resources change, this is often a substantial change in what was agreed to, and thus it requires a new agreement process. This seldom means a new contract, but perhaps a new version of the contract book, with a new agreement process. For example, Motorola places its contract books under formal change-control procedures. Without an established means of changing the agreement, it will tend to lose force as the inevitable changes in the project or its environment occur, thus making the original agreement less and less pertinent.

Be careful about the connection from one project to the next. If management drives a hard bargain, for example, or doesn't come through with what it promised, the next development team is going to be more wary about entering into the agreement process. The process will become more formal, and the participants more reluctant to sign up, the opposite of what we want.

    Do not tie the agreement strongly to rewards. In Chapter 7 we mention the pitfalls of relying on rewards for motivation. Although the agreement may contain criteria for measuring success and some kind of compensation or recognition for meeting the objective, going too far in this direction increases the level of caution everyone will have when entering into an agreement. This will lead to the difficulties mentioned a few paragraphs ago.

We do not know of an organization that is completely happy with its agreement process. It seems impossible to be satisfied with the dilemmas around which the agreement process appears to be built. Consequently, keep working on your agreement process, trying to get a balance that works well for you. The next chapter describes how you can do this in the context of continuously improving your development process.

THREE ESSENTIAL THINGS AN EXECUTIVE MUST DO

On one occasion when we were presenting the material in this book to a senior management team, the Chief Financial Officer, growing tired of the more technical aspects of time to market, simply asked, "What are the three things I need to do to accelerate development?" For the benefit of all impatient executives, we present below the 34-word version of time-to-market leadership as a summary of this chapter:

- Calculate the cost of delay and foster its use in making project decisions (Chapter 2).
- Religiously control the start-up of new projects (Chapter 11).
- Enable development teams to run themselves (Chapters 7 and 8).

SUGGESTED READING

Bartlett. Christopher A., and Sumantra Ghoshal. 1995. Changing the role of top management: beyond systems to people. *Harvard Business Review* 73 (3): 132–42.

These authors describe the needed shift from command-and-control behavior to that in which management helps subordinates to exercise their full potential. Managers doing this may spend half or more of their time coaching their people.

Kiechel III, Walter. 1988. The politics of innovation. *Fortune* 117 (8): 131–32. A clever lesson in the subtleties of mixed messages. Kiechel humorously illustrates how management unwittingly throws up roadblocks, such as the "no-special-treatment reflex."

Quinn, James Brian. 1985. Managing innovation: controlled chaos. *Harvard Business Review* 63 (3): 73–84. Innovation, compared to other corporate activities, is a chaotic process to manage, accelerated innovation being even more so. In this classic Quinn provides an exceptionally lucid account of innovation and its management.

C H A P T E R   15

Making Changes Faster

In Chapter 1 we attributed the "price" of faster development to a development system that is not as clean as a traditional sequential, functionally based process. In the intervening chapters we have laid out the tools of accelerated development. You may have observed that some of these tools—such as dedicated team members, co-location, intrinsic motivation, and saying "no" to a new project—are neither original nor a great intellectual breakthrough, yet they may still be hard to put into practice.

The reason that your competitors are not using these tools is that they cannot just buy them with money, as they might "buy" a talented employee or a CAD system. Most of these tools require organizational change to be effective and, unfortunately, some of the most powerful tools, the ones mentioned in the previous paragraph, for instance, require the most profound organizational changes.

However, the pleasant news is that there are ways to make these changes, and they are described right here. In a way, then, this is the most important chapter, because without these organizational changes, everything else in the book becomes just interesting ideas, great fodder for a debate.

THREE PATHS TO ORGANIZATIONAL CHANGE

Massive Process Redesign

Many companies have undergone business process reengineering in recent years, and similar massive reorganizations preceded BPR. The assumption behind such total redesigns is that every aspect of the current arrangement is fundamentally flawed, thus it should all be rebuilt. This may be true, but massive redesign has its weaknesses.

One weakness is that what usually impedes an organization is not so much its structure, which can be redesigned, but its underlying values and styles, which can't. Another difficulty is that because the redesign is massive, it is likely to be slow, which means that not only will the firm not see the benefits soon, but worse, that the change may lose momentum due to lack of apparent improvement for a while. Third, because this is an organizational megaproject, affecting the whole organization, the redesigners cannot afford to be wrong, so they tend to err on the conservative side. Sometimes the current structure is indeed so fatally flawed that total redesign is the best approach, but usually there are faster, surer ways to initiate change.

Organizational Prototyping

As suggested above, many of the impediments to rapid development have to do with values and styles; for example, the social resistance to co-location (Chapter 8) or management's reluctance to bet heavily on—and thus staff heavily—a few projects (Chapter 11). We cannot design the answers to these issues in advance. So we proceed as we would for a product concept that we are unsure will fit people's needs: we build an early prototype of it, put it into use with real customers, and then adjust it as indicated.

These organizational prototypes, or pilots, as we call them, are powerful because they leave room for discovering the answers as we go, and the answers can be far deeper than just the structure. With pilots we also start to see results sooner, and these fuel interest in going further. Finally, because we are not doing this company-wide initially, we can afford to try some things that wouldn't be thinkable on a larger scale. Consequently, pilots, although not as grandiose as redesign, can actually lead to more fundamental change faster and more surely.

Consider how Chrysler regarded its initial Viper project, as explained by President Robert Lutz: "Team Viper wasn't so much a 'skunk works' for us as it was a *test bed*—a test bed for our larger platform teams that are now in place. Aided by what we were learning from the Viper experience, we began making cross-functional teamwork the hallmark of *all* Chrysler product-development projects." (*Research-Technology Management,* March-April 1994, p. 16).

Continuous Improvement

Although pilots can initiate change quickly, they do not provide a means of continuously learning from what is going well or poorly so that our approach to product development does indeed get increasingly better. Thus, we need tools to learn from projects, and more significantly, to somehow institutionalize this learning.

In the long term, perhaps the greatest value of continuous improvement is that it yields a flexible, adaptable process. Even if we were able to get the process designed "right," it would not remain the best one, simply because of external changes in markets, technologies, and the political and regulatory environment. An established means of modifying the process can be used to make these adjustments as well as for internal tuning.

Notice that continuous improvement fits well with pilots, because both presume that we do not know all of the answers going in. But the fit with massive redesign is not as smooth, because redesign assumes both that there is a correct design and that we can develop it in advance through careful analysis.

A Combined Approach

Rarely is any of these three means of pursuing change used in pure isolation; nevertheless, there is value in explicitly planning combinations. Probably the most powerful combination is starting with one or a few pilots and then switching to continuous improvement once the initial gains are realized; see Figure 15-1. This may seem natural, but we have seen too many organizations with curves more like Figure 15-2. These firms seem to assume that once a better approach has been demonstrated through a pilot, people will just switch to the new approach. Unfortunately, reversion to old and comfortable ways is the more natural course. For example, Chrysler's journey looks more like Figure 15-1, as Figure 1-4 would suggest, but Ford's, following its highly successful Team Taurus project in the early 1980s has been less impressive.

We will not address massive redesign further, except to point out that there is value in combining it with the other two techniques. These

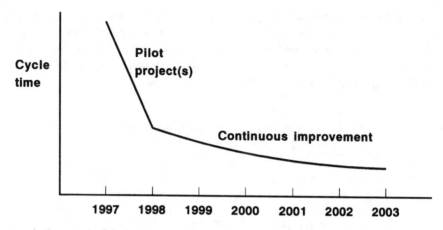

Initial pilot project(s) followed by the continuous improvement technique is an effective combination to drive down development cycle time methodically.

FIGURE 15-1

more fluid approaches help to move redesign thinking away from getting it right once and for all. With the combination approach, the new design is piloted on a small scale before rolling it out across the board, and throughout the process there is explicit emphasis on identifying the lessons learned and further tuning the new design.

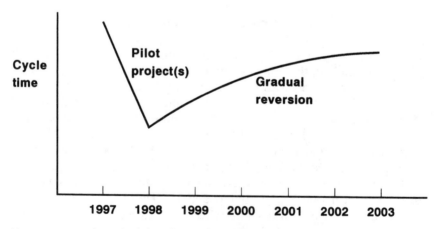

Many companies do not learn from their pilots or switch to continuous improvement, so they gradually revert to the familiar old methods.

FIGURE 15-2

Regardless of the approach you take, remember what someone once said about changes in human systems: people don't resist change, they resist being changed. Just as we promoted buy-in in a development project by giving those involved a say in being on the team, figuring out what customers need, and specifying the product, we foster ownership of organizational changes by including in the planning process those who may have to change.

Another general observation is that a total quality program is an excellent prerequisite for making the kinds of changes needed. There is nothing specific about total quality itself that is needed. But we have found, in working through such process and organizational change programs with many clients, that those with total quality programs have assimilated many of the basic tools they will need to shorten their development times. Such tools include running meetings, collecting and organizing ideas for change, joint problem solving, action planning, and mapping processes.

USING PILOT PROJECTS TO INITIATE CULTURAL CHANGE

Lasting changes in organization behavior ultimately require both the acquisition of new attitudes and associated changes in behavior. Psychologists have found that behavior and attitude are linked. Changes in attitude will normally result in changes of behavior. Nonetheless, attitudes can be inordinately difficult—and slow—to change. This psychological reality applies directly to accelerating product development. Large amounts of training, education, and executive pronouncements often result in only minor changes in behavior. The path of education simply does not produce change fast enough.

Fortunately, psychologists have discovered a shortcut: if you change behavior, attitude will usually follow along with it. The healthy mind works hard to bring its attitudes into alignment with its behavior, not just the reverse. This is the key to jump-starting organizational change. Schaffer (see Suggested Reading at the end of this chapter) explains the approach in general.

Just Get Started

If you want to change attitude and behavior, it is far faster and more certain to jump in and start trying it than to sit on the sidelines thinking about what it would be like or why it might not work. A highly decorated army colonel was once asked about his formula for battle-field success; his response was short: "Action is preferable to inaction."

This is not to say that we avoid training to give people the knowledge and the skills they need. Success requires an investment in skill building, which is valuable. A number of management tools have been discussed in this book, and education is a means for assimilating these techniques. However, intellectual training pales in comparison with the urgency created by pushing somebody out of an airplane and telling them, "The ripcord is in front; you should probably pull it!"

Avoid the Immunization Effect

Though we strongly favor the path of taking action, not just any action will do. Setting up for a major success on the first try is imperative. In organizations that have attempted behavioral changes and failed, there is a heightened "immune response" to a reintroduction of the program. "We tried that once and it was a disaster" is the classic complaint. Often, the initial attempt was poorly planned and executed, but the blame is placed on the idea, not its implementation. The "immunization effect" is this heightened resistance to change after an abortive first attempt.

This phenomenon is destructive, so it should be anticipated whenever attempting an organizational change. To use a biological analogy, to infect an organization with new ideas, be sure to use a strong enough dose of virus. If you do not, an attempt to reintroduce the idea will be much harder.

 To avoid the immunization effect, choose a relatively small problem, then attack it with more than enough resources to solve it. Normally, this is done by creating a small-scale pilot program and doing everything possible to guarantee its success.

This approach is quite different from the controlled experiment that would appeal to a good engineer or scientist. The scientific method suggests picking a representative project for the change program, because if we pick an easy one and endow it to ensure its success we cannot be sure the new techniques really caused the change to work. However, the sci-entific method is dangerous when faced with potential naysayers. If we fail the first time, we will not get another chance to repeat the experiment. If we succeed, we will build the organization's confidence and equip people with practical skills to take on more difficult projects next time.

Setting up the Project

 It is essential to keep in mind that, first of all, the pilot project is a means of making fundamental changes in *how* the organization develops new products. Many organizations have latched onto the pilot project concept for the wrong reasons. The Vice President of Engineering embraces it because it is an opportunity to slip in that new technology that she could not get approved by the executive staff. The Vice President of Marketing sees it as a way of getting an additional new product for a pet customer. These all miss the point: this project is being done, not for the product it will provide, but as a vehicle to create a new organizational style. If the focus is on the new process, you are likely to get both the process and the product; if it is on the product, that is all you will probably get.

With your basic motivation firmly in mind, it is time to select the project. Below is a list of project selection criteria that we have developed in helping many clients to set up pilot projects:

- The project should be an important one to the company, so that it is not likely to be canceled or delayed later for lack of interest or priority.
- On the other hand, do not select a project that is crucial to the survival of the company; management will have difficulty letting the development team run itself if this is a "bet your company" situation.
- The project should not be trivial technically, because potential naysayers should not conclude that the project was fast only because it was so simple.
- By contrast, avoid projects that require basic invention, for obvious reasons.
- Make sure the project is consistent with the accelerated management approach you wish to implant; for example, assure that the project will make good use of dedicated team members if you wish to move toward using dedicated team members.
- The project should be reasonably typical of your projects, encompassing the cost, timeliness, and political issues the business faces generally, so that the lessons learned will be as applicable as possible to future projects and the results obtained can be measured relative to past projects.
- Assuming that time to market is the motivation for the change, there should be a clear, believable, market-driven sense of urgency to the project.
- Pick a project that is of short duration, because you want to experience and apply the benefits of this experiment as soon as possible.
- Select a project that has not started yet, because there is a great schedule leverage in the very early decisions, such as team staffing and product architecture.
- On the other hand, choose a project that can be started soon, so that you can reap the benefits soon.
- Finally, select a project for which you already have the basic resources; there will be no time to hire people or build new facilities after you start.

Notice that the first and second items on this list are a contrasting pair; look for a project that provides reasonable balance. Similarly for the third and fourth items.

More generally, you will find that you cannot satisfy all of these criteria, and if you try, you will be searching for a long time. However, the trick is to avoid compromising so much that the success of the project, as a management innovation, is placed at risk. Therefore, rather than using this list as requirements, use it as selection criteria. If the project you select is weak in some areas, flag these as areas to watch for as you execute the pilot project. Do not wait until you have the "perfect" project.

Even before doing an economic analysis and creating the detailed product specification, select the project leader. As explained in Chapter 7, no other single decision has more influence on the chances of success. With the right team leader, most of the other steps that need to happen will take place. As with the project selection criteria, do not wait for exactly the right project leader to become available. The greatest shortcoming we have seen in organizations as they select a team leader for a pilot project is that they do not look broadly enough. Look outside of the department from which you usually select team leaders. Consider a functional manager, remembering the importance of this position to your future product development capability.

Enabling the Team to Move Quickly

As Chapter 14 emphasizes, the role of top management in rapid product development is less one of controlling than of facilitating progress. A Vice President at Xerox puts this well: management's job is more that of a police escort than of a traffic cop. Chapter 14 also suggests tools, such as MBWA, that management can use to keep up with a fast-moving team.

Support the team in its decisions, even if this requires making a substantial change from historical behavior. Nothing saps initiative more than someone's second guessing the decisions made. This is doubly true when that person correctly spots mistakes. Such second guessing must be controlled, and the team must be supported so that it will develop its own new operating style and the skills that go with it. A Native American proverb says that good judgment comes from experience, and experience comes from bad judgment.

Even when the team leader reports to general management (suggested in Chapter 8), conflict with functional managers can arise from leftover habits instilled by the familiar functional organizational. For example, top management usually understands that the team must be making its own decisions, but this is often new behavior for functional line managers, whose job in the past has been to make these decisions. Top management should ensure that middle management respects the team's authority. This may require making this policy clear directly to the team, so that it is in a stronger position to resist encroachments by well-meaning functional managers.

Cloning the Process

When a pilot project is nearly complete, begin planning the next few projects (clones) to make use of its techniques. Almost always, a gradual rollout is better than an explosive one. Do not get lured into scaling up too quickly. Logic might suggest that if one pilot project is good, several must be better. The fallacy is that we have a very limited pool of people experienced in the new techniques at this point, so we will have difficulty providing the caliber of resources needed for success in the second generation if we expand too quickly. It is tragic to succeed in the first generation only to fail in the second. Rather, continue nurturing subsequent projects with ample attention and resources until you have a pool of experienced people.

The most viable way to pass the virus of rapid product development is through direct contact, not simply by exposing people to the written word. Having people work on teams where development is done quickly lets them acquire the basic "soft" values, such as lending a hand to something on the critical path, that are the core of the techniques. Let them see what works and what doesn't. They will unconsciously be recording a set of behavioral options that they will be able to draw upon when they discover themselves in similar situations. There is just no substitute for on-the-job training in these techniques.

Once you have developed this pool of skilled rapid developers through a succession of rapid projects, should it take over the entire organization? Again, we warn against the illusory nature of universal solutions. Many development programs should not have development speed as their primary emphasis. An organization that cannot emphasize the other objectives described in Chapter 2, such as product performance or product cost, when these objectives are appropriate, will simply have exchanged one set of weaknesses for another.

Even if rapid development were best for all projects, there are still practical limits to the number of rapid development projects that can be supported simultaneously. These projects demand certain scarce resources, such as qualified volunteers and top management attention. Every organization must discover its own capacity for rapid development.

When you start your pilot project journey, you will have the luxury of ignoring some of the underpinnings for a while, things such as job descriptions, pay grades, and promotion policies that support your new organizational style. The pioneers are willing to work for a certain period without adjustments in these areas. However, discrepancies in these areas will wear thin after a "honeymoon" period. Unless systems are brought into alignment with your new operating style, people will eventually become annoyed with the discrepancy and revert to doing what the official "system" suggests they should do.

USING CONTINUOUS IMPROVEMENT TO BUILD A DYNAMIC CAPABILITY

Look back at Figures 1-3 and 1-4 (pages 5 and 6). These companies' impressive improvements have not come automatically; both firms have invested consistently in their product development process over the long term. They pay attention to their development processes and continually make them better. This section will show you how to do the same.

Expect Two Deliverables from Every Project

Most of us think of a development project as delivering only one item: the product itself. We are pleased if we get that as planned. But there is a second, valuable deliverable available: learning about the process that was used.

Companies at the higher levels of development-process maturity expect both deliverables. They do not consider a project complete until both are delivered. Expecting both is a learned style, a new habit. Just like other habits, you acquire it by practicing it, by reviewing every project consciously until process reviews become a habitual.

There is more to it, though, because there is a cost attached to process reviews. They take effort to conduct, and this effort comes directly out of your capacity to develop new products. In other words, it is a tax you place on every project to build a competitive asset for the future. This investment pays great returns later, but now it diminishes your ability to develop new products.

This investment in future competitive strength must be appreciated, or it will not be made. This is why most companies do not conduct process reviews routinely. Such reviews are easily seen as a luxury at the moment when the new product must be delivered. Then the in-

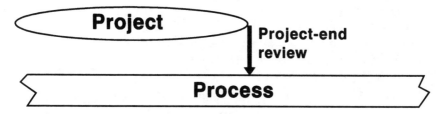

A basic process reviewing pattern. Many others are possible.

FIGURE 15-3

vestment never gets made, and the competitive asset never accrues. We have found that an effective way to get into this new mode of operation is to *expect,* from a high level in the organization, that there will be two deliverables from every project.

To make process reviews a normal occurrence, choose a pattern for reviewing them. The most obvious pattern is to review every project as it completes, as shown in Figure 15-3. Some companies want to gain the benefits sooner, so they conduct mini-reviews during a project as well as a full process review at its end. Other companies recognize that they make changes in processes annually, so they review every project underway at a certain time of the year, regardless of the stage of the project. Many other possibilities exist. What is important is that you pick a pattern that fits your company's needs and start using it as a normal expectation on every project.

Separate Process Reviews from Project Reviews

These reviews probably sound familiar, because you now probably conduct regular reviews of your projects. But the type of review needed to improve the *process* is quite different from the normal ones that focus on the *project.* Project reviews identify shortfalls or overruns in the project and take action to correct that project. In some cases, there is little that can be done to correct that project after problems have occurred, so it is a matter of accepting the overrun or schedule slippage and moving on. These reviews look backward at what has happened; they are not intended to prevent similar problems on other projects in the future.

Process reviews write off the project under review as a "sunk" event but look at it deeply for clues that will improve future projects. The questions asked include

- How did this occur (root cause)?
- How often does it occur?
- What could be done to prevent recurrence?
- Who will work on fixing the process?
- How will we know when it is fixed?

In addition to such questioning, which deals with difficulties encountered, a process review exposes items that went well in the project. These are the victories to celebrate, so that they will be repeated on other projects, and they also give the developers encouragement to take the next step.

Although such "good stuff" supplies the motivation to move ahead, it is the problems encountered that pinpoint where change is needed. To capture these "opportunities," the mistakes and misjudgments of all concerned must be allowed to surface risk-free. Focus on the system and process, and take the focus off of blaming individuals. Such a sysemic focus is important for getting to the root issues in a particular project, and it is essential for building an enduring environment in which individuals will feel comfortable exposing their mistakes.

Review Every Project

Do not review an occasional project that proceeded especially well or poorly but expect to learn from every project (above a certain threshold in size). There are practical reasons for this. Most companies do not have a large enough sample of projects to see patterns clearly; they need all of the reviews they can get.

More subtly, selecting certain projects for review makes them special. They turn out to be congratulatory exercises for the participants—or worse, witch hunts—which erode the learning and suggest to the participants that both they and the process are on trial. Selective reviews weaken the desired habit, which is that reviews are an expected and normal part of every project.

Institutionalize the Feedback Process

The only reason we conduct process reviews is to improve the process. While this may seem obvious, this final step fails to occur in all too many cases. Analyzing and discussing improvement opportunities is far easier than committing to actually improve.

In order to gain benefit from the effort expended on the review, establish a leak-tight system to convert significant findings into action. Those with the authority and resources to make changes in the process must initiate and monitor the change process. One difficulty with such changes is that some of them can be handled relatively informally at a low level, while others will require a massive effort led from the top of the company.

The resource issue cannot be overemphasized. Conducting effective process reviews will divert resources from activities, such as product development, with more immediate payoff, and taking action on certain findings will usually demand even more resources. Thus, an improved development process must be viewed as a strategic investment, just like a new laboratory. How much you are willing to invest depends on how quickly you wish to improve. Viewing the benefits as being free is a prescription for failure.

As with most cultural changes, a fundamental part of building the review-is-normal environment is assuring that it is supported by corporate expectations and rewards. For example, those who participate in the process should be given time to participate and compensated adequately for their involvement. At a practical level, consider providing a charge number for those participating in process improvement, so the time is not viewed as being stolen from other activities. Also cultivate intrinsic motivators, such as the satisfaction that one is making an important contribution to the company.

Don't Expect Perfection

One of the authors enjoys alpine skiing. Although he skis without ever intending to fall at the moment, he expects to fall, on average, twice a day. Many more falls than this, and it is time for reassessment and possible corrective action. Maybe he is tired or is skiing beyond his abilities. Interestingly, however, fewer than two falls a day also indicates a time for reassessment and possible corrective action; perhaps he is just cruising, not accepting the next off-piste challenge that will increase his likelihood of falling, thus improving his skills for the future.

Product development is the same way. Although you do not plan on making mistakes, if you are not making any, you may be too complacent. The goal is not "no mistakes"; instead, it is continual learning, which will require *some* mistakes.

GET GOING

The changes we have described throughout this book are additive. Benefits will accrue from any of the techniques we have described, if they are properly implemented. Because they are mutually reinforcing, they work best when used as an integrated set, but do not let roadblocks in one area prevent you from making changes in others. Any successful step in roughly the right direction will help.

The following two paragraphs, the last two in the book, also appeared at the end of our original edition. After working with well over a hundred clients in the intervening years to implement these tools, we now see that these words were perhaps the most profound ones in that book. As you close the book and consider implementation, let this story persist in your mind.

We are reminded of the story of the wise man who was approached by a youth who asked him how long it would take to walk to Athens. The wise man simply replied, "Get going!" The youth, disappointed, concluded that he would not get a straight answer and began walking in the direction of Athens. After the youth had taken about 20 steps, the wise man called out, "About four hours!" The youth turned and said, "Why didn't you tell me that when I asked before?"

"First I had to see how fast you walked," said the wise man.

SUGGESTED READING

Beer, Michael, Russell A. Eisenstat, and Bert Spector. 1990. Why change programs don't produce change. *Harvard Business Review* 68 (6): 158–66. This article further explains the approach suggested here, such as focusing on behavior rather than attitudes, starting with small projects, and continuously learning.

Kotter, John P. 1995. Why transformation efforts fail. *Harvard Business Review* 73 (2): 59–67. Kotter, who often writes on leadership, lists eight mistakes that leaders make in initiating change. For example, Error 1: Not establishing a great enough sense of urgency.

Schaffer, Robert H. 1988. *The Breakthrough Strategy.* Cambridge, Mass.: Ballinger Publishing Co. This book, a bit misleadingly titled, has nothing to do with building strategies but rather with getting things done in an organization through a sequence of small wins. These wins build confidence and ultimately develop the organizational capability to operate more effectively. A product development project may be a large task for Schaffer's small-wins tactic, but many of his ideas apply nevertheless.

Smith, Preston G. Your product development process demands ongoing improvement. *Research-Technology Management* 39 (2): 37–44. Provides additional details on continuously improving your development process.

Index